411

✔ KU-731-258

VM 30'

, F3. ALE

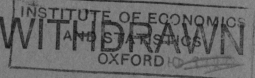
INSTITUTE OF ECONOMICS
AND STATISTICS
WITHDRAWN
OXFORD

ABG·

Fairfields

A Study of Industrial Change

———

K. J. W. ALEXANDER
and
C. L. JENKINS

WITHDRAWN

ECONOMICS LIBRARY AND STATISTICS

-9:

-9 SEP 1970

ALLEN LANE THE PENGUIN PRESS

Copyright © K. J. W. Alexander and C. L. Jenkins, 1970

First published in 1970

Allen Lane The Penguin Press
Vigo Street, London W1

SBN 7139 0108 X

Printed Offset Litho in Great Britain by
Cox & Wyman Ltd, London, Fakenham and Reading
Set in Monotype Times

Contents

Preface

THE authors wish to acknowledge the cooperation and help which was given to them by employees and management at Fairfields shipyard. They are particularly indebted to Sir Iain Stewart for his encouragement, to Mr E. O. T. Blanford and Mr J. D. Houston for the extent to which they allowed the full-time researcher to participate and probe in yard affairs, and to Mr Alex McGuiness, full-time convener of shop stewards, for his time and patience. The cooperation of a large number of trade-union officials was also of great assistance. The members of the Fairfields Central Joint Council were especially helpful.

Mr J. L. Steward, lately of the British Shipbuilding Research Association, was most generous with his time and expertise. Miss Margaret Pugh, Mr Frank Stephen, Jr and Mr S. Keppel helped with the research for short periods.

The points within the text at which we have drawn upon information provided by particular individuals are too numerous to allow specific attribution and thanks. We hope that all concerned will accept our general acknowledgement.

We are indebted to Professor S. G. E. Lythe (of the University of Strathclyde) and Mr James Jack (of the Scottish Trades Union Congress) for help in initiating and continuing the research work. Financial help from the Social Science Research Council is also gratefully acknowledged.

Secretarial assistance was provided by Mrs C. Sandell, Mrs Adrienne McCall and the late Miss Nan Skorpen.

An earlier version of a section of Chapter 8 appeared in the *Transactions of the Institution of Engineers and Shipbuilders in Scotland* and we are grateful to the Institution for agreeing to the publication of this amended version.

A list of abbreviations used in the book will be found on page 9.

Abbreviations

AEU	Amalgamated Engineering Union
ASB	Amalgamated Society of Boilermakers, Shipwrights, Blacksmiths and Structural Workers
CJC	Central joint council
CSA	Clyde Shipbuilders' Association
DATA	Draughtsmen's and Allied Technicians Association
EMC	Executive managers' committee
ETPS	Estimated target payment scheme
MDS	Measured daywork scheme
MTPS	Measured target payment scheme
NUGMW	National Union of General and Municipal Workers
PSD	Productivity services director
PSM	Personnel services manager
PSO	Productivity services organization
PTU	Plumbers' Trade Union
ROWP	Relaxation of working practices
SITB	Shipbuilding Industry Training Board
SMW	National Union of Sheet-Metal Workers, Coppersmiths and Heating and Domestic Engineers
UCS	Upper Clyde Shipbuilders Ltd

Chronology

1835   Charles Randolph and Richard S. Cunliffe found a small engine shop in Glasgow.

1852   John Elder enters the firm.

1853   The firm builds its first marine engine.

1854   Elder patents his compound engine which halves the amount of bunker coal a ship needs to carry.

1860   The decision to move into shipbuilding is taken.

1864   Fairfield farm near Govan village is acquired and a composite shipbuilding and engineering establishment begun.

1868   The first ship is launched at Fairfield.

1869   John Elder dies.

1870   John Elder & Co. is formed with William Pearce as shipbuilding partner.

1871   Fairfield shipyard is completed.

1879   S.S. *Arizona,* the first of Pearce's many Atlantic record breakers, is launched.

1885   Sir William Pearce elected first MP for Govan.

1886   The *Victoria* is built for the London, Chatham and Dover Railway Company on a contract specifying that the ship need not be accepted if she fails to maintain a one-hour-each-way service every day for a month on the Dover-Calais run, which she does.

1886   The Fairfield Shipbuilding & Engineering Co. Ltd is established.

1888   Sir William Pearce dies. Sir William George Pearce becomes chairman.

1907   Sir William George Pearce dies and Dr Francis Elgin becomes chairman (output of yard in this year = 48,000 gross tons).

1909   Sir Alexander Grant becomes chairman.
        Shortly after the First World War Lady Pearce, widow of Sir William Pearce, dies and there comes on the market a large block of shares which are bought by the Northumberland Shipping Company of Newcastle-on-Tyne, which company thus gains control of the Fairfield Company, backed by the Sperling Group, merchant bankers of London. A new chairman, Mr R. A. Workman, takes over.

11

1930	Sir Alexander Kennedy becomes chairman.
1935	Sir James and Mr Henry Lithgow take over the company.
1937	Sir James Lithgow becomes chairman.
1951	Sir Jackson Miller becomes chairman (Sir James Lithgow becomes president).
1954	Major reconstruction of shipyard is begun. Lord Elgin becomes chairman.
1957	Sir John Erskine becomes chairman.
1963	Fairfield Shipbuilding & Engineering Co. Ltd purchases David Rowan & Co. Ltd and Fairfield-Rowan Ltd is formed.
1964	Mr J. E. Boyd becomes chairman.
15 October 1965	A receiver is appointed for the Fairfield Shipbuilding and Engineering Co. Ltd.
1966	Fairfields (Glasgow) Ltd is incorporated, with Mr Iain M. Stewart as chairman.
1968	Fairfields becomes the Govan Division of Upper Clyde Shipbuilders Ltd.

CHAPTER 1

The Background to the Fairfields Experiment and the Research

THE financial collapse of the Fairfield Shipbuilding and Engineering Company Ltd in October 1965 was one further dramatic reflection of the acute crisis which faced the British shipbuilding industry, and which had brought about the closure of seven yards in four years.

In February 1965 the President of the Board of Trade appointed a Shipbuilding Enquiry Committee

to establish what changes are necessary in organization, in the methods of production, and in other factors affecting costs, to make the shipbuilding industry competitive in world markets; to establish what changes in organization and methods of production would reduce costs of manufacture of large main engines of ships to the lowest level; and to recommend what action should be taken by employers, trade unions and Government, to bring about these changes.

The establishment of this Committee, under the chairmanship of Mr (now Sir) Reay Geddes, reflected government recognition of and concern with the critical situation in British shipbuilding. Recognizing the seriousness of the situation and the need for speedy remedial action, the Geddes Committee tackled its work vigorously, finally reporting within a few days of the first anniversary of its appointment. The financial crisis which hit Fairfields Shipyard in Govan came about two-thirds of the way through the working life of the Committee.

Recognition by the government of the seriousness of the crisis would not, by itself, have supported a case for keeping the yard open. Indeed there was much talk of 'rationalization' within the industry at the time, and a widespread belief that the findings of the Geddes Committee would be followed by a phase of 'planned contraction'. It seems very possible that the optimistic forecasts which Geddes finally made regarding the expanding potential market open to British shipbuilders were being shared by the government some four months before the report was completed. In the absence of such forecasts, and their implications for the level of capacity which British shipbuilding could use in the future, government support to keep the yard in production would not have made economic sense. The criticism of government support for Fairfields at the time of its threatened closure* was made without appreciation of the influence which such optimistic forecasts had on the decision.

The prospect of a rising demand for shipbuilding capacity would have established a case for keeping the Govan yard open more or less without managerial or other change until Geddes reported, and then allowing the recommendations of that Report to dictate the pace and character of change in the yard thereafter. With hindsight and the knowledge that the merger of yards on the Upper Clyde came within two years of the publication of the *Geddes Report* it is clear that the period for which such a policy of propping-up would have been necessary would have been around two and a half years. This was not the basis on which support was forthcoming, however. The statement by Mr George Brown, as First Secretary of State at the Department of Economic Affairs, was quite explicit about the 'proving-ground' aspect of the new Fairfields exercise.

I am sure the House will welcome our actions as a quite new partnership not only between Government and private enterprise, but now between Government, private enterprise, and the trade unions, the motive being not merely to save a recently modernized Scottish shipyard from extinction, important as that would be, but in addition to provide a proving-ground for new relations in the shipbuilding industry which could change the whole image of our country.†

*For example, 'The wrong sort of intervention,' *Financial Times*, 10 December 1965. 'The shipbuilding industry suffers, among other things, from a surplus of capacity. Some firms will inevitably have to merge with others in the early future and some capacity will have to be scrapped.

'The first to go should be those who, for one reason or another, are least capable of standing up to foreign competition.'

†House of Commons Debates, Vol. 722, Col. 2103, 22 December 1965.

The set of circumstances, the various pressures and the ideas of the main parties and persons involved which together produced this unique formula deserve examination. The political background of the time was itself important. A Labour government was in office, with a very small majority. Although responsive to job-protection arguments from shop stewards, trade-union leaders and local members of parliament, there was little support in the Government for full-scale public ownership as a means of keeping the yard in production. Without the support of private capital it seems unlikely that the government would have felt able to offer its help. Without government help, on the other hand, it is unlikely that private capital would have been forthcoming in sufficient volume. Commercial considerations alone would not have induced private capital into shipbuilding at that time. Shipbuilders on the Clyde would probably have been interested in 'picking up the pieces' once the yard closed, but not in preventing the closure. There was equipment of above-average quality and below average age at Govan which would certainly have attracted local buyers. Scarcity of labour at the time meant that local employers saw opportunities for expansion following on a closure of Fairfields.

The campaign by the shop stewards to keep the yard open was vigorous and unrelenting, but the Government was unsure of how it could help in the situation of the time. The catalyst was Mr (now Sir) Iain Stewart, a Scottish businessman of high repute and wide experience, who had for some years previously been campaigning for 'new look' industrial relations, based upon security of earnings and a considerable extension of retraining facilities. Immediately prior to the financial crisis of the Fairfield Shipbuilding and Engineering Company he had been exploring with local business and trade-union leaders the possibility of forming a consortium of engineering, building and shipbuilding firms within which greater security of employment could be offered in return for greater flexibility amongst skilled tradesmen. His reaction to the threatened closure of Fairfields was that a mass pay-off affecting 2,500 workpeople would destroy any possibility of building better industrial relations on Clydeside. In addition, he saw the possibility that

15

to avert such a mass pay-off the Fairfields workers might be willing to change attitudes and labour practices within that yard in response to a fresh approach by a management itself resolved upon change. With such thoughts in mind he let it be known that he would be prepared to play a part in helping the yard back to commercial health again, given that there was an unequivocal assurance of cooperation from the employees. For their different reasons, both Sir Iain Stewart and the government were anxious to avoid majority ownership by the government. Sir Iain frequently declared his political sympathies to be Tory, and was unwilling to be party to any 'back-door nationalization' arrangement. The government, too, partly because of its delicate parliamentary majority, and partly because it did not want to join issue on the nationalization question when the Geddes Committee was at work, was keen to have the cooperation of private capital as well as the support of private entrepreneurs. That the idea of public participation in shipbuilding was attractive is illustrated in a comment later by a member of the Government:

In shipbuilding public participation by the acquisition of equity was made possible under the Shipbuilding Industry Act, and Fairfields was acquired to guarantee its role in the industry.*

Sir Iain used his powers of persuasion on a number of businessmen to convince them to invest in a new company to buy the shipyard. The arguments used were heavily weighted on the side of the need for change, particularly in the related fields of industrial relations, manpower utilization and productivity, although commercial viability and a reasonable return on capital in five years was suggested as a target which could probably be attained. Interestingly, all of the private investors who responded to this approach had strong Scottish connections. (They included Lord Thomson, Sir Isaac Woolfson, Mr Hugh Stenhouse and Mr C. Salveson.) Investment by trade unions was the truly unique feature of the voluntary association of public, private and trade-union capital which combined to form Fairfields (Glasgow) Ltd. This investment arose out of a

* A. Wedgwood Benn in *Tribune,* 8 September 1967.

suggestion made in the process of discussion between the Government, trade-union representatives and Sir Iain Stewart about 'saving the yard'. In response to an outline by a government member and Sir Iain of the difficulties of raising adequate capital one national trade-union leader interjected that had he any money he would be keen to invest. This triggered off the question: why not investments by trade unions from their accumulated funds? A number of trade-union leaders agreed to propose such investment to their executive committees. One union, the ETU, was opposed to holding equity in a company in which it organized members, but agreed to put up debenture capital. This opposition was a reflection of the same attitude that has made the ETU an opponent of 'workers' participation in industry' and in particular of any idea that trade unionists should serve on the boards of private companies. Any such participation – or profit-sharing through equity-holding – would blur the interests of company and trade-union members, and weaken a clear-cut understanding of the trade union's independent function. One other union found that its rules prevented any such investment. The unions which did hold equity in Fairfields (Glasgow) Ltd were the Amalgamated Engineering Union; the Amalgamated Society of Wood-workers; the Clerical and Administrative Workers' Union, and the National Union of General and Municipal Workers. In addition, and for the reasons given above, the Electrical Trades Union had a debenture holding. The route by which trade-union investment occurred suggests that it was not of central importance other than as a means of mustering the necessary capital at the outset. Some of the private investors were themselves encouraged by the promise of trade-union capital to support the efforts of Sir Iain Stewart to raise the private capital on which government was insisting. Nevertheless, as shall be seen, this investment by trade unions did influence developments within the yard, not always favourably.

The enthusiasm of Mr George Brown for making Fairfields a pace-setter within shipbuilding and a laboratory for exploring the possibility of improving industrial relations and manpower utilization more widely, played a major part in establishing the new company. This enthusiasm can be seen as a particular reflection of the task for which the new Department of Economic Affairs had been established – to improve the efficiency of the British economy 'from the ground up' in contrast to the approach of economic management exercised by the Treasury through fiscal and related measures. The DEA approach had to rely very substantially on exhortation, committee work through the National Economic Development Committee and 'the little neddies' set up to cover specific industries, and there was a natural attraction – particularly to a minister of Mr Brown's pragmatic turn of mind – in the idea of a practical grass-roots exercise to see what changes could be brought about in an industry reputed to be particularly resilient to change.

Once the concept of a proving ground had been proposed by Sir Iain Stewart and adopted by the Government, trade-union leaders, local shop stewards and private investors, and with the capital required assured if the proving-ground concept were endorsed by workers in the yard, Sir Iain addressed a mass meeting of all yard employees. He had declared in advance his willingness to take over as chairman of a new company which would run the yard if he had an assurance from the workers of full cooperation including a removal of restrictive practices and an undertaking to forego strike action during the proving period. After Sir Iain had outlined his proposals and his conditions these were put to the mass meeting by a local trade-union leader and overwhelmingly endorsed. This meeting was the first of five such mass meetings which Sir Iain addressed as chairman, establishing a position of trust and leadership with the workers and becoming something of a symbol representing a 'new deal' in Clydeside shipbuilding.

The emergence of Sir Iain Stewart as chairman of the new Fairfields added to the opposition which in any event would have existed to keeping the yard in being, even without 'pace-setter' implications. His campaign for change, particularly during his term of office as President of the Institution of Engineers and Shipbuilders in Scotland, had caused offence amongst those who equated his vigorous advocacy of change with at best implied criticism of the management extant. One leading shipbuilder complained about the offering of unasked-for advice and the presumptuousness of an outsider claiming to have the answers to the industry's problems. Another less defensive about the need for change but fearful of the apparent alliance between the local critic and a Labour government, and of the effect of the new Fairfields on the Clydeside labour market, stated bluntly 'I know we need a blood transfusion, but is it sensible to cut our throats in the process?' These local attitudes contributed very substantially to the 'siege mentality' which affected the new management for part of the life of Fairfields (Glasgow) Ltd, but such opposition also encouraged workers and trade-union leaders to place their hopes for the reform of the industry on the new company. In this there was an element of conflict with the intention of Sir Iain that the fifty per cent public ownership formula should not be exceeded, for many of Fairfields trade-union supporters reasoned as follows: 'The failure of Fairfields would strengthen the opposition to all forms of public ownership and control of ship-building and its success would strengthen the case for public participation in one form or another.'

The idea that the Fairfields experiment should be the subject of research arose naturally out of the proving-ground concept. The new chairman proposed the research and linked this to the proposal that one of the researchers join the board of the new company to ensure full and untrammelled access to information within the company. Observation began on a part-time basis in February 1966 and the research was conducted on a full-time basis from 1 April 1966.

The research at Fairfields had a number of interesting features. First, it was continuous 'on the spot' research in contrast to most industrial research by academics which usually explores the causes of industrial development after the events, and in a spasmodic way. Secondly, we were guaranteed full access to the information necessary for the research, with the right to publish. Thirdly, and as an inevitable consequence of its 'on the spot' character, we were involved in developments in Fairfields. We could not avoid inter-acting with the subjects of our observation and analysis. Fourthly, the involvement and inter-action was not only with top management but with all levels of management and trade-union organization within the yard. This is in sharp contrast to a 'consultancy relationship' in which the results of observation and analysis are the property of top management and only made available to other groups on the initiative of top management. Our findings, usually in the form of reports, were made freely and equally available to all interested sections within the yard. We also invited individuals and representatives to suggest topics for research examination, although making it clear that a decision about whether to pursue a particular suggestion must remain with the researchers. It was disappointing that despite close contact and good relations with all groups in the yard very few of such research requests were in fact made.

The first task was to overcome the inevitable barriers of suspicion and uncertainty in the yard regarding the aims and purpose of the research work. This was done by holding meetings with all groups in the yard, shop stewards, foremen and managers, to explain and invite questions on the purpose of the research work. When the approval of the yard's workers had been given through the shop stewards, the full-time research worker began to establish contacts with all groups in the yard. Attendance at meetings, and many informal conversations and much social contact expedited the process of gaining yard cooperation with the research work.

The first research task was to make an assessment of the attitudes of the work-people towards various aspects of industrial practices and conditions in the shipyard. This survey, and others concerning foremen and shop stewards, was done on a questionnaire and interview basis. Wherever possible, interviews were held with those participating in the surveys. These interviews were 'guided' so that a basis for comparison could be established. In some cases, e.g. the foremen survey, the numbers involved were too large and each foreman was given a questionnaire, to be completed in the presence of a research worker. Interviews and questionnaires were covered by a guarantee of anonymity. No information or names were divulged without the permission of the interviewee. Very early in the project management and workers came to accept that the research work was confidential, and we enjoyed a full and free flow of information.

Much of the information was gained by attending meetings. The research worker had permission to attend any meeting in the yard, if no objection to his presence was raised by any of the participants. During the period of the project this veto was never used, and the research worker's presence at meetings and other gatherings became regarded as part of the proving-ground concept. In addition, much of the basic research information derived from informal and social contacts.

The free flow of information was never jeopardized because one of the researchers was a director of the company. Although it was obvious that the two researchers became privy to much of the policy-making and planning of both management and shop stewards, information was never withheld on this account, nor were attempts made to have the researchers break a confidence. These relationships were highlighted on one occasion when at a time of high tension in industrial relations in the yard management and shop stewards met for a confrontation, with one researcher attached to each side as observer and taking part on 'his' side in all of the pre-negotiation discussions. The knowledge that ultimately the researchers would be publishing their findings did not seem to inhibit people in the yard. Neither researcher was ever given a piece of information with the qualification that it could not be used. The problem of what should be published and what is best left unsaid has been left entirely to the discretion of the researchers. Given the controversy which has arisen about the outcome of the Fairfields experiment the participants have shown remarkable forbearance and restraint in not seeking to influence the character or content of this report on the research in any way.

The extent to which both management and labour at Fairfields allowed us to observe and probe into the affairs of the yard made it probable that their actions would be reported on and commented upon, and that this could expose weaknesses and cast shadows over the performance of individuals and groups. This was the intention of the research – and particularly

21

was it the intention of the chairman who initiated and encouraged it. It is to be hoped that managers and others who have never been exposed to outside observation and published comment will avoid adopting a 'holier than thou' attitude to those who have.

The approach adopted in this report is largely descriptive.* Given the substantial accumulation of misconceptions which have grown up around the Fairfields experiment, we have felt our main responsibility to be to set out the principal facts as we see them. Inevitably this process has to be selective. We have tried to combine reasonable brevity with comprehensiveness. The process of selection can merge, almost imperceptibly, into interpretation and evaluation. We have tried to keep subjective judgements to a minimum, and here to some extent we have been able to check each other. The heroic, if not improper, attempt to generalize on the basis of one observation has not been made. The 'lessons' which are drawn are drawn tentatively and must be related back to their environment by anyone seeking to apply them under different circumstances.

*Other aspects and views are found in Oliver Blanford, *The Fairfields, Experiment*, Industrial Society, 1969, and S. Paulen and Bill Hawkins *Whatever Happened at Fairfields?*, Gower Press, 1969.

CHAPTER 2

Shipyard Economics

A MAJOR theme of this book is that shipyard production does not differ so widely from production in heavy manufacturing industry as to exclude it from benefiting from the experiences of the rest of industry and from applying proved techniques of management. Shipbuilding is not a world apart, a world unknown and unknowable as far as the mainstream of industrial management is concerned. Nevertheless, the economics of shipbuilding does differ in a number of quite significant ways from that of most manufacturing industry. A comparison with the building and civil engineering industries suggests some strong affinities as far as marketing and the broad organization of production are concerned, whereas the specific processes of production are those of both manufacturing and of building. Parallels are less helpful than a detailed examination of the characteristics of the industry itself, and this chapter makes such an examination. In it the demand and supply sides of shipbuilding will be examined and there will be a brief discussion of the relevance of economic theory to shipyard economics. The influence of industrial structure on the efficiency of the industry will be discussed, and the case for and consequences of mergers in shipbuilding analysed.

The demand for ships is characterized by four main features: first, it is derived largely from the growth and expected growth in the volume of international trade; second, it is subject to very marked fluctuations; third, at the level of the national industry, it tends to be influenced by government decisions as well as commercial ones; and fourth, at the level of the national industry and the shipyard, it is strongly affected by competition from alternative producers.

The derivation of the demand for ships from the volume of international trade has been very fully commented upon elsewhere.* A first consequence of this derived quality is that marketing ships is almost exclusively a competitive exercise. Salesmanship cannot expand the demand for ships, only for the ships produced in a particular country or shipyard; that is, the character of demand encourages competition, quite apart from the impetus to competition given by the internationally mobile character of the product. A second consequence of the derived character of demand is that it is more than usually difficult to forecast future demand trends. Underlying any such forecast there must be forecasts of production trends for both manufactured products and raw materials, shifts in the pattern of international demand and consequently the movements of goods, trade and aid policies of governments and international agencies, and of many other influences on trade. Forecasting the future demand for ships is made especially difficult not only by the derived character of demand but by each of the other three major features influencing demand listed above. The existence of sizeable fluctuations complicates forecasting because of the difficulty of disentangling what is short-run and what long-run in the factors influencing demand at any one moment of time. Government intervention (or its withdrawal) can also introduce unpredictable shifts in the long-run demand trend. Most difficult of all, when it comes to estimating the demand situation of a particular yard, the high degree of competitiveness inevitably introduces major sources of possible error in estimation. It is difficult enough to estimate future changes in productivity, efficiency and costs in one's own yard, more difficult to estimate such changes for other yards in the same country drawing upon similar sources of supply for manpower and bought-in factors of production, and difficult almost beyond the bounds of credibility to make firm estimates of changes in foreign competitiveness.

The difficulties of forecasting demand are compounded from the derived demand characteristics and the extreme vulnerability to fluctuation in demand of the market for ships. Writing in 1960 Parkinson estimated that demand for tankers might, on

*See, for instance, J. R. Parkinson, *The Economics of Shipbuilding in the U.K.,* Chapters 5 and 6.

optimistic assumptions, run at around 3,000,000 gross registered tons in future years,* that is about 5,250,000 dead-weight tons (DWT). By 1966 the actual demand was 8,200,000 DWT and the forecast commissioned for the *Geddes Report* expected an increase in demand of 7·2 per cent per annum, resulting in a total demand by 1975 of 16,600,000 DWT. A separate forecast made by the Board of Trade expected 1975 demand to range between 6,000,000 and 9,500,000 DWT (based on an annual growth rate of 5 per cent after an initially slower rate) and a private estimate made by consultants considered 11,500,000 DWT a more realistic figure for 1975. In estimating future demand for dry-cargo vessels Parkinson concluded 'Thus a demand of 3,000,000–4,000,000 GRT [approximately 4,500,000 –6,750,000 DWT] per annum is more likely to err on the side of optimism than pessimism.'† This forecast made in 1960 has to be compared with the 1966 world output figures of over 11,000,000 DWT (covering both bulk-carriers and other dry cargo vessels which appear to be covered in Parkinson's dry cargo or 'non-tanker' categories for which the 4,500,000– 6,750,000 DWT figures were quoted), an estimate for 11,400,000 DWT by 1975 for the Geddes Committee, and an independent estimate of 9,700,000 DWT for 1975. Different estimates again for 1975 were made at about the same time by the Dutch Shipbuilding Commission and the Economic Studies Office of the Italian Ministry for the Merchant Navy.

Ships deserve their honoured place in economic texts as an example of a commodity subject to wide fluctuations in demand, mainly as a result of substantial drops in demand when either financial stringency or gloomy expectations about the demand for shipping space encourage ship owners to postpone replacement orders. Changes in the value of scrap have been known to accelerate or postpone replacement, and this is one of the least influential of the possible influences. Thus even for quite short periods of time it is not possible to predict demand with any degree of certainty. For example with nearly 1,500 Liberty Ships due for survey in the years 1967–70 it was not possible at

* Parkinson, op. cit., p. 71.
† Parkinson, op. cit., p. 57.

the beginning of that period to predict with any degree of accuracy what replacements might take place. Such fluctuations also encourage over-capacity in shipbuilding when judged against the longer term level of demand. This tendency to over-capacity is distinct from that which can arise in a country failing to meet international competition and, therefore, faced with a long-run decline in demand. This has been Britain's recent experience.

The influence of government policy on the demand for ships operates partly indirectly through government policies affecting the level of economic activity and of trade, but mainly directly through policies aimed specifically at the demand for ships. A fairly recent international survey of such policies* brings out the extent and the variety and the magnitude of such intervention in the industry. Amongst the measures in operation are: customs duties, import restrictions, preferential treatment for home-built ships, direct subsidies (ranging from 9 per cent of contract price to 60 per cent of estimated cost), tax preference, easy credit facilities, public purchasing – of which naval purchases are the most important, regional subsidies, and finance to stimulate remedial measures. Against such a background it is obviously necessary to qualify the notion that the shipbuilding industry is competitive. International competition between shipyards is supported by very substantial subventions in the case of many countries. The fierceness of competition has in some cases exerted upward pressure on the magnitude of these subventions rather than the downward pressure on costs (or capacity) normally assumed in economic theory.

Interventions by governments in industry are usually a re-action to economic adversity rather than positive attempts to improve an already strong commercial situation. British ship-building has been no exception; indeed it might be regarded as the prime example of such government reaction to adversity. Because of this, successive subventions have not had the effect of maintaining either the absolute or even the relative share of the industry in a rising world demand. The strength of inter-

*The Situation in the Shipbuilding Industry, OECD, 1965.

national competition – most also supported by government aid, though to very different degrees – has cut sharply into the position of the British industry as Table 2.1 indicates. When the output of an industry declines absolutely as the international demand for its product rises substantially, and this despite successive injections of government aid to the industry, it is clear that its position is critical and that the solution must depend primarily on whether it can improve its productive efficiency.

By far the most important impact of market factors on the economics of shipbuilding is the tendency to encourage over-capacity. Fluctuations in demand and government intervention together tend to create and sustain world capacity above the level at which full utilization can be approached. The difficulties of forecasting long-run demand may also bring into being capacity destined to be surplus (or push other capacity into that category). In a period of expanding demand the effects of these tendencies need not be acute, but in a period of stability or only slowly expanding demand this tendency to over-capacity can cause waste and hardship.

The ability of a shipyard to build a given tonnage in a given period depends on the fixed resources at its disposal and the efficiency with which it can use these resources. The nature of the shipbuilding process, the several very different processes and stages of building involved, means that there are several distinct 'fixed factors of production' within one shipyard, any one of which may prove the limiting factor to expanding production, as a result of the particular composition of the building pro-gramme at a given time.

If an invariable labour force, constant pace of work and fixed time span for work (i.e. a given system of shift working, say single-day-shift only) are assumed in each separate stage of production, then the main variability of output over a given period would arise from the extent to which the product-mix and its phasing enabled the fixed resources required for each stage of production to be utilized as fully as possible. If varia-tions in labour input are possible then fuller utilization of each of these several sets of fixed resources becomes possible. Thus the combination of 'fixed' and 'variable' factors of production in shipbuilding is very much more complicated than in most manufacturing industries, as a result of the several distinct stages and processes of which shipbuilding production is composed. The ability of a firm to keep unit costs of production low depends upon its ability (or good fortune) in achieving the optimum product mix, and the optimum combination of fixed and variable factors in each distinct process of production. Thus achieving an order book which makes full utilization of the different 'fixed factors' possible is part of the planning process in shipbuilding which should be regarded as an integral part of the total production process. The variability and unpredictability of demand greatly complicates this ideal approach.

The main fixed resources used in shipbuilding are: stockyards, prefabrication and plating shops, berths, basins, and joinery, sheet-metal and pipework production shops. In addition the handling facilities impose an upper limit on what may be produced, and by what methods, in a particular yard; the maximum tonnage of the available cranes and the areas within which this cranage is operational are key factors determining upper limits to the output of a shipyard. Berths and cranage are crucial. Other stages of production can be farmed out, so that particular bottle-necks may be overcome despite limitations on the capacity of a yard to carry them out, although this is likely to be costly. Human limitations have meant that drawing and design facilities have had to be regarded as factors of production in fixed supply in certain periods.

The cost of expanding facilities in a yard can also be very great and usually time-consuming so that sharply rising costs are often experienced when full utilization of fixed resources is reached at one or more of the distinct stages of production. Such full utilization can occur when the total output of the yard falls short of maximum under conditions of optimum product mix. Thus the fact of under-utilization does not, in shipbuilding, necessarily mean that unit costs of production are falling or even constant. When production programmes fall behind schedule the problem of bottle-necks and rising costs in a few sectors despite an overall under-utilization of capacity can be particularly serious.

The flexibility which a variable labour input allows can also push costs up – either as a result of the payment of overtime or shift premiums. Such variability may also be limited absolutely, for example, by employee opposition to shift work or to farming out processes normally carried out in the yard, e.g. the pre-fabrication of steelwork.

The existence of a series of possible cost-increasing bottle-necks complicates the estimation of the probable total cost of building a given ship. The fierceness of competition for orders in recent years has led many British yards to quote prices unrealistically low given their costs, but even without this fac-tor it is possible for actual costs to exceed estimated costs by substantial amounts as a result of such bottle-necks.

Tendering systems are usually evolved to improve the bargaining position of the buyers of large, once for all type commodities produced by a few suppliers who may not always engage in genuine competition with each other. Such a system does not by itself ensure competition for business but it makes it more likely, partly by bringing pointers to its absence more clearly into prominence. In the market for merchant ships the tendering system appears to heighten competition, partly by keeping shipbuilding in the dark about the prices being quoted by competitors before the shipowner's closing date and partly by making at least the successful price known so that an approximation to 'perfect knowledge' is achieved without encouraging collusion.

From the shipowner's point of view such a system appears ideal. He is provided with a number of prices which give him a better idea of the appropriate price range than he would have by approaching one or two builders only, and he may also be given ideas for incorporation in his ship which he might not otherwise have had. From the builders' point of view the system is expensive and time-consuming, frequently involving the use of scarce design resources which could be deployed on design work required for ships already on the order book.

An enquiry from a shipowner or broker may contain only

the minimum of information about the size and type of ship or it may contain a very detailed specification. Many more enquiries are received than tenders are prepared for. Enquiries may be discarded because of doubts regarding the credit-worthiness of the prospective buyer, because insufficient detail has been provided and the enquiry is thought not to be serious, or because the type of ship is unsuitable – it would not suit the yard or its current building programme. Over four years of the old and new Fairfields, 146 estimates were sent out, an average of thirty-seven each year.

The basis on which tenders are prepared in shipbuilding has tended to be historical costs and experience gained in connexion with ships built in the past. In addition prices and delivery dates for auxiliary machinery and other major bought-in materials and components will be sought. Once the individual departments have compiled their separate estimates these will be aggregated by a chief estimator who may make adjustments before passing the estimate to the accountant or financial comptroller who will check, adjust and add amounts for recovery of overheads and a profit rate calculated on costs. Managers with long experience in shipbuilding will claim virtue for intuitive adjustments in tenders at this stage, but it is vital that the reasons for all changes be made explicit and recorded. The tender may then go before the board, or to the managing director, when further adjustments may be made, perhaps in the light of a conviction that to win a certain order is necessary to establish a connexion, or even to stay in business. As the length of time between making the tender and completing the ship is likely to be at least eighteen months, probably over two years and can be as much as four years* it is plain that there is an element of forecasting involved in the tendering process. This is accentuated when the many pitfalls and unforeseen complications which can arise in shipbuilding are taken into account. For example, what escalation in wage costs should be allowed for over a thirty-month building cycle when negotiations for 'a substantial increase in wages' are in process while an estimate

* Over nine consecutive vessels, the average time-period between tender and completion was two and a half years.

is being prepared? What increase in material costs? Will productivity remain the same, or rise or fall? In a fiercely competitive situation would it be legitimate to allow for expected increases in productivity in making an estimate of labour costs, or would it be 'wiser' to ignore such possible gains and lodge a tender which has little hope of success because of this? Decisions such as this, which can make or break a shipbuilding company, must be made by the board or chief executive, and the basis on which they are made must also be quite explicit.

At Fairfields approximately twenty-five people were directly involved in this tendering process and the efforts of many more were involved indirectly and for part of their total working time.

Tables 2.1 and 2.2 bring out very clearly the failure of such a tendering system to predict actual costs incurred at all accurately. The tables illustrate how far actual productivity and costs matched the expectations built into the original estimates, which in turn were the basis of the tenders which secured these orders. The figures are based on the performance in four ships, all orders gained by the old Fairfields, though one was completed under the new management. The average length of time elapsing between estimate and delivery was approximately eighteen months. The 'failure' is not necessarily the fault of the estimators. The estimate of the labour hours necessary in a particular department may have been realistic, but actual performance may have fallen short because of (say) poor management. It has been very common for shipowners to ask for many changes in their vessel as building has progressed, usually without adjustment to the contract price. Such changes explain a small part of the gap between estimate and performance. The major part has to be explained by a combination of faulty estimating (sometimes deliberate underestimating induced by a low order book and by strong competition) and poor performance. A comparison between the real and money labour inputs shown in Table 2.1 brings out very clearly that a substantial part of the total gap was due to an underestimation of wage movements and the extent to which departments would have to rely on overtime and week-end work to cut down on late deliveries.

Table 2.1

Gap between estimate and performance: Man-hours and wage costs
(difference expressed as percentage of estimate; better = +, worse = −)

Department	Ship							
	A		B		C		D	
	Man-hours	Wage cost	Man-hours	Wage cost	Man-hours	Wage cost	Man-hours	Wage cost
Steelwork	− 14·82	− 63·11	− 0·63	− 5·51	+ 5·69	− 24·09	+ 15·46	− 2·3
General smith-work	+ 37·54	− 62·67	+ 7·31	− 12·32	+ 22·57	− 0·78	+ 16·27	− 7·48
Loftwork	− 26·47	− 78·73	+ 18·8	+ 7·83	− 11·01	− 9·31	+ 3·21	− 3·39
Joinerwork	+ 2·97	− 12·08	− 1·57	− 18·97	+ 106·13	+ 29·43	+ 6·78	− 20·49
Plumberwork	+ 6·51	− 50·26	− 8·9	− 23·55	− 30·17	− 17·72	+ 33·54	− 40·6
Sheet-ironwork	− 105·78	− 172·24	− 5·42	− 20·00	+ 11·46	+ 39·45	+ 14·59	+ 1·71
Paintwork	+ 43·47	+ 18·59	+ 15·51	− 18·83	+ 18·98	+ 14·76	+ 22·91	+ 0·89
Riggers	− 26·00	− 58·83	+ 1·7	− 43·2	− 41·25	− 75·66	+ 56·91	+ 36·6
Cranemen	− 70·86	− 104·52	+ 49·5	+ 41·94	+ 1·69	− 20·67	+ 24·36	+ 16·85
Draughtsmen	+ 75·49	− 90·18	+ 11·95	+ 15·04	− 31·19	− 46·21	+ 44·91	+ 47·64
Electrical work	− 92·55	− 86·94	+ 15·94	+ 8·11	+ 2·11	+ 66·07	+ 12·22	− 2·23

Table 2.2

Gap between estimate and performance: material costs
(difference expressed as percentage of estimate:
better = +, worse = —)

Department	Ship			
	A	B	C	D
Steelwork	+ 8·55	+ 3·37	+ 10·09	+ 6·66
General smithwork	− 8·41	− 24·00	− 28·28	− 55·95
Loftwork	−43·40	+ 22·71	+ 8·85	+ 63·00
Joinerwork	+ 1·28	+ 4·89	− 15·77	+ 0·94
Plumberwork	−51·46	− 7·95	− 20·3	+ 1·29
Sheet-ironwork	−41·92	−106·16	− 96·64	−108·35
Paintwork	−16·21	−121·26	+ 3·69	−181·61
Riggers	+ 8·47	− 22·4	−188·75	+ 15·71
Electrical work	−51·67	+ 2·28	− 9·33	− 1·3

When the outcome of a contract can vary so substantially it is clear that companies can run into financial difficulties, and that financial reserves are of great importance. The factors which make estimating so inaccurate can now be summarized. The first is the fact that most ship orders are once for all, orders for large and intricate bespoke commodities which require an immense number and range of bought-in components. The second is that the estimate has to forecast eighteen months and more ahead. The third is that estimating techniques rely too much on historical data and that quantitative data on which more accurate forecasts could be built is rarely available. The fourth is that the shipbuilding process itself is difficult to predict accurately, partly because of component delivery difficulties, design and assembly difficulties, but also because of poor management control. A fifth is that estimating processes often have an intuitive element which encourages price cutting to meet competition. A sixth is that attempts to determine and analyse the cause of wide divergences between estimates and outcomes in specific sectors do not seem to be made as a regular part of a management learning-process. It is not possible to separate the issue of improved management in shipbuilding and improved estimating. More accurate estimating requires, for example, more work study data and better programming. The computer makes possible considerable improvements in the related processes of design, estimating and programme planning – but without the quantitative data which only work study can provide there would be serious gaps in any such computer-based approach.

The relationship between estimated cost and the achievement of target launch and delivery dates within a building programme is obviously a close one, with planning and management providing the link. Failure to keep to programme for one ship may push up the cost of another, probably delaying it and requiring the application of expensive 'remedial' labour. 'Every ship is the enemy of every other' was used by the general manager at Fairfields to describe a situation of this sort. It is doubtful whether with the most rigorous system of planning, closely integrated with the actual process of production, it would ever be possible to fulfil the building programme of a shipyard to a fine degree of accuracy for all of the time. When the estimating and planning processes are fairly unsophisticated, however, the unavoidable bottle-neck generates a whole series of consequential problems which could be avoided if a more sophisticated planning programme existed. Again, the use of a computer in association with a flexible network programme could iron out many of the self-imposed bottle-necks which shipyard managements have had to deal with, and at least reduce the extent of late delivery and the upward push of costs which such late delivery usually involves.

The breakdown of the costs in shipbuilding differs considerably between countries, shipyards and, of course, ships. Differences in labour costs between countries are as much the result of differences in man-hour productivity as of wage rates. Japanese labour costs are especially low as a result of both influences. There are also differences in materials prices between countries, differences in the price of steel being an especially important factor. Between yards in our country the main influences are the type of ship being built and shipyard efficiency.

A general idea of the broad breakdown of UK costs is given in Table 2.3 from Census of Production figures for 1954. These

Table 2.3

Breakdown of UK shipbuilding costs

	(1) 1954 all	(2) 1960 Large shipyards		(3) 1965–7 Specific vessels		
		Tankers	Dry-cargo vessels	Tankers	Bulk carriers	Naval vessels
Materials	55	71·0	72·6	60	66	36
Labour	35	20·8	19·9	26	27	40
Overheads and profits	10	8·2	7·5*	14	7	21

Sources: (1) Parkinson, op. cit., Table 20, p. 199.
(2) *Productivity in Shipbuilding,* The Shipbuilding Conference, 1962, Table VII, p. 62.
(3) Fairfields.
* 'Shipyard changes'.

are set alongside average figures from large shipyards in 1960, and examples for three different types of ship in the 1964–6 period.

The experience of British shipbuilding in recent years has been one of falling profits and under-recovery of overheads. Table 2.4 illustrates the profit situation. A similar picture of

Table 2.4

Profitability of shipbuilding and marine engineering, UK, 1958–64

	1958	1959	1960	1961	1962	1963	1964
Sales (£m)	496	466	422	427	432	382	372
Profit (£m)	32	30	22	21	12	10	9
Profitability	6·5	6·4	5·2	4·9	2·8	2·6	2·4

Source: *The Shipbuilding Industry,* survey produced for private circulation by Hoare & Co., in 1966.

depressed shipbuilding profits is given for 1963 when shipbuilding gross profits (before depreciation) were less than 4 per cent of the turnover, a performance bettered by all but one of twenty-eight British industries.* The under-recovery of overheads was commented on in the *Geddes Report* (Paper 108): 'Certainly British yards are not earning a sufficient surplus over current outgoings to meet capital costs on the scale required for an expanding and prosperous industry'. An attempt has been made to illustrate the real costs of shipbuilding by charging all overheads to a building programme. The heroic assumption of a one type vessel programme has been made, so that a crude supply curve may be produced and the effect of volume changes on average cost illustrated. The figures used are based on an analysis of experience in recent years and on estimates; the allocation of costs between categories is fairly accurate. No more is claimed for the following illustration in Table 2.5 than

Table 2.5

Shipyard costs of production: an illustrated example

Number of ships in building programme	0	1	2	3	4	5	6
Overheads:							
fixed (£m)	1·1	1·1	1·1	1·1	1·1	1·1	1·1
variable (£m)	0	0·25	0·5	0·75	1·0	1·25	1·5
Materials (£m)	0	1·3	2·6	3·9	5·2	6·5	7·8
Labour (£)	0	0·6	1·2	1·8	2·8	3·5	4·2
Total cost (£m)	1·1	3·25	5·4	7·55	10·1	12·35	14·6
Cost per ship (£m)	0	3·25	2·7	2·52	2·52	2·47	2·42

Notes: These figures are illustrative only. A building programme made up of one type of vessel has been assumed. It is not assumed that each vessel is identical, i.e. no 'learning' benefits are assumed. Similarly no purchasing economies of scale have been assumed in determining materials cost. A shift premium of one-sixth has been used to calculate the extra labour costs when more than three ships are completed in the year.

*D. C. Upton, 'Expanded provisional input-output tables for 1963', *Economic Trends,* No. 178, August 1968.

that it provides a crude estimate of an unrealistic situation. It will be noted that with three vessels being built the broad breakdown of costs is: labour 24 per cent; materials 52 per cent and overheads 24 per cent. The figure for overheads is substantially higher than that for overheads and profits illustrated in Table 2.2 and therefore than the contribution to overheads actually achieved. Such a figure is likely to become fairly representative of British yards as these adopt more 'management-intensive' methods.

Two other influences on costs should also be noted. The first is the very pronounced tendency for costs per dead weight ton to fall as the size of ship increases. The cost per ton of a 70,000 dead weight ton bulk carrier would be about 20 per cent below that of a 30,000 ton carrier, so that a ship of two and a quarter times the tonnage would cost only 60 per cent more than the smaller vessel. The second influence is that of the cost-reducing effect of multiple orders for closely similar ships. Some of this reduction is due to economies of scale, for example, on design and in the purchase of materials, whereas a further reduction is due to experience gained on the first ship helping to avoid snags and to develop a more efficient programme for the second ship. Spread over two or more ships the reduction in cost can be around 10 per cent on unsophisticated ships and 15 per cent or more on sophisticated vessels.

These cost figures throw considerable light on the problems facing the industry. The contribution which higher productivity could make to reducing costs and increasing competitiveness is obviously important but limited. If productivity per man-hour could be doubled without adding either to wage costs or overheads, total costs would fall by 12 per cent. It is obvious, and experience at Fairfields reinforces this, that both wage and overhead costs would rise, so that the reduction in total costs would be much less: a reduction of 5 per cent from this source would seem to be a realistic expectation. The existing differences in productivity per man-hour suggest that a halving of labour input would be possible, and both detailed work studies and activity sampling at Fairfields confirmed this. International comparisons are shown in Table 2.6. Comparisons* showing the comparative situation in UK yards for steelwork only for 1967 show man-hours per equivalent ton ranging from sixty to around 100, with an average of approximately eighty.

Table 2.6

Productivity in national shipbuilding industries
(man-hours per weighted steel ton)

	1960	1961	1962	1963	1964	1965	Average 1960–65
USA	221	157	124	124	202	220	164
Sweden	102	98	84	75	82	62	82
Japan	109	104	76	77	62	39	70
Germany	158	163	171	139	169	135	155
UK	218	206	223	151	180	140	187

Source: An Economic Analysis of U.S. Naval Shipbuilding Costs, by H. Williams *et al.*, Institute for Defense Analysis, Virginia, USA, 1966.

N.B. These figures refer to all shipbuilding, not merely naval shipbuilding. The productivity index covers all output. The weighting makes adjustments for the different types of vessel produced in each year in each country to allow for comparison.

The possibility of spreading overheads by increasing output through shiftworking has been suggested.† The cost structure illustrated above would suggest that there was little scope for cost reduction by such means. In Table 2.5 the normal building programme involving the completion of three vessels per annum has been extended by a further three as a result of double shifts. Wage costs have been adjusted upwards to take account of the shift premium which would be paid under such circumstances. The reduction in costs per ship is only £100,000, or 4 per cent, and this does not allow for the higher rate of depreciation which more intensive use of capital equipment would require. It

* Made and circulated privately by the British Shipbuilding Association.
† An attempt to introduce double-day-shift working at Fairfields was abandoned as a result of trade-union opposition, arising from fear of the precedent which would have been set on a matter of such major importance for all of the industry's employees.

would seem to be more promising to increase output in day-time shifts, thus spreading overheads without incurring the additional wage costs which shift work involves. A combination of increased productivity, more effective planning and above all a reduction of building time in the berth (partly by increased efficiency there, and partly by more pre-berth fabrication) could reduce costs by more than a straight switch to shift work. It may be that both policies should be adopted; certainly the additional reduction in costs of around 4 per cent which shift-working could contribute might make the crucial difference between viability and continued decline. At least it should be clear that by itself such a change could not bring about cost-reduction of the required magnitude.

Wages in UK shipbuilding are not high by international standards, as Table 2.7 illustrates. The problem is to increase

Table 2.7

International comparison of wage costs per hour
1965 (in deutschmarks)

USA	Sweden	Belgium	Denmark	Norway	Finland	France
15·62	8·83	6·87	6·795	6·665	5·83	5·79

Germany		Netherlands	UK	Italy	Japan	Malta
5·79		5·67	5·295	4·825	3·46	2·79

Source: Wages, Wage Costs and Purchasing Power in Shipbuilding, 1960–65, International Metalworkers' Federation, Geneva, 1967.

productivity per man-hour, not to depress or even stabilize wages. A wage system which can remove the very considerable 'slack' in British shipyard productivity can also yield higher wages, though the increase in productivity must exceed the increase in wages if a contribution is to be made to reducing costs.

Shipbuilding has been much cited as an example of over-manning, and the general view appears to be that this is primarily due to restrictive practices imposed by workers, in particular by rigidly drawn demarcation lines. Such restrictive practices have played a part in creating over-manning, but although it is not possible to quantify the various causes it is doubtful if restrictive practices have been the main cause. It is important to establish this point, as otherwise it may be too readily assumed that the erosion of restrictive practices now in progress in shipbuilding will remove the bulk of the over-manning problem.

Theoretical economists have treated the over-manning problem in terms of the concept of 'disguised unemployment',* and most people with experience of other industries who had an opportunity to make observations in British shipyards would not quarrel with the application of the term to that industry. A distinction must be made between the pace of work when the work is being done, and the proportion of the total working day which is spent doing work. It is in the second area that shipbuilding in Britain earns its reputation for over-manning. The description of disguised unemployment runs 'It is not that too much labour is being spent in the production process, but that too many labourers are spending it.'† This has to be expanded to read 'It is not that too much labour is being spent in the production process but that the time intervals between spending it are frequently too long.' These time intervals are frequently so long that if they could be reduced the effect on costs could be substantial enough to expand sales and thus keep in employment some at least of the labour who otherwise would have been displaced by the increased productivity per working day.

The causes other than restrictive practices which have produced over-manning are the fluctuating demand for shipbuilding labour in association with the generally high demand for scarce skills both from other shipyards and other industries, and the special importance of keeping to the programmed time-table for building ships. The importance of maintaining programmes, and particularly of meeting promised delivery dates, is especially

*See for example, Jacob Viner, 'Some reflections on the concept of disguised unemployment', *Contribuções a analise do desenvolvimento economico,* Rio de Janeiro, 1951.

† A. K. Sen, *The Choice of Techniques,* 1960.

important in shipbuilding. One reason for this is that the method of payment for a ship under construction is for a number of substantial instalments to be paid to the builder when distinct stages of the building are complete. Thus for a building programme to fall behind does not merely tie up fixed capital equipment and materials for longer and increase the probability that overheads will be under recovered, it can affect the cash flow forecast by substantially reducing the availability of cash until the stage of the programme at which the instalment does become payable is reached. This can create a willingness amongst shipyard boards to sanction the employment of additional men even when their addition to output is less than the cost of employing them. This action is economically motivated, although it does not fit the traditional view of economic theory as expressed by Jacob Viner:

> Unless one assumes non-economic motivation on the part of employers, there is difficulty also in conceiving why they should hire at any wage rate additional units of labour beyond the point at which they know the labour will add less in value to the product than the wage cost, to say nothing of the case where the labour will add nothing to and may even subtract from the product.*

This view takes no account of the possibility that marginal productivity may have a time dimension in which the product is measured against a scale other than the revenue to be derived from the additional units produced by the additional labour hired. Diagram 2.1 illustrates a shipbuilding case.

If employment is expanded beyond OL_1 men the marginal revenue product of the additional men employed (MRP_L) is less than the ruling wage rate (W_1). The necessity of achieving a given stage of the building programme by a certain date is taken into account by the addition of a scale showing the contribution to programme achievement made by having additional labour shown by the MCP-AL curve. A shipyard management will be motivated economically in expanding employment from OL_1 to OL_2 even although the contribution to revenue of the additional men employed is less than the wage bill incurred (by

* Viner, op. cit.

41

Diagram 2.1

Contribution to Programme-Achievement

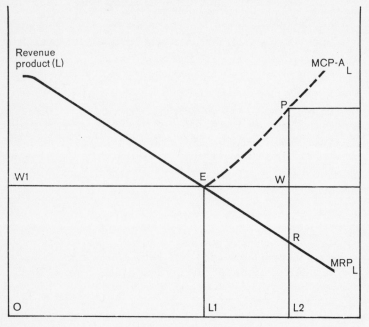

Labour input

E W R) because the advantages (liquidity, goodwill, survival) of meeting the programme by a given time are greater than the cost of having the additional men required to achieve this (by E W P). The ultimate effect on profits of the gain from programme achievement should be compared with the loss of revenue product, for example by assessing the additional interest charges which would have had to be borne if a cash instalment were postponed because of delayed programme achievement. If such a comparison is made, the economist's profit-making assumption would fit the behaviour of shipyard management, although this behaviour could not be explained in terms of the simple revenue or 'value product' model Viner was using. However, in many cases, because of the sense of

42

urgency which a decision associated with the time factor can have, or because a management may pay too much attention to the absolute size of the instalment payment and not enough to its cost in terms of interest, or because the matter is seen even more sharply in absolute terms – the difficulty of remaining liquid or the effect on future orders of a failure to achieve a programme – shipyard management will not make an accurate assessment of gains and losses. There will be cases where such behaviour is rational in economic terms even although it is not profit-making. This pressure for programme achievement and the associated sense of urgency it can introduce into the behaviour of shipyard managements has implications for industrial relations and particularly for shifts over time in relative bargaining power which will be considered in Chapter 8. The more strictly economic impact of these influences is to accentuate the tendency to over-manning in shipbuilding, by giving such over-manning a managerial rationale.

This link between efficiency of production planning, programme achievement and the degree of over-manning in shipyards provides one further illustration of the ramifications of production planning for the economic efficiency of a shipyard. This link suggests that if manpower utilization were integrated with production planning through a system of payment based on measurements derived from work study, the contribution to shipyard efficiency could be very considerable, and certainly much greater than the straightforward relationship between output and payment would, by itself, suggest.

The major recommendation made in the *Geddes Report* was that existing British shipyards be merged into larger groupings. The structure of British shipbuilding at the time of the Inquiry is shown in Table 2.8. The basis for the recommendation to merge rested quite substantially on a comparison between the share of total tonnage built by large groups in Japan, Germany and Sweden, and the much smaller share produced by large British companies. This evidence is reproduced in Table 2·8. Whereas in Britain there were forty-nine firms launching under

43

Table 2.8

Proportion of tonnage launched in shipbuilding countries by size of shipbuilding group
(Ships of 100 gross tons or more in 1964)

In groups of firms with annual launchings of gross tons	JAPAN		GERMANY		SWEDEN		UNITED KINGDOM	
	Gross tons (in thousands)	Percentage of total launchings	Gross tons (in thousands)	Percentage of total launchings	Gross tons (in thousands)	Percentage of total launchings	Gross tons (in thousands)	Percentage of total launchings
Over 750	1,576	38·6	—	—	—	—	—	—
250–750	1,336	32·7	—	—	720	70·5	—	—
100–249	508	12·4	458	51·5	230	22·5	440	42·2
Under 100	361	8·8	397	44·6	63	6·2	597	57·2
Unspecified yards*	304	7·5	35	3·9	8	0·8	6	0·6
Total	4,085	100	890	100	1,021	100	1,043	100

*Not individually recorded
Source: *Report of the Shipbuilding Inquiry Committee 1965–1966* (Appendix P).

100,000 GRT per annum and accounting for 57·5 per cent of total British output, in Japan and Sweden much smaller yards accounted for only 8·8 per cent and 6·2 per cent, respectively, of total launchings.* In addition to this argument the *Report* listed a large number of improved facilities required by British shipbuilding, and argued that 'in most cases it will not be practicable to make these resources available unless yards are grouped'.†

These resources and facilities can be classified into:

1. Improved managerial techniques, the provision of which would place too heavy a burden of overheads on small and medium sized companies (marketing, development, design and drawing offices, purchasing and progressing, production engineering and planning, personnel and safety and welfare services, training and re-training for all levels of employees, accounting including management accounting, organization and system-analysis including computer techniques).

2. Advantages of scale which could not be achieved by smaller yards even if it were possible for them to carry very heavy overhead charges (yard specialization without the attendant risks which such specialization involves for single yards; better balanced building programmes, helping to iron out the fluctuations in demand for labour of different trades; avoidance of inter-yard competition for labour; closer relationship between the costs of training programmes and the benefits to the company because a majority of shipbuilding employees on an estuary would become employees of one company).

The above classification of the expected benefits of grouping makes it clear that a substantial part of the benefits are secondary, in the sense that they do not derive directly from the act of

* *Geddes Report*, p. 89. An EEC Commission study of the shipbuilding industry made similar comparisons to the disadvantage of member countries. 'In the EEC about forty firms build ocean-going vessels compared with fifteen in Japan (of which nine account for 80 per cent of production) and six (96 per cent of production) in Sweden.' *Problems of the Shipbuilding Industry*, EEC, 1966.

† *Geddes Report*, p. 87.

grouping (as, for example, would elimination of duplicated facilities and the consequent reduction of overheads) but arise from managerial and other innovations which larger units make financially possible. The quality of management is crucial and the process of merger accentuates the need for improvement. A mediocre management will make a worse job of a large-scale enterprise than of a smaller scale one. The evidence suggesting that smaller British yards are more efficient than the larger ones* may be explained by management's incapacity to cope with the problems of scale. Although the *Geddes Report* did not stress the point there is no doubt that the Committee saw as one of the advantages of grouping a possibility of shedding or demoting some of the less capable amongst the top management of British shipyards, and bringing to the industry new managerial blood. Both the weak financial state of the industry and the powerful position within it of substantial shareholders exercising managerial authority suggested that government financial help and pressure would be necessary to bring about mergers, and this provided a means by which changes in management could be encouraged. The probable advantage of such changes can not be quantified, but the potential is certainly great. Several of the other changes recommended are also difficult to quantify, and this accentuates the case for encouraging grouping from outside the industry. There is an element of faith in the argument that the provision of better management will yield not only benefits substantially greater than its additional cost, but benefits great enough to reduce the unit costs of shipbuilding by 15–20 per cent, the reduction required to make the industry internationally competitive again. By way of illustration the possible impact of a merger of three medium-sized yards into a group employing around 8,000 is given in Table 2.9.

In addition to these reductions – the quantification of which is necessarily dependent on assumptions regarding the size and composition of total output – there could be a further saving in labour costs due to the elimination of inter-yard competition for labour, and leap-frogging induced by yard

* Parkinson, op. cit., p. 214.

Table 2.9

	Percentage reduction in total unit costs
1. Reduction in overheads due to elimination of duplicate facilities (purchasing: design and tendering: some physical facilities – e.g. joinery shops)	8·0
2. Reduction in cost of bought-in materials (improved efficiency and bargaining power)	2·0
3. Planning and industrial engineering:	
(a) Reduction due to improved planning and programme achievement	2·0
(b) Reduction due to increased productivity based on work study, after allowing for increased wage rate	6·0
4. Cost reduction stemming from more economical design and value engineering, in association with more effective liaison with customers	2·0
5. Improved manpower utilization due to larger unit, greater flexibility, and improved personnel policies	2·0
6. Reduced costs due to specialization and increase in building of two or more similar ships	2·0
	24·0

bargaining.* An additional benefit from grouping would show in higher prices rather than in lower costs, if grouping reduced the pressure of competition upon prices. It might seem that, because, after grouping, five or six major shipbuilding companies in

* The rapid shifts in the pattern of demand for labour in adjacent shipyards has made such competition and leap-frogging a particular preoccupation of shipbuilding employers: the task of the employers' organization in this situation is concerned 'not with protecting employers against trade unions, but often with protecting employers against themselves. The easiest thing in the world for any employer to do is to cave in to a situation in which he is under threat and thereby put all his fellow employers in a very difficult position, to filch labour by increasing wages, and so on'. Edward M. Taylor, MP (an ex-official of the Clyde Shipbuilders' Association), *Hansard*, Vol. 768, No. 156, Col. 1328, 16 July 1968.

Britain would remain to compete with each other and with foreign yards, the benefits from the mitigation of competition must be negligible, but this overlooks the effect that the elimination of the keenest and most desperate of tendering by marginal yards would have on the average level of prices tendered. If these additional benefits of merging are expressed as cost reductions an additional 2 per cent could be added to the 24 per cent giving a total reduction in cost of 26 per cent. There is a substantial element of faith in such calculations of cost reduction, and some estimates could be more and some less optimistic. A deduction has to be made for the increased costs of the improved services which grouping makes economic and which have contributed to the reductions in cost. Again, a range of estimates is possible; an addition to costs equivalent to 5 per cent of the unit cost of ships to be built by the group is a tenable assumption, bringing the final estimated effect of merger on unit costs to a reduction of 21 per cent.

The possibility of achieving such substantial benefits makes a very strong case for grouping, although it has to be noted that even with such cost reductions British shipyards would have found competition from Japanese and Swedish yards very keen in 1965–6. The position has somewhat improved in 1967–8 partly due to rising costs and full utilization of capacity in foreign yards,* partly to world demand (the closure of the Suez Canal played an important – and unpredictable – part in this), partly to improvements in British performance, but mainly to the devaluation of sterling. The margin on which to base long-run viability is clearly not a safe or comfortable one, however. Even after grouping and the introduction of new techniques the British shipbuilding industry is likely to remain in a keenly competitive situation and to be subject to continuing financial difficulties.

This prospect is complicated by additional transitional costs which arise from the merger process, and by the difficulty of estimating the time period for which these additional costs would be incurred, and the time required for all of the benefits

* Wages were rising by as much as 15 per cent per annum in Japan, and losses were being made on ships to be delivered in 1968 and 1969.

to become fully operational. The redeployment of management within a larger group usually raises costs for some months, while both newly recruited and existing managers settle in to new responsibilities. Securing mobility of labour between yards will be costly, both because of the effect of settling in to new routines on efficiency, and because a levelling-up of wage rates will be the necessary price of securing such mobility. In addition a new grouping would be likely to embark upon a programme of capital investment which would introduce new financial overheads and cause some temporary disruption, reducing efficiency and increasing costs.

The disturbances to production which can be caused by a merger complicate its attainment. The difficulties of estimating the value of work-in-progress in shipbuilding are compounded when changes in management and methods are introduced. There is attraction in the idea that such difficulties could be circumvented by letting the profits or losses on existing contracts lie with the original companies, the new company taking over the fixed assets and goodwill. Such an approach would mean that the separate managements and methods must be left until the existing order book is completed, and this is unlikely to be in less than two years and could be considerably longer. It would thus postpone the benefits of the merger as the price of bringing it about without major financial complications, and seems both undesirable and impracticable (in the sense that it is difficult to envisage any form of guarantee which could prevent disruption).

This survey of shipbuilding economics underlines the critical situation of the industry in Britain, a situation highlighted by the failure of the old Fairfield Shipbuilding and Engineering Company Ltd in November 1966. With costs high in relation to major competitors the British industry had failed even to maintain its level of output in a situation of rising world demand. Over-capacity and over-manning were related features, part cause and part result of the failure of the industry to compete. Modern methods of management were slow to percolate into the British industry. Indeed there was some positive resistance to them, buttressed by the belief that the nature of the

49

production environment and processes in shipbuilding would keep their effectiveness below their cost.

The labour market situation looked bleak. Workers were uncertain of their future in the industry. Shipbuilding was located in 'development areas' which increasingly provided alternative employment opportunities, so that wage rates were certain to rise as traditional sources of supply thinned out. The need to increase labour productivity was – and is – not just a reflection of the short-term weak competitive position of the industry, but also reflected the longer-run need to pay higher wages if an adequate labour supply was to be maintained.

The recipe recommended by Geddes could be reduced to three constituents: mergers to achieve economies of scale, a managerial revolution and an attempt to reconstruct the foundations on which the industry's bad industrial relations had grown up. The establishment of Fairfields (Glasgow) Ltd three months previously was based on a similar diagnosis. The attempt was to be made to see how far within one yard the second and third of these constituents could restore competitiveness and profitability. Ironically the third constituent – merger – was to cut short the attempt before the contribution of the other two to success could be fully established.

CHAPTER 3

Management: Reconstruction and Problems

THIS chapter discusses the adaptation of the management structure to meet the needs of the new company, and how this structure helped, through various committees and new techniques, to improve communications. The productivity services organization is examined and the work done by its departments described. An assessment is then made of management at Fairfields with particular reference to the problem of management morale.

The building of a new management team was the first priority of the company. The existing management had been a legacy from the previous company. It would take time to assess the abilities of these managers, and very largely a new team had to be developed around the existing management structure. A potential source of recruitment was the adjacent Fairfield-Rowan engine works which was being run down. Some managers were already leaving the works and Fairfields' general manager interviewed all the remaining managers and the technical staff, and recruited those he wanted. In some respects the misfortune of Fairfield-Rowan was beneficial to the new company as it allowed it to recruit some very able managers.

The new company recruited managers from many industries and from different parts of the country – it was seeking management ability rather than shipbuilding experience which it already had available. As the recruitment of managers continued, some of the problems of the company became obvious. There was a low morale among all managers and employees largely as a result of the traumatic events of October 1965. This low morale reflected itself in absenteeism figures and also in the level of yard productivity, particularly in steelwork which had been declining since July 1964 and was to continue the downward trend until the introduction of the estimated target payment scheme in June 1967. Because steelwork production largely determined the pace of work for the rest of the yard, management regarded the raising of productivity in the steelshed as a priority.

The task of raising productivity could not begin without a fact-finding investigation to reveal any weaknesses and suggest a policy to increase productivity. There was no absence of information about the company or its operations; but often the information was badly coordinated or not available in a convenient form. The management emphasized the need for quantitative thinking without which it would be difficult to make good decisions or formulate policy. The absence of monthly departmental budgets, proper capital expenditure authorization procedures, up-to-date stores records, etc. illustrated the *ad hoc* nature of the management only too common in shipyards. It would be unfair to assume that the Fairfields situation was untypical of other shipyards – company accounts and similar statistics indicate that this was not so. Shipbuilding is an industry with a significant amount of technical expertise but with limited professional management ability. The Fairfields experiment was probing the possibility of using new management skills and expertise to revive a yard whose problems were a microcosm of those of the industry.

The management were soon to identify the main problems and begin to implement changes. One of the problems was the inadequacy and indeterminacy of the existing company structure. The structure was not clearly defined and had a blurred system of management deputies. Diagram 3.1 illustrates the structure of the company at the time of the take-over in January 1966. The diagram is necessarily abbreviated because it was difficult to determine the lines of authority leading to the shipyard manager, who was responsible to the managing director for all manufacturing. The new management considered this structure to be unsound, and changed it to that shown in Diagram 3.2.

From this new organization structure developed the executive managers' committee (EMC) made up of all the executive managers. The convenor of shop stewards and two other stewards were invited to attend these meetings. A prepared agenda was discussed and the meetings usually included a

Diagram 3.1

Organization structure
Old company

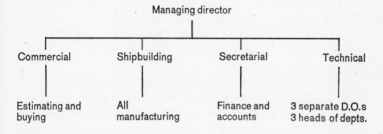

Managing director

Commercial	Shipbuilding	Secretarial	Technical
Estimating and buying	All manufacturing	Finance and accounts	3 separate D.O.s 3 heads of depts.

Beyond this level it is difficult to distinguish any further pattern.
Source: Information supplied by the productivity services department.

Diagram 3.2

Organization structure
New company June 1966

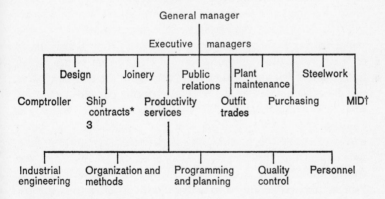

General manager

Executive | managers

Comptroller Design Ship contracts* 3 Joinery Productivity services Public relations Plant maintenance Outfit trades Steelwork Purchasing MID†

Industrial engineering Organization and methods Programming and planning Quality control Personnel

* Three ship contracts managers, one in charge of each ship during construction.

† Machinery installation department, formerly part of Fairfield-Rowan.

report from one of the managers on his department. In the discussion that followed and in all other matters, the shop stewards were equal in rights to all other members. This allowed them to extend their knowledge of company affairs and to inform their colleagues of wider issues which they would usually have little or no knowledge of. On some issues the shop stewards were asked to respect confidentiality of information, and this was done. Without ever compromising their positions and responsibilities as shop stewards these men played a useful role on this EMC.

The management were determined to improve communications with the workers. Before this could be done, it was necessary to ensure that management communications were good. Within three months of the company's formation, a week-end course on 'communications' was held for managers and foremen. The course was organized and conducted by the Industrial Society, with assistance from the company's senior managers. Most of the managers attending these courses were already working late two nights during a week and on Sundays, and they were not pleased to give up Friday evening, Saturday, and most of Sunday for the course. However, senior management was adamant that communications had to improve and these week-end courses certainly did emphasize this importance.

One side-effect of the emphasis on communications was that managers were constantly being reminded by their subordinates of their failure to communicate. To ensure that issues which management felt should be widely known in the company were rapidly disseminated to all levels, the 'briefing group' technique was used. The general manager would write a brief which was read to and discussed with senior management. The latter would continue this process with departmental managers, foremen and shop stewards. This chain of communication was speedy and effective, except when managers for reasons of work, time or negligence, failed to distribute the brief to their departments. When properly used, the briefing system allowed major announcements, e.g. regarding a contract, to reach all levels of the company within hours.

The briefing group procedure was important in a number of

ways. It provided the men with information which they were coming to regard as rightfully theirs. It also made them feel part of the company, which it was difficult to do when they obtained their information from public newspapers rather than within the company. This system was an important means of short-circuiting the 'grape-vine' which was largely responsible for the low morale of the foremen in the first year of the company. Often the foremen had been in the invidious position of having to ask a shop steward for information on what was happening in the company. Very properly, the foremen felt that this undermined his position vis-à-vis the men. The value of the briefing system is supported by a survey of foremen taken in August 1967 when 68 per cent of them considered that 'communications had improved during the last twelve months'.

Perhaps the most remarkable manifestation of the efforts made to improve communications at Fairfields were the mass meetings at the local Lyceum Cinema. On five occasions the yard's workers met at the cinema at 7.50 a.m. to hear a report from the chairman. These meetings were probably unique in industry, but it was felt by management that they had a duty to report to the workers taking part in the proving ground, on the state of the company. After the chairman's report, questions were invited from the workers. With such an audience it might have been expected that questions and contributions to discussions could have been influenced by political factors internal to the trade unions, and been of a demagogic character. In fact the contribution was almost all of a probing but constructive character, showing concern with the effects of yard practice on the viability of the company.

For example, at the meeting on 27 April 1966 management were asked their attitude to mergers in light of the publication of the *Geddes Report*. Another questioner wanted information on the company's prospects for future orders. These meetings provided an opportunity for the yard worker, as distinct from the shop steward, of questioning management. At the meeting of 11 November 1966, one questioner wanted to know why there were 'so many non-productive workers in the yard'. The build-up of the management team was a constant source of discussion among the men. One former shop steward described the build-up in the following way: 'at Fairfields – the Government, private enterprise, and trade-union financed yard – they were reaching the nil production stage. Yet the number of coloured hats, representing different departments meant that, at a launch when you look down on the heads, it looks like a tulip field, or some say a billiard table'.* The management were thus given the opportunity to explain their 'high overheads – low costs' philosophy to the yard workers. Similar questions were asked at all five cinema meetings. The coverage of these mass meetings is illustrated by that on 12 May 1967 which was attended by 83 per cent of those employees eligible to attend.

These meetings were important as a means of reporting progress and re-emphasizing the role of the proving ground. They were certainly not a cheap form of communications with an average of 2,000 workers being paid for approximately one and a half hours.

The shop stewards were unhappy about some aspects of communications in the yard, in particular they felt that the board were not kept in touch with yard opinion. This had been emphasized at the time of the N U G M W dispute. Arising from this the chairman met the shop stewards on 5 May 1967 to 'find out exactly what is going on'. He had arranged a meeting with all the yard workers at the local cinema and wanted, before addressing that meeting, to get a 'feel' of the yard situation. He had agreed to the shop stewards' request for a meeting from which the management was excluded. The stewards had insisted on this exclusion because they felt their presence would 'likely inhibit the free flow of discussion'.

The shop stewards recognized Sir Iain as the prime mover behind the proving ground concept. They had a great respect for him and a certain loyalty towards him as an individual. They felt that he should be in closer touch with yard opinion: 'There is a great need for a regular meeting between yourself and the shop stewards. You will get the truth from us: otherwise you will receive only the polished boardroom version'. As a result of this meeting the chairman was made aware of certain failures

* *Morning Star,* 27 November 1967, p. 7.

in communications in the yard, and he agreed to meet the shop stewards monthly.

This regular meeting with shop stewards never took place. The chairman had considerable commitments other than those at Fairfields, but more important he had to retain the distinction between the board and executive management.

My object was to try to establish a climate within which management can operate. I am not a manager. Managers were introduced to the company on the understanding that they would have freedom of operation. I cannot come closer to the yard without undermining management.

Despite the failure to hold the proposed meetings, the shop stewards succeeded in highlighting some major grievances, e.g. poor communications between the central joint council and the yard workers, which although not always directly the fault of management, had an effect on management-worker relationships.

The company was reorganized into four main production divisions. An interesting feature was the position of ship contract managers. These managers were in charge of a contract and had overall responsibility for all matters relating to the contract, including liaison with shipowners, and the coordination of building activities. In their work the ship contract managers were delegated with the 'authority' of the general manager to facilitate coordination of the building work. In practice, certain difficulties arose because of the broad-based structure of the new company. The ship contracts managers felt wary about managing another departmental manager's men – and there was no clear delineation of the authority to manage. Despite these weaknesses the innovation was particularly successful in developing closer relations with the shipowners and as a means of improving the coordination of building.

Unlike the previous company, the new management gave prime consideration to the monitoring of the company's progress. A financial comptroller of considerable experience was recruited, and given responsibility, amongst many other things, for the introduction of budgeting controls and management accounting which would provide considerable and essential information for management. Departmental budgets, prepared and monitored monthly, would help avoid some of the losses incurred by departments under the previous company. If careful budgeting itself could not prevent losses, it would at least ensure that any losses were investigated, which was not previously the case.

In addition to the introduction of budgeting controls, the comptroller was very much involved in the preparation of contract tenders. The process of preparing a tender or estimated building price for a shipowner is very much an inexact exercise. Much of the tender can be fairly accurately costed, but much also depends on the experience of the chief estimator and the general financial knowledge of the comptroller. The chief estimator was given a larger staff and more help from newly established departments such as programming and control.

The purchasing 'system' inherited from the old company was badly in need of reform. There appeared to be little formal control over purchasing and over twenty people placed orders with outside suppliers. Delivery dates were often unreliable, stock levels uncontrolled, and the service provided by suppliers was often indifferent. For a company buying-out approximately 60 per cent of its final product, this situation could not be allowed to continue. An experienced buyer was recruited from another industry, and he was given the task of reorganizing and coordinating the purchasing system, the stores, and introducing inventory controls.

The buyer set about re-organizing the stores – a not inconsiderable task considering much stock dated pre-1914. In addition to building stores and sub-stores, a materials control section began the job of introducing inventory controls. The centralization of records helped avoid wasteful duplication. The new methods provided stricter control of stock, allowed a better assessment of trends to be made thereby reducing inventory by 33 per cent of the former financial level. Further reductions in stock and therefore in money tied-up in the section were anticipated. Further cost savings will come from the computerization of stock.

The progress unit was responsible for the prompt delivery of orders to the yard – a previously neglected area. This unit developed close links with the central programming department and with production control to establish priority needs which could hold up production. The links with other departments, particularly quality control, enabled a close watch to be maintained on the standard and quality of material bought.

The buying department recorded considerable savings on their estimated contract prices. There is little doubt that this department made a substantial contribution to the reduction of costs and to the overall production process in the yard.

Undoubtedly the main departure from the previous company's structure was the introduction of the productivity services organization (PSO). The structure of this organization is illustrated in Diagram 3.3.

Productivity services included most of the usual departments found in management services organizations. The organization was given the title it carried to emphasize the importance of productivity to the company. The idea of the PSO and its initial development preceded the similar recommendations of the *Geddes Report* by some six weeks. The PSO was to spearhead the drive towards increasing productivity and among its main tasks was the need to stimulate and develop quantitative thinking in the company.

There was wide-spread scepticism in the yard among management and men regarding the feasibility of the techniques proposed for use in a shipyard. Most of the managers had not worked outside shipbuilding and many of them believed that a certain 'mystique' attached to shipbuilding. They did not consider that a shipyard could be successfully run by senior management who were not experienced in the industry. The new managers challenged this view. They felt that professional management could operate in any industry. Many of the managers coming to Fairfields regarded as part of the challenge of a proving ground the need to disprove the 'shipbuilder's myth'.

There is no doubt that the self-confidence of the new managers in their own abilities as professional managers, and their disregard for the traditions of the industry, was one source of

Diagram 3.3

Organigram: Productivity services

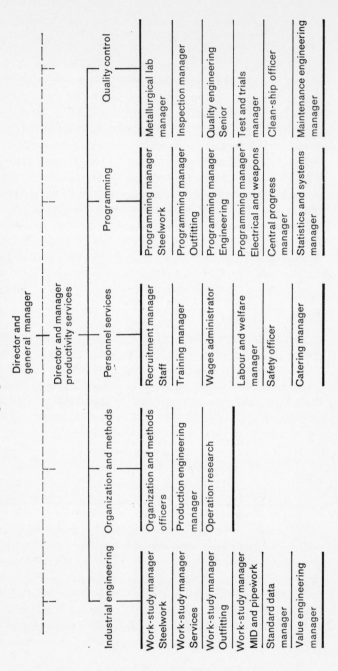

the animosity of management in other yards on the River to Fairfields. The constant publicity surrounding the yard and the condemnation of management in the industry – either directly or by implication – by Fairfields' protagonists further deteriorated relationships with other shipyards. As a proving ground, Fairfields became isolated within the industry. Rather than dispirit the new management, this increased their determination to succeed, and to pursue radical change as vigorously as possible.

Within the PSO the first department to be established was industrial engineering. The main work of this department centred on cost control, planning, estimating, measurement and the collection of work-study data. The development of this department has been described elsewhere* but its great importance in the overall policy of the company was the collection of data to begin a work-study-based incentive scheme. The management believed that the introduction of work-study techniques as a means of providing control and incentive would be directly beneficial to productivity. These proposals increased the scepticism among middle management and foremen, few of whom believed that work study had any relevance to shipbuilding.

This attitude towards work study was not based entirely on unfounded prejudice. Some two years before the formation of the new company an attempt had been made to introduce work study into the steel fabrication shed. The experiment ran about nine months before being abandoned as impractical by the former management. There were difficulties in applying standard data, and the workers were not kindly disposed to accepting time studies. The new management's proposals to introduce work study to all areas of the yard considerably increased the number of sceptics. The challenge was not only one of implementation, but also a larger one of education, of both management and workers.

A major part of the proving ground concept was the need to educate and alter opinion and attitudes about change in the yard. It was necessary to inform people before they would become

* See Chapter 10, on productivity.

involved in change. Informing the workers of the proposed changes and probable consequences was necessarily time-consuming. Much of this work devolved on to the industrial engineering department, primarily because it was responsible for the introduction of the measured daywork scheme. Work study, with its emotional overtones, had to be explained to and discussed with the workers, who had to agree to the making of time studies. The proposed revolution in shipyard work methods, although initiated by management, had to be sanctioned from below. Careful preparation was essential to ensure acceptance and application of the scheme.

Most of the data for the scheme and for other projects was collected by the industrial engineering department. This work was supplemented and complemented by the four other departments within the PSO. One of these departments was programme and control, responsible for the planning and allocation of labour resources in the yard and involved in coordinating all aspects of the building programme from preparation of tender to sea trials. The department had most of the modern programming techniques available, and made extensive use of network analysis. As a coordinating function, the department was responsible for the feed-back of information to line management. It occupied a key position in the shipbuilding process and was certainly one of the most important sources of information for all other sections of the company.

A section of this department carried out statistical analysis on data which allowed the build-up of records for future programming. This is specially important for meeting demands for tendering information – usually required relatively quickly. The records and statistics available allowed a picture of the forward-load of labour to be projected against known commitments or other restraints. This resource allocation exercise was done on the company's own computer, and was an invaluable source of management information.

The department also had considerable importance in the field of budgeting control. There are various progressive stages in breaking down the total labour allocation for a trade working on a contract. By checking that each stage of contract is not over-spent in terms of man-hours relative to the programmed time, a monitoring of performance will allow a check to be made against budget. There are difficulties of operating this system – not least the accurate recording of job times on job cards – but it has been developed and should prove to be a very useful management tool.

An important aspect of the changes prepared by management was the standardization of commercial systems. There was a wide range of commercial practice and documentation in use in the company, and this was reviewed and where necessary altered by the organization and methods department. This department was responsible for introducing the documentation supporting the measured daywork scheme. It was also involved in the preparation of teaching aids which were used to explain the plans and proposals of the company.

The department was also responsible for the provision of systems that feed information to management, and it also had a cost-control function. An example of this was a project under-taken in the drawing offices. This project was aimed at investigation of drawings and specifications to ensure that drawings gave all the information that was required, but nothing more. A common fault in the yard was for the workmen to provide more quality, or the draughtsmen more information, than was required – or paid for. In the drawing-office project, the organization team were concerned with this aspect of work, but were equally concerned with the communications between drawing office and production planning. These communications were not as reliable as they might have been, and investigation indicated several areas for improvement.

The quality control department was set up essentially as a cost-saving department. The new management could not afford to jeopardize the goodwill the company had acquired from some shipowners; quality considerations could not be neglected. On the other hand, the high cost of rectifying work and replacing defective parts had to be reduced. In some cases the company was losing money by providing workmanship at a quality higher than specified or required. There was a need for checking quality and adherence to work specification.

The hub of the quality control system was the central records office. All reports passed through this office. A quality control manual was drawn up to specify certain standards and procedures which had to be adhered to. A special system was designed to meet Admiralty standards. This particular system was a break-through for the company and was certainly the best and most comprehensive of its type in the industry. Much use was made of the radiographic facilities which the company expanded. This is a large section, and did a lot of work on materials testing.

Inspection of work for quality and specification was a new procedure for the yard. The workers had not been used to having their work scrutinized but soon became used to inspection. The inspection function was integrated with the manufacturing cycle to ensure that faulty work and uncompleted operations were detected early in the manufacturing process.

The fourth department within the PSO was the personnel department. The reasons for its inclusion, and the role of the department are examined elsewhere.*

The development of the PSO was continuous. A later development was a value engineering unit. This unit scrutinized components and materials to discover if there was a cheaper way of constructing the part. Value engineering usually produces quite substantial savings over the cost taken to set up the unit. At Fairfields the company offered shipowners an option of having a value engineering clause in their contract, the savings resulting from any suggestion being apportioned between company and owner, depending on who made the proposal.

The forms of controls and systems introduced to the yard were well known in industry – they were innovations only in the shipbuilding industry. What the company wanted to prove was that such techniques could be introduced to shipbuilding and successfully used to stimulate productivity and achieve cost savings. It is against this background that the Fairfields 'innovations' need to be assessed; without these innovations the infrastructure could not have been developed which gave rise to productivity gains.

* See Chapter 5, on labour relations.

Despite its success in creating a basis for future profitability, and its achievements in the field of human and labour relations, the company was characterized by continuing managerial dissension and disunity which considerably affected its performance. One of the main problems facing the senior management was that of the foremen.

In the early days of the company the management concentrated much of its efforts on getting the support of the workers for their proposed changes. Foremen were regarded as part of management and as such, were assumed to support the changes. This assumption, while understandable, was invalid. The foremen were dispirited, and had little idea of their own part in the proposed changes. They did not feel part of management, and when the workers' representatives were constantly being consulted by the senior managers, they felt that they were being ignored. Like many of the workers, foremen expected great changes under the new management and were disappointed when these were not immediate. Senior management reassured foremen about their status and their place in the company, but foremen wanted a more tangible form of recognition – increased salaries. Senior management had other priorities and resentment built up around this issue which affected the performance of the management function.

Foreman selection was arbitrary, and exhibited a degree of favouritism as well. Foremen were 'made-up' without any training. They were paid weekly and were paid for over-time working. Often they were paid less than the men they supervised, and this was not only a potent cause of discontent, but limited the number of good craftsmen who were prepared to accept foremanships. Their jobs were regarded in a narrow technical sense – they dealt with e.g. the solution of problems arising from work, the allocation and supervision of work, and the authorization of material requisition for their men. Their spans of supervision were irregular, but often involved supervision of thirty to seventy men – an impossible number to control, particularly on board ship. All these factors contributed to low foreman morale.

This situation could not be allowed to continue. The overall effectiveness of management policy depended on good first-line supervision. Senior management examined the foremen's pay structure, evolved a rational salary structure and established the foremen as monthly-paid, salaried employees.

The foremen were sent letters in January 1967 indicating the salary they would be paid. Unfortunately, the proposed increases had not been cleared with the Ministry of Labour. The letters intimating an increase were sent on a Friday and had to be revoked on the following Monday. The increases could not be paid until June 1967. This incident, arising from the good intentions of the company, obviously had a serious effect on the morale of foremen.

Some training was given to the foremen. All were given one week's full-time on work study appreciation. Extra courses were arranged at the training centre for selected foremen. A foreman selection procedure was adopted which eliminated the charge of favouritism which had tarnished previous appointments. By and large the company had to work through the foremen they had. Some appointments were made, but the overall quality of foremen was low. Basically the foremen at Fairfields were no better or no worse than those in other yards.* What made them appear incompetent was the nature of the demands made upon them.

For the first time the foremen were asked to regard their jobs in a wider sense. They were expected to pay close attention to lateness and absenteeism records, to work quality, and most important, to cost targets. Emphasis was placed on quantitative thinking and on the managerial aspect of their job, as they were assumed to possess the requisite technical knowledge. Many of the foremen were not able to meet this challenge. They had little knowledge of, and little liking for, the new methods. Work study and the ETPS imposed as much control on the foreman as it did on the worker. For the first time it became possible to monitor the performance of the foreman.

The foremen were essential to the successful implementation of the ETPS. But they required careful 'nursing' and some industrial engineers were seconded to production areas to assist

* See Appendix II, on foremen.

the foremen. To facilitate supervision, the senior management planned to reduce each foremen's 'span' to a team size of fifteen on a ship, and twenty-five in the shops.

Despite these improvements in salaries, training and the reduction in team sizes, foreman morale was a continuous problem. One major difficulty was the disunity of the foremen. The steelwork foremen had an unofficial committee which met irregularly. The other foremen had no similar meetings and could not express to senior management the corporate grievances and opinions of all the yard foremen. The foremen felt that they had only spasmodic and tenuous contact with senior management. To overcome this problem, a system of foremen representation was devised and introduced.

The foremen elected representatives from each department to a foremans' yard committee which met once a week. From this committee three foremen delegates were elected who together with the two senior managers formed the foremen's consultative committee which met once a month to discuss a prepared agenda. These committees could discuss issues affecting foremen generally; individual issues had to be referred upwards in accordance with the usual procedure. The system of foremen's representatives is seen in Diagram 3.4. These changes did lead to an improvement in foreman morale, but morale is a transient thing, and the morale of foremen was subject to wide fluctuations over quite short periods of time.

Low morale was also found in some areas of senior management. The publicity given to the yard and the claims made for it, had also conditioned the managers to the idea of, and necessity for change. From change improvements were expected, but these did not necessarily or immediately follow.

By February 1967 eight of the thirteen executive managers were worried about the future of the yard; they were pessimistic about the future and their morale was at a very low ebb. There were various reasons for this but broadly they could be grouped into factors affecting productivity and factors affecting general management in the company.

Productivity, particularly in the steelwork division, was of concern to all management. The increased payments to

67

Diagram 3.4

Foremen's representation

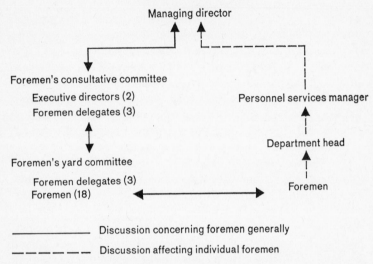

Managing director

Foremen's consultative committee

Executive directors (2)
Foremen delegates (3)

Personnel services manager

Department head

Foremen's yard committee

Foremen delegates (3)
Foremen (18)

Foremen

———————— Discussion concerning foremen generally

— — — — — — Discussion affecting individual foremen

steelworkers resulting from the ASB agreement of 2 June 1966 had seriously affected labour relations throughout the yard. Management needed to use the agreement to its fullest to obtain an increase in productivity. This they could not do.* They had incurred a substantial rise in costs without any immediate benefit. The general indices of production produced by the divisions were usually regarded by management as unreliable. Failure to increase productivity was as apparent to the men as to management. This fact, coupled with the foremen's attitude, produced a general air of despondency in the company towards the end of 1966 and in the early months of 1967.

Most executive managers were of the opinion that there had been little increase in productivity. One was concerned with ' ... the absence of any productivity – there are too many gimmicks and too little attention given to the problem of increasing productivity'. Another felt that 'the drive has gone out of the place'. Later evidence was to show that these opinions

* See Chapter 6, on labour relations.

were correct; since the beginning of the company steelwork productivity had fallen by February 1967 by 9·5 per cent. Although the failure to increase productivity was concerning most executive managers, others were equally worried about the way in which the company was being managed. The discontent about the management of the company stemmed from the organizational structure and from managerial personality.

The management structure was broad based, with the general manager assuming responsibility for production. The number of executive managers reporting to the general manager was excessive. There was no screening of access or information. He became too closely involved in the minutiae of daily operations, and this placed limitations on the time available for formulating policy. The number reporting to him made access difficult and often important and urgent matters were delayed.

There was a gulf between the two executive directors on the one hand, and the majority of executive managers on the other. Some executive managers felt that they were not given sufficient opportunity to discuss important aspects of company policy – 'there is an absence of opportunity for open discussion on relevant aspects of company policy such as finance and productivity'. The phrase 'relevant aspects' was significant. The critics believed that all important aspects of company policy were decided exclusively by the executive directors. One executive manager put his grievance succinctly – 'there is not enough time given at the executive managers committee to real issues – too much time is spent on peripheral matters'. Other managers felt that the presence of shop stewards at these meetings inhibited free discussion. The situation was summed up by a manager who said that there was 'a growing lack of faith in the company'.

Although some of these problems were closely associated with the structure of the company, others were more attributable to the rapid development which took place in the company, and to managerial personality.

That senior managers were prepared to talk among themselves about these matters was cause for concern. The tremendous pressure on senior management in the first twelve months had put managerial communications under strain and the executive managers were not as well informed on certain matters as they should have been. The difference in status and ability between the executive directors on the one hand and most of the executive managers on the other accentuated the problem.

These difficulties were compounded by the extent to which the company was caught in the full glare of publicity. In some cases the chairman and the executive directors had made pronouncements about the company's success, e.g. on productivity increases, which had the effect of inhibiting frankness and creating cynicism within the yard. Some executive managers felt that to express doubts would be to contradict what the chairman and executive directors had publicly committed themselves to – 'I don't want to be the first to rock the boat.' Thus frankness became disloyalty in the minds of some managers, and this inhibited the flow of fact and opinion to top management. A siege mentality had developed which forced discontent to remain as a discussion point among executive management groups, rather than be aired in free debate.

In their attitudes the managers crystallized into three main groups. Firstly there was a group of managers who were closely identified with the previous company. This group of 'traditionalists' were sceptical of much of the change introduced to the yard, and believed that somewhere in the top strata of management there should be a person with a sound knowledge and experience of the shipbuilding industry. This group believed that top management failed to understand fully much of the information given to them. They felt that much of their work was being frustrated by lack of understanding by top management. They complained of the difficulty in obtaining decisions, particularly when these affected important and urgent matters relating to ship contracts and similar issues.

In the second group were largely new managers in the company who lacked confidence in the executive directors, and had little personal liking for them. At the top level of management, schisms had been evident for the six months before February 1967. For a number of reasons, not least being the failure of the executive directors to involve more executive managers in the policy-making of the company, relationships began to deteriorate. This deterioration was exacerbated by personality clashes.

Thus the first two management 'groups' were similar in having a lack of confidence in top management, and a common dislike of the persons involved. The third group of managers were largely new recruits and had a very close personal allegiance to the productivity services director, a man with a very strong personality capable of inspiring enduring allegiance in some managers and dislike in others. The nature of the PSO function caused upset to many line managers. As a spearhead for the productivity drive, it was unpopular in some areas of the company.

The disunity among management posed a serious threat to the future of the company. On 28 February 1967 the general manager convened a meeting of his executive managers to discuss the situation.

The general manager dealt with the problems as he saw them. He defended his chosen organization structure and clarified the position of the PSO vis-à-vis line management. On productivity he felt that the 'imperfect indices available tended to show an upward trend. Steelwork remained a problem because management seriously under-estimated the job to be done – particularly with the welders. Over 75 per cent of the welders failed to reach a commercial standard on trade tests. The best Dutch yards were able to get 98 per cent of the welding past Admiralty standards first time; the best figure for our welders is 20 per cent'. He then pointed out that he expected constructive criticisms from his managers – which he had not received – and spoke of his own shortcomings in relation to communications.

The meeting should have developed into an open discussion which might have resolved some of the outstanding problems. No open discussion took place for during the course of his talk the general manager had said that 'this meeting is basically concerned with loyalty – to me, the board, and to the company'. The mention of disloyalty was sufficient to inhibit free discussion. New restrictions on passing information to non-executive directors of the company (without first being cleared by the general manager) hardened attitudes, and effectively nullified the general manager's appeal to his managers for candour. The groups went to ground again.

As in most companies there was a formal as well as informal chain of communications. Because of the origins and short history of Fairfields there were close ties between individual managers and individual board members which would not normally be found in long established companies. This meant that information about the operations of the company passed to board members without always passing through the general manager's office. This increased management tensions.

One factor which increased tensions among management was the growing importance and influence of the PSO in the yard. Although never formally designated as such, the PSO director, by reason of his seat on the board, was to all intents and purposes recognized in the yard as being deputy to the general manager. This situation bestowed an authority on the PSO which a service division does not usually possess. The movement of some PSO personnel into senior line management jobs further created an image of a company within a company. It was not unnatural that the PSO should eventually supply some line managers. The appointments reflected the abilities of the men concerned. But it increased the suspicions of those managers who believed a 'jobs for the boys' policy operated against those managers associated with the old company.

The situation in the spring of 1967 was uneasy. Some of the criticisms had registered. On 20 April 1967 the company structure was reorganized with the appointment of a production director who took much of the responsibility and burden from the general manager. The new organization is shown in Diagram 3.5. A new company, Fairfields (Glasgow) Management Ltd was formed. It was a nominal Company composed of the two executive directors and the production director, purchasing director and comptroller. These five men formed the executive directors' committee and met, on average, three times weekly. It was anticipated that this committee would, subject to the dictates of the main company board, decide executive policy.

In theory the concept of a management company was work-

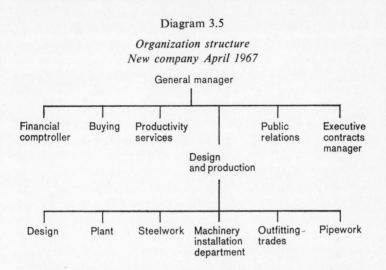

Diagram 3.5

Organization structure
New company April 1967

able. Discussions were certainly more worthwhile than they ever had been in the executive managers' committee. Various aspects of planning, e.g. manpower and recruitment, tendering strategy, were discussed. As a forum for discussion it was an improvement on what had previously existed, but one of the participants described it as 'a fake – a device to elevate our status while safeguarding the powers of the original executive directors'. This committee had no regular direct contact with the main board of the company where overall policy was decided. The schisms in top management had gone too far, little confidence or trust remained. Even at this level complaints were voiced about failure to communicate instructions and decisions.

It was during the months of June–July 1967 that the possibilities of mergers on the Clyde were discussed. Within the company, top management made clear to the employees that a merger would only take place if the Fairfields management with its skills and expertise were to predominate. Discussions with two other yards broke down. By late August 1967 the probabilities of broader merger, in line with the *Geddes Report* seemed strong, affecting the attitudes of everyone in the yard, management and men.

73

The new management, particularly the group associated with the P S O, reiterated their belief in the progress made by Fairfields and felt that the yard should be allowed to continue as a proving ground. This sentiment was strongly supported by the workers. On the other hand, if the yard could not continue alone, then the Fairfields management, by reason of their achievements, should be predominant in any group.

The two other groups viewed the possibility of a merger in different ways. The 'traditionalists' wanted shipbuilding experience at the highest levels of management. The other group believed in the inevitability of a merger, and also held the opinion that many of the claims made by Fairfields would be found to be insupportable. They thought that the traditional shipbuilding interests on the Clyde would effectively block the ambitions of the Fairfield management. Divisions within management were now greater than ever; in particular, relationships at the highest level were strained. The possible implications of the merger exacerbated these tensions; everyone was trying to secure his own position.

By October 1967 it had become too late for the general manager to control the dissension. One senior manager described the situation as one of 'managerial anarchy'. The shadow of the merger and the committees which the Clyde shipbuilders were organizing as a prelude to the formal merger, began to stem the initiative and dull the incentive of the proving ground. Although the management occasionally reiterated their positions on merger and their conditions for participation, the inevitability of merger was there for all to see. On 7 February 1968 the merger formally took place.

Thus the path of management within Fairfields was not smooth. There was always debate and usually conflict. It would not have been a proving ground without it. One cause of debate was undoubtedly the broad-based management structure which was not amended until May 1967. Because of the structure, the general manager was too concerned with trivia. This concern with detail certainly curtailed the amount of time devoted to important issues, and caused a good deal of discontent among subordinate management. A 'screening' process was required to separate the superfluous from the essential. This situation, together with a failure to delegate work, was a potent source of strain.

The proliferation of committees did not assist management. Most of the participants would have spent their time better elsewhere, a fact readily appreciated by most managers. A hierarchical management structure was required to facilitate delegation of work. It was not until the production director was appointed in April 1967 that shipbuilding experience was again represented at the higher levels of the company. There is no 'mystique' attached to shipbuilding – but experience of an industry is a valuable asset to management. In Fairfields the deployment of this special knowledge should have come sooner than it did.

The position of the PSO was a curious one. Certainly it was essential to the proving ground. Without doubt it made a great contribution towards the improvements in the company's fortunes and towards the establishment of quantitative thinking. At the time of the merger it employed 218 people – a very high number for a relatively small company. Because of its development role in the company it provided opportunities for the company's own work people. Despite its weaknesses, it was essential for the company's progress.

The problems of Fairfields were made sharper by the personalities of those most closely involved. The great deal of publicity surrounding the yard seemed, occasionally, to seduce some managers from the realities of the situation. The two executive directors had very different temperaments, and this was to cause a growing strain in their relationship. Their ranges of abilities differed quite considerably, but instead of proving complementary and thus strengthening the top management duo, the differences proved incompatible. If a merger had not taken place this situation would have had to be resolved by the board.

Despite the setbacks and management problems, a tremendous amount of good work was done in the two years of the company's existence. In many ways it was run as an open laboratory, with visitors and experts alike being given freedom to observe, question and discuss. The first and outstanding achievement was to survive. In the early months of the company this seemed improbable and the certainty of survival was never assured until the merger was complete. Real progress was made towards attaining profitability. The merger removed the time necessary to consolidate the gains achieved and to put right the mistakes and breaches which the pace of change had revealed.

CHAPTER 4

Decision-taking at Board Level

AN assessment of the Fairfields board must begin with an analysis of the company's function, in as much as this differed from that of most other companies. The concept of an 'advisory board' will be discussed, together with the bearing this concept had in determining the distinctive composition, character and working methods of the Fairfields board. The role of the directors nominated by government and trade unions will be examined. The extent to which the board functioned effectively as a policy-maker and check upon executive management will be examined in relation to the main areas in which it had impact: finance, orders, programmes and delivery dates, labour, new methods and merger negotiations.

Although in practice the Fairfields board came to see its prime objective as commercial viability and profitability in the shortest possible time, this was never unambiguously declared to be so. The shift in emphasis from 'profits in five years' to 'profits as quickly as possible' was not consciously willed, but arose indirectly out of the very tight liquidity position from which the company suffered for most of its life and which was recognized within a few months of the take-over. The non-availability of funds made it clear that failure to break even within two years and to make profits in the third could involve extinction. There is no reason to expect the costs of experiment-ation in management methods and industrial relations to be lower and to spread over a shorter period than the costs of research and development in science and technology. It would seem likely that the unprofitable period of gestation would in fact be longer. Yet at Fairfields the board eventually saw the logic of the company's cash position and of the criteria which were being used in pre-merger discussions and bargaining as imposing upon it a drastically foreshortened time-scale for achieving profitability. There is an obvious conflict between achieving profits in as short a period as possible and the notion of running a company as a proving ground.

This foreshortening of time-scale was made easier by the fact that the elements and aims of the 'experiment' had never been precisely set out, either publicly or internally within the company. Indeed, different directors and managers attached different meanings to the concept of 'experiment' and 'proving ground'. Had the objectives of the experiment been on record in clear-cut terms, conflicts between one or more of them and the speedier achievement of profits would have arisen. Even then, however, the conflict probably would have been resolved in favour of the profitability aim, as for the great part of the company's life the imminence of merger strongly affected policy discussions. Another factor which would have favoured short-term profits over 'the experiment' was that there was general agreement that profitability must eventually be achieved; in fact it would probably be correct to regard profitability as the one agreed common aim to be achieved in the proving ground: what was in question was the length of time within which profits were to be made.

The concept of the proving ground began with the chairman, Sir Iain Stewart. Reference to his speeches, lectures, articles and pamphlets both prior to and during the lifetime of the new Fairfields suggests that he saw it as having the following aims: the improvement of industrial relations by the provision of high and stable earnings, these to be achieved by a combination of modern management techniques, better utilization of labour, manpower planning, a retraining revolution, the erosion of restrictive practices and the voluntary abandonment of the strike-weapon. He was also frank enough to admit publicly that he saw Fairfields as a platform from which to campaign for the expansion of retraining facilities (including guaranteed earnings) by the government. The chairman also attached great importance to communications, as is evidenced by the mass-meeting at the local Lyceum Cinema at which he addressed all of the 2,500–3,000 employees. His desire for an effective channel of communications led to a detailed exploration of the possibilities of installing closed circuit television in the yard. No installation was made, partly because there were reservations about the desirability of a one-way system of communication, and partly for financial reasons. The general manager was also a strong advocate of good communications, emphasizing the importance of two-way communication and of employees' participation in the decision-taking process, and his ideas had considerable influence in establishing the public image of the proving ground. The two directors with trade-union backgrounds favoured this approach, while on the other hand expressing some doubts about the likelihood of the no-strike pledge being fully implemented, and of the dissolution of restrictive attitudes and practices being accomplished quickly. One director saw the no-strike pledge as the central, perhaps even the exclusive, element in the proving ground. This diversity of emphasis partly explains why no unambiguous statement of the aims of the proving ground was ever made, and it also helped remove the possibility of a head-on clash between proving-ground aims and the pressure for short-run profitability.

With the pressures of illiquidity and of impending merger forcing the company to emphasize profitability as a short-run aim opportunities for far-reaching industrial and managerial experiments were missed, particularly in the field of employee-participation and 'single-channel' collective bargaining cum consultation, for which the isolation of the yard from the rest of the industry made it an ideal laboratory. The pressures did not come from shareholders (private, government and trade union) insisting on financial orthodoxy. All of the shareholders had put their money into an experiment knowingly, and most if not all were more interested in the outcome of the experiment than in the outcome of their investment. It was the pressure of financial circumstances and, more important, the combination of local attitudes, and the merger situation created first by the *Geddes Report* and the ensuing Shipbuilding Industry Act which narrowed the board's room for manoeuvre and limited the range of experiment carried out in the yard. What was done was noteworthy enough, and is covered in other chapters. Nevertheless, it fell short of the expectations generated by Mr George Brown's statement to the House, the early speeches of the chairman and the pledge of the employees, and the very extensive newspaper coverage of the new company's establishment.

Financial survival overshadowed all other aims of the company, but this preoccupation did not block the costly build-up of specialist management services, or prevent other expenditures which were believed necessary for commercial success. The board's aim was to carry through these significant though limited changes in management and industrial relations, yet at the same time to strengthen the company commercially, with emphasis on the second if the first appeared likely to threaten it. Thus the board's aim differed very little from that of many companies going through a period of rapid managerial change and upheaval.

The composition of the board stemmed partly from the chairman's support for the concept of an advisory board and partly from the unusual sources of capital tapped by the company. Originally the chairman's intentions had been that only one executive manager would serve on the board – the general manager. The purity of this intended structure was quickly modified as the price of recruiting the executive manager in charge of productivity services, and in effect the second-in-command. The effect of this on managerial structure is discussed in another chapter. Its effect on the board was to give the non-executive directors access to a wider and fuller range of information. A major defect of the non-executive board is that it dangerously narrows the channels of information available to it, unless great care is taken to provide regular contact between it and at least the top echelon of executive managers. The Fairfields board partly met this difficulty by hearing reports from individual executive managers on the evening before board meetings. A more effective contact could have been maintained through regular meetings between the non-executive directors and the board of Fairfields (Management) Ltd, but such meetings did not take place.

The original board was made up as follows: chairman, Iain Stewart, an industrialist of great experience serving on around eighteen other boards; E. O. T. Blanford (general manager) –

a professional manager (ex-consultant with one of the 'big four') with wide managerial experience including management of a shipbuilding machine shop, although not at the level of managing director; J. D. Houston (productivity services manager) with considerable experience in light engineering and electronics; J. M. Lenaghan, managing director of the previous Fairfields shipyard, who resigned after a few months; D. J. Palmar, merchant banker, with industrial experience and at that time serving as industrial advisor at the Department of Economic Affairs – appointed by the government to the board; K. J. W. Alexander, academic economist. This board was obviously open to the charge of inexperience in shipbuilding. Partly to meet this and partly in the hope of overcoming the very strong local antagonism to the new company amongst other Clydeside shipbuilders two prominent members of established shipbuilding families were invited to join the board. Both declined, as did a member of a shipowning family who was also invited to join.

The investing trade unions took some months to select their nominee for the board – Andrew Cunningham, the regional officer of the National Union of General and Municipal Workers in the north-east of England, with much experience of labour problems and negotiations in shipbuilding. Two other representatives of shareholders joined the board. First, Hugh C. Stenhouse, a Scottish financier and insurance broker with wide company experience gained through management of a holding company, and second Sir William (later Lord) Carron, at that time general president of the Amalgamated Engineering Union and a director of the bank of England. Because the AEU (now AEFU) was one of the investing unions there was some public confusion about his position on the board; in fact, he was the nominee of a substantial private shareholder and not of his union. A further appointment – that of Jack (later Sir Jack) Scamp – completed the board, bringing to it quite exceptional knowledge and experience of labour management in large-scale industry and conciliation and mediation in industrial disputes.

At full strength, therefore, the board numbered nine. After the resignation of James Lenaghan not one of these nine had previous board experience in a shipbuilding company. This was a weakness, but not a very serious one. The notion that shipbuilding is unique, distinctive, an industrial world on its own, was not born out. The specialist background of board members overlapped somewhat. Main interests were general management (three), financial management (two), labour and industrial relations (three), industrial economics (one). In addition board members had secondary background experience, mainly in general management, engineering and industrial relations. The spread of specialisms was probably rather narrow and out of balance. Marketing certainly ought to have been there; this was recognized but no satisfactory appointment could be made. Engineering and production might appear to be a weakness, but expertise in general management compensated for that. Expertise in labour and industrial relations was heavily represented, but as this was a major area of activity and change in the company which held a substantial place on board agendas, this representation was not seriously out of proportion.*

The chairman's commitment to the part-time, non-executive board concerned with policy making had produced a board heavily weighted against the full-time executives, with the consequence that executive power in the company was firmly concentrated in two pairs of hands. This was resented by some other executive managers, not only on personal grounds but because the uneven distribution of discretionary power at the top level of executive management created bottle-necks in the decision-taking and command processes, which at times created frustration and reduced efficiency. A shipyard is a complex industrial process, and its operations cannot be reduced to routine. Of all industrial processes shipbuilding is the one least suited to control by a simple authority structure with discretionary powers concentrated in a few hands at the top. The Fairfields board was aware that the management structure was not well matched to its complex functions, but did not change it radically. The reasons for this were threefold: first, the concentration of

---

* In the importance it placed on evolving personnel policies for the company, the approach of the Fairfields board can be compared with that advocated for boards by the Royal Commission on Trade Unions.

executive power stemmed directly from the composition of the board; secondly, it was believed that during the period of rapid change and transition power should be concentrated, particularly while the new top management was making its estimate of the managers it had taken over from the old company; and thirdly, it was believed that the over centralized control structure would be compensated for to some extent by a free and frequent communication process amongst managers. By the time that the force of these arguments had weakened, the board did not feel inclined to push through a fundamental review of its top management structure, mainly because by then the prospect of merger looked strong. Had the company been continuing independently the case for a shift towards a less mechanistic and more organic structure, capable of managing the complex ship-building process, would almost certainly have been accepted.

A feature of the Fairfields board which affected its working was that its members were men of considerable standing in other spheres of life, well used to having their say and, frequently, getting their way. It was not a board of 'yes men' – or even of 'maybe if men'. The possibility of sharp clashes, both of opinion and of personality, was heightened by the very different backgrounds of directors and the prejudices they brought to the board room from those backgrounds. A board on which sat a member of the National Executive Committee of the Labour Party, a TUC general councillor, the treasurer of the Conservative and Unionist Party in Scotland, and another who frequently boasted he was 'so far to the right I'm off the edge' was likely to require careful handling.

If to this personality situation is added the crisis atmosphere in which the company functioned the crucial role of the chairman can be seen. Whether by design or by inclination the approach of the chairman was very well suited to these characteristics of the board. There was no attempt to pre-judge issues, to use the board as a rubber stamp or to rush decisions. Frequently the atmosphere was more that of a seminar than of a decision-taking body, yet decisions were taken which usually reflected the general view of the board after such free-ranging and sometimes very heated discussions.

For the first few months the board met fortnightly and thereafter monthly, meetings generally lasting for around three and a half hours. On the evening before each board meeting, there was an informal meeting at which broad policy issues were aired, and usually, a report from an executive manager discussed. Thus the board devoted around six to six and a half hours per month to running the company. In addition, of course, the chairman and some individual members of the board spend considerable time on company affairs. An advisory board which is to do more than offer the most general advice and be more than a rubber stamp must spend considerable time – both as a board and as individuals – on company affairs. The one weakness which arose out of the character of the board and its way of working was that issues tended to be seen rather too broadly. This is almost certainly a feature of advisory boards but Fairfields' experience probably accentuated the tendency. Not that this was accidental; it was very much the philosophy of the chairman that the general manager be left free to run the yard. Nevertheless it does seem – in retrospect at least – that there was a tendency to paint the wide canvas somewhat at the expense of the vital detail.

The role of the directors nominated by government and the investing unions deserves special mention. There was a general insistence that 'all directors are equal' and for most of the time and on most issues this was so. There was fairly general agreement that it was not the job of Fairfields to anticipate government wishes just because the government had a 50 per cent shareholding and had provided loan capital. For example, on 'incomes policy' there was no pressure exercised to make the company behave in accord with government policy any more than an entirely private enterprise company would have done.

The greatest single difficulty with the government director arose out of his responsibility to report regularly to the Ministry of Technology on the progress of the company. There was a very strong feeling that his written report ought to be made available to the rest of the board. On the other hand there was a realistic recognition that such a procedure might simply produce additional 'secret' reports, although perhaps only of a verbal nature. It seemed to be tacitly recognized that a shareholder owning 50 per cent of the stock would under any circumstances expect to be kept regularly informed about company progress, and that this was even more understandable when the money invested was 'public'. No clear resolution of this difference of opinion was made, and no report of the government director was ever circulated – either before or after submission to the Ministry. This issue apart, however, the government director did not exercise special powers or claim special responsibilities.

The trade-union director made his main contribution to the work of the board in the field of labour relations, but not by advocating 'soft' labour policies. On occasion he was able to assure the executive directors that their plans were compatible with trade-union thinking and that certain local opposition was unrepresentative and probably transitory. Both he and Lord Carron helped evolve company policies (e.g. on working practices, redundancies, and wage differentials) which had at least a chance of making their way through the labyrinthine tangle of shipbuilding trades-unionism. The presence of trade-union directors enabled the executive directors to take soundings on trade-union attitudes which prevented the presentation of policies which would have been rebuffed or proved unworkable in practice. What was remarkable was that neither the workers in the yard nor their stewards sought to bring pressure on these trade-union leaders who were influential in the company's councils. One might have expected lobbying when the board met at the yard, but nothing of the sort took place. It would be wrong to believe that the presence of these trade-union leaders on the board gave the workers at Fairfields any sense of 'participation' at the top, and this was never suggested as a reason for their presence. But it did create a certain confidence that the top management had nothing 'up their sleeves' which could be seriously damaging to the interests of the workpeople. That top trade unionists were privy to the key papers and influenced company policy made some contribution to the general atmosphere of security and cooperation which infused industrial relations at Fairfields most of the time. That such confidence was not misplaced may be judged both from the conditions of employment in the yard and from the attitude of the trade-union directors themselves. Their attitude was certainly one of concern that no situation should arise which could be held to be a breach of the best possible employment practice and thus provide legitimate grounds for criticism of their participation in the management of the company. By way of illustration one of the trade-union directors made it very clear to the chairman that if he thought the Fairfields board was taking a decision which would be to the disadvantage of his members he would inform the chairman of his intention and then make a public statement of his reason for resigning.

The role of the academic director also deserves brief mention. As has been explained in the introduction his place on the board arose out of the chairman's wish that the proving ground be studied and written-up. Board status was accorded to ensure complete access to all papers and personnel, but was not limited to this. The academic director played a full part in the work of the board, also functioning in extra-boardroom capacities, e.g. as chairman of the company team in the first round of merger negotiations, as chairman of a joint trade-union and management working party on job evaluation and as a management representative on the Scottish Conference which decided upon issues in dispute between employees and the company. At board meetings he was very much and very openly 'a chiel amang them, takin' notes', but this was never the cause either of inhibition or of pleas for 'off the record' status for particular items or statements. The chairman claimed that the knowledge that behaviour of management and employees at Fairfields was open to scrutiny and eventual public display provided a certain discipline. At board level this was probably so, though only to a very limited extent and as far as broad policy issues were concerned. But on more immediate questions and above all on questions involving personalities there was no sign of window dressing. At times the limits of frank and brutal personal and policy conflict were reached, quite unaffected by the scrape of at least one director's pen.

In exercising its control over the company's finances a major difficulty for the board arose from the fact that the company had taken over work-in-progress from its predecessor. The difficulties of assessing work-in-progress are discussed in Chapter 2. The attempt to estimate the value of the work-in-progress in the hectic atmosphere of pressure and negotiation which preceded the establishment of Fairfields (Glasgow) Ltd faced many more difficulties than the usual extremely complicated task of estimating work-in-progress in shipbuilding. On the basis of this estimate a payment was made to the receiver on the assumption that a given volume of work was completed and therefore a given volume remained to be completed. The cash flow of the company depended upon the correctness of this estimate, which determined both the likely calls upon cash to complete contracts and the probable timing of instalment payments. Within three months it was obvious that the estimates of the state of the building programme taken over had been over-optimistic. It is, of course, possible that some part of the short fall in completion stages was due to poor performance by the new company. In Chapter 10 we discuss the difficulties and disappointments in the area of productivity during this period, difficulties encountered not only at Govan but fairly universally throughout the industry. However, the speed with which the new management had to report to the board that the ruling programmes must be extended and the evidence they presented at this time, and in succeeding months, indicated quite clearly that a substantial part of the trouble lay with over-optimism regarding the state of building programmes at the time of take-over. This critically altered the company's cash position for the worse, probably by as much as £600,000. Early hopes that half of the company's liquidity might be deposited on three months' call were abandoned and the board were forecasting a substantial overdraft within four months of take-over. Shortage of cash and of reserves then characterized the company's finances for the remainder of its life. Hopes that the value of work-in-progress might be re-negotiated downwards and a substantial cash repayment ease the situation were nurtured but never fulfilled. As costs mounted – both wage costs and overhead costs associated with the establishment of the new management techniques – the position could only be eased first by borrowing and secondly by bringing programmes forward again as a result of increasing productivity. Earlier plans for raising more private capital were abandoned once the report of the Geddes Committee put the structure of shipbuilding on the Upper Clyde in the melting pot. These plans had been mainly dictated by a drive to reduce the proportional share of the government below 50 per cent, to counter the charge of 'back door nationalization', but the money so raised would have provided most welcome reserves. Thus to the other major pressure to raise productivity in the short run – the pressure for money wage increases – was added the pressure of financial stringency, removing from management any possibility of a longish period of gestation, a long-haul to increase productivity, and making success in the short period an imperative. Although from time to time the board consoled itself that this 'financial discipline' had a healthy effect (as it had, e.g. in forcing the pruning of some inflated budgets which might otherwise have been treated more leniently or even survived intact) on balance it was damaging in leaving the management very little room for manoeuvre and creating a crisis atmosphere with its attendant tensions. Its impact, for example, in the field of industrial relations was a confusing one: on the one hand the management would enunciate and stand firm on the policy of 'nothing for nothing' but on the other there was the recognition particularly in the last year of the company, that the company's lack of reserves meant that it could not survive a major industrial clash. This inevitably produced fissures and dichotomies in its labour policies which were at least as much due to this underlying financial situation as to more proximate policy differences and the management structure through which labour disputes were handled, which we discuss in Chapter 7.

From its inception the board was determined to have full financial information and to exercise firm financial control: the experience of its predecessor was fresh in everyone's mind.

With the help of the job cards to be used in the measured day-work scheme the intention was to develop a much more precise estimate of work done and cost incurred, which when related to the total contract would give a firmer basis from which to translate the projected state of the building pro-gramme into a cash-flow estimate. Because job cards were only in operation for approximately the last six months of the company's life, and then as part of an estimated target payment scheme rather than a full measured day-work scheme, the full rigour of this system of financial control was never applied over a period long enough to test it adequately. It was beginning to make improvements in estimating the state of building pro-grammes and in tightening financial control, and given time such a system could remove one of the weakest links in manage-ment control in shipbuilding. If the old Fairfields company had had such a system the difficulties over the value of work-in-progress would have been much less. Even if such a system could have been introduced by the new company in the early months of 1966 the more precise information on the production programme and finance would have allowed the board to get its priorities in better order and the management to avoid costly errors – for example greater emphasis would certainly have been given to steel-work productivity and to the planning of space in relation to steel production.

As it was, the volume and quality of financial information provided to the board was high, contrasting very favourably with the machinery for financial control at the time of take-over. Although initially it had been thought that it might take at least a year to get a team together and introduce an effective system, in fact this was achieved in eight months. This provision of financial information was invaluable during the negotiations which preceded the merger, and its very high quality was com-mented upon by several of the independent professionals involved in pre-merger studies.

The distinctions made by Professor Woodward between the 'task' financial function – 'the keeping of accounts and the determination of financial policy' and the 'element' function of 'management accounting; . . . part of production adminis-tration concerned with production and control'* would be

*See Joan Woodward, *Industrial Organisation: Theory and Practice* 1965, pp. 112–13.

quite impracticable in shipbuilding, even in a company with a more generous margin of reserves than had Fairfields. Financial policy and production administration are so closely inter-dependent that any attempt to separate these functions would either prove dangerous to the company or lead to many loops and links in organizational practice not shown on the organiz-ational chart. Experience at Fairfields certainly bore out Professor Woodward's finding that 'people concerned with works accounting . . . saw their role as a controlling and sanctioning one rather than a servicing and supporting one. Line managers resented this attitude and retaliated by becoming aggressive and obstructive.'* However, in shipbuilding there can be no solution to this problem simply by separating the 'task' from the 'element' function.

The board was closely involved in marketing. As there was no top executive manager specializing in marketing, marketing activity was undertaken by a number of board members and in particular by the chairman, the two executive board members, Mr D. J. Palmar and the financial comptroller. Selling in ship-building is an amalgam of long-established connexions, price competitiveness, 'efficiency-credibility', especially regarding delivery dates and, quite frequently, the ability to arrange credit to help the potential owner finance the building of the ship. In a sense, therefore, it is not one specialism but a combination of several. Because of this the board of a shipbuilding company should always keep very closely in touch with the marketing situation. This was certainly done by the Fairfields board, although there was a weakness in the lack of central responsi-bility and attention at top level to the specialist aspects of marketing. Next in importance to liquidity a preoccupation with orders characterized the first year of the new company's activity. Although it took over a substantial order book there was an obvious need to add to this if commercial viability were to be established (it should be remembered that the board began with the aim of making the company profitable in five years) and if the speeches about greater security of employment and a long-run guarantee of high and stabilized earnings were to be

*Woodward, op. cit., p. 113.

turned into hard fact. There were also important psychological reasons why it was important to secure new orders. A new company must always establish its own commercial viability if it is to attract and retain high-quality management. This is particularly so if the company is the object of criticism and operating in a traditional minded industry. 'I'll give them to the end of the year' was a remark not limited to merely one critical shipbuilder, which found its way into circulation and even in to the press. In addition – and indeed of even more importance – it was recognized that there would be a brake upon rising productivity unless the state of the order book made it abundantly clear that there was no risk of men working themselves – or others – out of a job. The relationship between order book, productivity and employment was a constant preoccupation. Unknown to the board there was an even stronger reason why new orders were necessary if morale in the yard was to be raised. It seemed that the old suspicions were so deep-seated that some workers and foremen suspected that the new company had been set up merely to complete existing orders, particularly for the Navy. To the top level of management and the board, intimately involved in planning radical changes in the operation of the yard, such a suspicion was so unreal as never to have even occurred to them, so that no reassurance or categorical denial was given. As the months went by and no new order was announced the suspicion spread its roots, undermining the confidence required for the change in attitude which in turn was a necessary element in the overall changes in performance which were being planned. Thus the winning of the first new order in August 1966 had important psychological as well as commercial advantages.

Winning an order may be a long-drawn-out process, from initial soundings, through design, tendering and the arrangement of credit. Board members can be concerned with a particular potential order over several months, during which very detailed negotiations and examinations will take place at several levels within the company. In one sense every marketing decision can have repercussions affecting the future of the company. With each unit of commodity so large, and with past experience indicating the possibility of loss on one contract being larger than the reserves of a shipbuilding company, this is obviously so. In addition, however, there are particular marketing decisions which are of an even more obvious significance. One such was Fairfields' negotiations with the Admiralty regarding the possibility that the yard would build a 'lead' ship, first of a line. Such a contract would have been profitable, would have provided stable employment over a lengthy period, and would have greatly enhanced the company's bargaining power in merger negotiations because of the implications for the future of naval work. After extensive 'vetting' the Admiralty were ready to award the contract to the company. On the company side there were reservations. Design and 'debugging' problems are notoriously difficult with a 'lead' ship and the yard had not built such a ship for the Admiralty in over two decades. Eventually after detailed examination and cross-examination of the relevant managers by the board, the board was satisfied that the company's design capabilities could be made adequate for the task. One difficulty remained – a gap of six months between the delivery date the Admiralty required (and there were important strategic considerations involved) and the date that company planning suggested it could achieve. In a contract which was to run over a minimum of four and a half years this six months was obviously a pretty fine calculation. Certainly to exclude oneself on such grounds was to set very high store on one's planning precision and on establishing a reputation for meeting delivery dates. There were voices (not within the board) which urged that it would be realistic to cut the Fairfields' estimate of time required by the necessary six months – realistic in the sense that other difficulties would eventually arise, such as late delivery of components outside Fairfields' control, which would allow the company to operate within its own time schedule without any ignominy attached. Naturally the planners were pressed to see whether they could reduce the time period, but the more the issue was explored and discussed the more the longer time span seemed the only one the company could operate within. Eventually the board decided to make the lengthening of the building period an integral part of its final approach to the Admiralty, and on that basis the contract was lost.

Most other marketing decisions to be taken by the board had rather narrower implications. For example the existing enquiries which appeared likely to yield an order and which might conflict with each other and be incompatible on the company's order book had to be assessed to decide which the company would prefer and would therefore put more effort into getting. Inevitably with shipbuilding's business-getting procedures such an exercise could be frustrating and appear academic, as after much sifting of the relevant information the preferred enquiry could be lost and the less preferred become a firm order, or both alternatives might fail to materialize on the order books. Whereas the highest rate of profit, or contribution to overheads and profit, should be the main commercial criterion in determining preferences as between potential orders, in practice at Fairfields at least equal weight was given to the desirability of providing long-run stability of employment. Estimates of future demand for the different trades and grades of labour would be adjusted for the change in demand which each additional potential order would impose, and the contribution to stabilizing or expanding employment would be taken into account. In the process adjustments would be made for expected increases in labour productivity, and estimates would also have to be made regarding the supply of skills on the river at relevant times in the future. The advantages both for manpower planning and for decision-taking regarding the balance of the order book which can arise once merger has centralized the decision-taking for an entire estuary are obvious. The nature of the raw data with which decision-takers in shipbuilding have to deal means that the more normal approach to achieving the optimum product mix is inappropriate. More once-for-all methods are required, almost treating each potential contract as if it were a decision to set up a subsidiary plant. The techniques of operational research are obviously relevant here. Unfortunately, during the lifetime of Fairfields the data for decision-taking was of insufficient quality and quantity to allow such a technique to narrow the scope for judgement and reduce the risk of error. The company financed a research fellowship as a means of establishing the best ways of applying operational research to such problems in shipbuilding.

That there is considerable overlap between decision-taking about the order book and information about the state of the building programme has been indicated clearly. The possibility that a projected building programme may fall behind has also to be taken account of. On occasion it may be possible to bring the programme for a particular ship forward so as to make room for some other change, either in the existing overall programme or in the order book. Advancing a ship is usually an expensive business, not only because of the high over-time premiums involved but because of the need to re-phase all the other processes which dovetail together. Most changes in programme are the result of failure to keep to target dates rather than of conscious decisions aimed at gains which otherwise would not accrue. At board level the most important function is to keep watch on the state of the programme (the relationship between this, the payment of instalments and the state of the cash flow has already been commented on), to maintain pressure for the fulfilment of targets, to explore very critically the reasons given for any falling behind and to decide when changes must be made, having regard to the consequential changes involved. There is a natural tendency for executive managers to blame falling behind either upon colleagues, upon labour or upon outside suppliers. If unjustified 'buck-passing' succeeds slackness will escalate, and bad relations will be generated which, in time, will make their own contribution to poor performance. Responsibility to prevent this lies with the general manager, and ultimately with the board. The two executive managers on the board would sometimes disagree there about where blame should be allocated; usually this arose from their different estimates of the capabilities of individual managers. Whether there was agreement or not the non-executive directors were not in a position to form a more accurate judgement, but were limited to stressing the seriousness of any delay and, on occasion, deciding upon contingency steps to meet a threatened delay. With the reputation of the industry for late delivery, the large sums of money involved and the wide range of possible causes of delayed programmes, any management system in shipbuilding must provide an effective means of allocating responsibility and improving performance. At a minimum a non-executive director should be charged with exploring particular cases. The representatives of owners in the yard are a valuable source of information which can be independent of yard influences, and the non-executive director should have free access to these representatives as well as to all employees in the yard. The need for an independent yet fully informed assessment of managerial performance in industry is, of course, not unique to shipbuilding. In that industry, however, there is a combination of circumstances which suggests the need for special attention to the problem. Again the shift from single-yard to multi-yard operation can help, as executive management not themselves directly responsible for the operational efficiency of any one yard emerge at 'group' level. Even there, however, both the nature of the various possible causes of delay in a building programme and the magnitude of the consequences of such delay are such as to suggest the need for specialist machinery.

Labour problems and industrial relations problems occupied a good part of the board's time, which was natural given both the characteristics of the employment relationship in the industry and the declared intention of the new company to bring improvements in this field. The main crises are fully covered in chapters 6–7. The impact of the board on labour matters was considerable. Quite apart from the importance of these problems the specialist interest of a number of board members in them ensured very full attention and discussion. Each board meeting received papers on the level and distribution of employment between departments; wage claims; procedures and disputes were fully discussed and the limits – usually narrow – within which settlements could be reached, decided. The position of those directors with trade-union connexions was difficult here, but there was no case in which their integrity in either capacity could be said to have been compromised. They were able to explain to management when their plans were in conflict with trade-union principles, or where they might prove unacceptable on other grounds. This was not done in a way that strengthened the negotiating position of management but in a way that shifted its thinking into ways more likely to be acceptable to trade-union objectives and thinking, yet without cutting across the company's objectives.

The much publicized no-strike pledge caused some difficulty for the board when strikes took place and were very fully publicized. The chairman was faced not only with the usual pressure from owners and potential buyers, but on one occasion at least with a *démarche* from a private shareholder to the effect that a settlement of a particular type would result in a strike of capital by withdrawal of his. A few members of the board felt that the first strike was the virtual end of the experiment. The chairman was emotionally involved in the no-strike pledge which had been given to him and which he had used to raise capital to save the yard from closure, and his own enormous enthusiasm for 'the Fairfields experiment' was considerably dampened when strikes took place. He quickly adjusted to the realities of the situation, recognizing the limitations which any such pledge must inevitably have in practice. One of these limitations was the fairly substantial rate of labour turnover, but more important was the pull of outside loyalties – derived from trade-union organization, and the heavy weight of traditional reactions. As these difficulties became more fully appreciated board members took a more sombre view of the possibilities of removing loss by strike from the shipbuilding industry. The chairman adjusted to the view that one of the issues the 'proving ground' would put to the test was the extent to which trade unionists could carry through their expressed intention not to strike in a management situation unusually sympathetic to trade-union aspirations.

A major objective and concern of the board was the introduction of new managerial techniques. In this the board was not initiating but providing the environment within which the new management could put their ideas to the test, subject only to the financial balance between costs and revenues being estimated to be advantageous to the company. On the provision of an atmosphere strongly favourable to managerial innovation the board never wavered, although many attempts were made from outside the company to convince individual members of the board that the new methods were inapplicable in shipbuilding. Remembering the lack of shipbuilding expertise on the board and the great confidence with which the traditionalists set out their views that – for example – work study methods had been tried and found impracticable in the industry – the support of the board for very wide ranging managerial innovation was in itself a considerable contribution. In this the board was encouraged by the *Geddes Report* which set out in general terms the case for the application of new methods in an industry in which that committee's investigations had shown them to be notably absent. The main credit, however, must go to the enthusiasm of the new managers for this task of innovation and in particular to the energetic advocacy of the two full-time directors. The executive managers' enthusiasms fructified when they found that at the top of the firm their ideas encountered not a sceptical and hidebound attitude but met with encouragement and support. Several of the new men in management had been attracted to the firm by its reputation for a willingness to experiment and introduce new methods.

Obviously in this atmosphere there was a risk that particular projects would be adopted which were not appropriate or designed to fit the circumstances of shipbuilding. The check imposed by the board was a financial one, not in terms of the total cost of an innovation but in terms of the savings which it would make possible. The usual criterion was that the estimated savings should be at least five times as great as the salary cost of the innovation, a criterion which left room for adjustment if there was under-estimating of costs or over-optimism regarding gains. Proposals for managerial innovation came before the board very frequently, and their overall impact on costs could be assessed from the detailed breakdown of overhead costs made in connexion with the annual accounts and the budgeting process. With the pace of change a very rapid one the build-up of the overhead costs of improved managerial methods was rapid. As a result of the speedy establishment of an effective system of financial control the magnitude of this build-up was recognized early and the board kept up to date on significant changes. There was no substance in the suggestion or criticism made from outside the yard that this increase in costs was taking place without its full magnitude or its implication being recognized by the company. A criticism which could reasonably have been made was that the presentation of improvements in management techniques as separate items at successive boards made it possible for some double counting of estimated savings to be made. Low efficiency left a great deal of slack to be taken up and potential savings to be made. The attack on some aspects of the low efficiency could be made from a number of directions; for example, a small part of the savings estimated as resulting from the work of the organization and methods department in labour utilization would overlap with savings shown as productivity gains arising out of work study and the introduction of the new payment scheme, and it was possible that double counting took place. This was quite innocent and accidental, but it highlighted the importance of the detailed analysis of submissions by individual managers and departments first by general management and then by the board. A board which is substantially non-executive should ensure that departmental proposals go through a check filter of financial and general management control before being presented for decision.

Ex post analysis of innovation can also be most valuable, both in the taking of decisions about the continuation of new methods and in determining the future pattern and pace of innovation. Unfortunately, the time span of the Fairfields company was too short to allow much of this. Continuing reports were received on the results of some managerial innovations (e.g. productivity bargains; quality control; value analysis) and in the last months of the company judgement on the value of particular innovating proposals was building up on the basis of past experience.

It might appear that a weakness in the approach of the board to management innovation arose out of its composition and the impact this had on management structure. Mr J. D. Houston's

position as one of only two executive directors and head of
productivity services inevitably blurred the distinction between
the executive and advisory roles. At particular times and around
particular issues it certainly appeared that this was an organizational error. For example, how far was productivity services
to be responsible for the implementation as distinct from the
design and introduction of the ETPS? On balance, however,
this structure probably met the needs of the situation better
than the originally intended structure which would have had
only one executive director, the general manager. It has been
argued already that shipbuilding is too complex to be operated
effectively by a highly centralized control system. Two full-time
directors were on this score alone better than one – although
four or five would probably have been more effective. In
addition, the extra authority which an executive director could
give to the process of managerial innovation was probably
necessary given the reservations and outright opposition felt by
some of the lower levels of management who had been inherited
by the new company. When a company is carrying through
such radical changes the case for representing 'management
services' on its board is very strong. It is vital, however, that
the ultimate power to decide on applications is seen to lie with
the general manager. When difficulties arose at Fairfields it was
not because the executive and the advisory roles overlapped,
both personally and to some extent departmentally, but because
the friction which the overlap could generate was not resolved
by the provision of a *specific* means by which conflicts of judgement could be resolved. To say that conflict of any sort must
ultimately be resolved or referred to the managing director is
not enough when there is a built-in overlap of this sort likely to
generate conflict. When a director has become *de facto* assistant
general manager (and a very good AGM it should be said) and
yet at the same time has an advisory role to play, it is the duty of
the board to make clear by what means the inevitable policy
conflicts which arise may be resolved without damaging
management morale and further blurring the line of control.
This the Fairfields board failed to do, and although no very
serious consequences flowed from this the signs of potential

damage were clear enough, and once the first wave of the managerial revolution had subsided it would have been wise to make some alterations.

The most important single issue which the board had to deal with was whether or not and on what basis Fairfields yard should be merged with other yards on the Clyde. It had, that is, to decide on its own demise. The mixed feelings with which the board approached this issue did not, however, arise from a sense of self-preservation but from the board's very strong loyalty to 'the Fairfields experiment'.

The economic case for merging was accepted by the board. That more effective manpower utilization would reduce the need for berths; that stability of employment could be increased and leap-frogging wage drift reduced if manpower planning was on an estuarial rather than on a yard basis; that economies in design and tendering could be achieved by merger and that there were considerable economies to be made by rationalizing purchasing, all of these convinced the board that the Geddes prescription was the right one. The view that size by itself would not solve the industry's problems was also advanced, not as an obstacle to merger but as a reason for pushing ahead with the radical changes in management already begun at Govan. But this was the point in the argument at which doubts emerged: would a merger provide a wider and more promising area within which to put into practice the Fairfields approach or might it not result in a slowing down of change, and an end to the experimental approach?

In addition to the logic of the economic case for amalgamation there was the influence which government wishes must have on Fairfields' capacity for survival as an independent unit. The matter was put fairly bluntly in the *Geddes Report* (paragraphs 334 and 335). 'We accordingly sought and received confirmation that . . . the Government would not undertake commitments or authorize long-term plans which would make it difficult for Fairfields to be included in some structural reorganization of the industry.'

As soon as the publication date of the *Geddes Report* was known the board decided to meet four days thereafter to consider the implications of the *Report* for the company's future. The arguments for merger, taken together with the encouraging fact that the general recommendations made in the *Report* regarding a new approach to managing the industry were very closely in accord with the changes being introduced at Govan, encouraged the Fairfields board to make a public declaration of its readiness to discuss merger with one or more of the other yards on the Clyde. From that time onwards Fairfields never dragged its feet in the approach to merging, despite the reservations, heart searchings and indeed fears which individual directors – including the chairman – had as to the possible outcome and the opportunities which might thus be missed for carrying the changes through to a demonstrably successful conclusion.

The disdain and dislike of much of the rest of the industry for Fairfields had, naturally enough, hardened the sense of its uniqueness amongst the people most closely associated with the experiment. If you are told that you are bound to fail and you have any sense of pride and confidence at all you will be all the more anxious to demonstrate without any possible doubt that you have succeeded – and the prospect of being denied that opportunity by a self-inflicted act of merger was a bitter and unpalatable one.

The approach to the other companies was not warmly received, the first positive reactions being that the time was not ripe for talks. The increasing financial difficulties of some yards plus the clear insistence by the government that mergers should take place (although the Shipbuilding Industry Bill was not published until February 1967) resulted in the 'three and two' pattern, in which Fairfields began talks with John Browns of Clydebank, and Connels, Stephens and Yarrows announced that they were to merge. A meeting between Fairfields and this 'CSY' grouping made it clear that the then view amongst the group was that Browns and Fairfields were the vulnerable 'lame ducks' of the river and that it would be best if the other three yards consolidated and made a success of their mini-merger before exploring the possibility of bringing the five yards together. In addition there was the possibility of bringing the two yards on the lower reaches of the Clyde into some upper reaches combination.

The technical, financial and managerial implications of a merger with John Browns were very fully explored, but the approach was overtaken early in 1967 when the Shipbuilding Industry Board made its preference for a single grouping uniting at least all of the yards on the upper reaches. The companies came together and set up an independent working party to explore the basis for such a merger and for some months the initiative for merger passed out of the hands of the board. When the report of the working party was presented at the end of July 1967 it seemed that some of the companies were not enthusiastic about proceeding with negotiations to merge at that time on the basis outlined. At this stage the initiative passed back to John Browns and Fairfields.

The board background to developments at this time was that whereas the majority of members favoured immediate consideration of a decision on the proposals of the working party, to the extent of arranging a full board meeting in London on the evening of the day on which the report of the working party was presented to chairmen there, one member vigorously advocated a less hurried approach. The matter was one of judgement: it could not be decided on the basis of the known facts and reason alone.

From the decision to meet to give immediate consideration to the report flowed the decision to go with representatives of John Browns to the Shipbuilding Industry Board with proposals for a merger between these two companies. This approach helped the Board encourage the companies reluctant to merge to change their minds, and a more broadly based process of merger was set in motion, eventually to produce Upper Clyde Shipbuilders Ltd in February 1968. Thus the timing of the John Brown-Fairfields initiative made a valuable contribution to establishing the full merger quickly. From the point of view of the narrower Fairfields' objectives it seems likely that a less hurried reaction to the working party report would have been best.

The relative position of Fairfields in August 1967 was

certainly strong. The order book was healthy; the ETP scheme had just been introduced and substantial increases in productivity had been achieved; the working party report had endorsed the objectives of the Fairfields experiment and declared that these 'must ultimately be achieved throughout the group's operations'; and the working party had made it clear that the technical facilities and resources of Fairfields were necessary if a viable group on the upper reaches was to be established. Taking a narrow company view – and it is the duty of a board to take such a view – it may be doubted whether the ultimate characteristics of the February 1968 merger reflected the strength of the company's relative position in August 1967. What were the objectives of the board in this merger process?

It might be expected that a board with a substantial majority of non-executive members would, when involved in merger negotiations, put the interest of shareholders well ahead of the interest of managers and employees. The Fairfields board, however, gave first priority to whether or not the Fairfields approach to managing the industry would continue, and it formed the opinion that this would be most effectively achieved by the redeployment of Fairfields top management in key posts in the new group. Although the board fulfilled its duty to shareholders throughout the merger negotiations, with conspicuous success in the financial terms finally agreed, the successful placing of top management was its prime concern. In this the board was not successful, certainly not judged by the ambitious results it had earlier hoped for. The reasons for this failure are complex. Objectively, the board's ambitions may have been unachievable given the still strong opposition to Fairfields management and objectives. Endorsement of their objectives by the working party was not followed by immediate conversion to them by all of the parties concerned. Those who no longer doubted the objectives doubted the ability of Fairfields' management to achieve them. The atmosphere was still hostile, although the foundations on which this hostility rested were shifting. Even those who had from the outset regarded the company as set on a disaster course, had now shifted round to arguing that 'Fairfields has yet to prove itself'. This attitude was, in a way, a compliment to the 'proving ground' concept, but it was galling to Fairfields to be thus 'put in the dock' by representatives of an industry which had, for the most part, proved itself incapable of meeting competition, even in a rising market.

When Fairfields, together with John Browns, provided a lever by which the Shipbuilding Industry Board would lift the merger negotiations out of the impasse into which they appeared to be settling after the report of the working party, the board probably undercut its own bargaining position. Its willingness to progress a merger was not hedged around with any reservations. Because of the fundamental strength of its relative position at that time Fairfields might, by marking time, have found itself courted to initiate or take part in fresh merger talks. Instead it took the initiative itself, and without conditions. This initiative was in character with the approach to mergers taken by the board from the publication of the *Geddes Report* onwards. Nevertheless, it arose specifically out of the decision to meet on the same day as the working party report was presented. The board judged that 'the time in the affairs of men' had arrived, but its decision might have been different had some weeks elapsed and had it been left to others to take initiatives. A time-table dictated by a desire to grasp initiatives may sometimes encourage a board to compulsive action when calm inaction is more appropriate. Even with hindsight it is not possible to be certain that this was such an instant, but it provides an interesting illustration of such a possibility.

Its determination to see the Fairfields approach carried forward in any new grouping led the board to approach negotiations with the following questions in the forefront: Can a satisfactory management *structure* be agreed? Will the disposition of personnel in that structure ensure that the new methods continue to be applied? In the event, Fairfields men were not at the top of the new grouping, although a few occupied key positions at the level below that of executive directors. All that concerns this study is why the end result should have differed so materially from the aims of the board. That a possible explanation is a failure to exploit a strong bargaining position has already been suggested. Even in a merger situation, however, it need not be assumed that bargaining power alone determines the outcome. This should certainly not be the case when an independent body, charged with bringing about mergers which will re-establish the industry as commercially viable, plays an influential part in the negotiations.

The Fairfields management, as pioneers, had been aggressive and assertive. Other shipyard managements had been criticized, at least by implication. The pioneering process results in more mistakes being made than by a management set in unadventurous ways. The use by Fairfields of publicity as a management tool ensured that its mistakes were widely known; and there were many ready to read the signs of error and failure where these did not exist. A cool assessment of the chances of Fairfields men of emerging at the top of a grouping would not have rated the chances very highly. That this was not clearly seen was a reflection of both the strength and the weakness of the Fairfields board. Strength because it was a mixture of commitment and loyalty which prevented the difficulties being fully recognized and frankly discussed; weakness because judgements were thereby affected and decisions less realistic than they might have been. In the final stages of the negotiations the financial basis for a merger became the central consideration. This was probably inevitable; there were intricate matters to be resolved which were crucial if the necessary support of shareholders was to be achieved. Given that the Fairfields board set such high store upon a satisfactory outcome of the management question it was probably mistaken in not tabling its views on this clearly and unambiguously. Although its general attitude was known and presented vigorously in the pre-merger discussions no unambiguous terms were specified. This was a major failure of the Fairfields board to achieve objectives it had set itself. In as much as these objectives were unrealistic and the causes for failure beyond the board's control, the board's failure could be regarded as one of judgement rather than of performance.

The weaknesses of failures of the board were ones of omission rather than commission: a failure to set out clearly the essential elements of 'the Fairfields experiment'; a failure to remedy weaknesses in the company's managerial structure once the major changes had been introduced; the failure to achieve its managerial objectives in the merger negotiations, and a tendency to concentrate on the broader issues sometimes at the expense of important matters of detail. The successes were the successes of the company: to have survived, achieved a strong order book and carried through major changes across the whole range of shipbuilding management, despite extreme financial stringency; to have built up and enthused a management team capable of carrying through these changes, partly from outside the industry and partly by changing the approach of men already in ship-building. These successes were achieved by a board which itself was experimental, drawn from and partly representing interests not normally involved in running a company. Here a number of firmly held views about the impracticability and undesirability of such representation were not borne out by Fairfields experience. The board was an effective instrument for bringing about much needed change – in the boardroom as well as in the shipyard.

CHAPTER 5

Labour Relations 1

Attitudes: Communications: Institutions

WITHIN the old company, labour relations were much neglected – it was an area regarded as peripheral rather than central to the well-being of the company. Effectively, responsibility for labour relations lay with the shipyard manager, who was also responsible for the day-to-day operation of the yard. Pressures of time and events often forced the shipyard manager to deal with matters relating to labour relations in an *ad hoc* fashion. Nominally the company appointed a personnel manager but he was given little authority or support and largely acted as a welfare officer. In a shipyard employing 3,000 people it may appear surprising that labour relations were given so little attention, but this was not unusual for the River or the industry.

The period between October 1965 and January 1966 was one of activity and lobbying by workers, shop stewards and trade unions to avert the closure of the yard. This fight to avert closure was seen by Sir Iain as a means of introducing into a traditional craft industry modern management practices and at the same time improving the basis of industrial relations.

The need for cooperation and support to ensure the survival of Fairfields was made clear by Mr George Brown when he made his announcement regarding Fairfields in the House of Commons. 'In setting up this tremendous new format in British business, all the partners, the Government, private enterprise, and the headquarters of the unions are relying on the man in the yard to unreservedly cooperate in working the yard as efficiently as possible, and in particular achieving the flexible manning arrangements and interchangeability of workers which are essential. If this cooperation were not forthcoming, the whole scheme involving the combined support of government, the trade unions, and private enterprise would fall to the ground and the yard would have to close.'*

Similar sentiments were expressed by Sir Iain Stewart when he addressed a mass meeting of the yard workers on 27 April 1966, at a Govan cinema. He regarded a proving ground as 'primarily ... to demonstrate that given a new element of unreserved cooperation between management and men, with good management professionally trained and being given full authority to apply their modern trends and techniques, it will be possible for shipbuilding and indeed other industries where productivity is low, to regain their former competitive status in world trade'.

Procurement of this 'unreserved cooperation' could not be immediate despite the 'pledges' exchanged with Sir Iain at the Lyceum Cinema, Govan on 27 December 1965. The management had to overcome the suspicion and scepticism of the workers. Concessions were bargained over, and not merely given. Against the background of the recent history of the industry it was not surprising that the workers retained suspicions of management's intentions. Consequently, there were differing attitudes among the workers to the idea and aims of a proving ground.

The neglect of labour relations had an adverse effect on the attitude of the workers. In April 1966, a cross-section of employees was surveyed to provide some indication of the type of yard attitude towards management and company which had prevailed before January 1966.

Eighteen long-service employees were randomly selected; on average they had given twenty-two years unbroken service to the old company. Many of these men remembered the years when a man was considered fortunate to have a regular job. Others were perhaps suspicious of being interviewed by a researcher newly arrived in the yard. A combination of reasons made this group guarded in their comments, particularly with reference to general management. However, the majority of them considered that they had never been given enough information about the company or about its prospects; they had

* *Hansard*, Vol. 722, Col. 2102, 22 December 1965.

felt very isolated within the company. They were disappointed by the slow improvement in working conditions and amenities in the decade before 1966. As a group they strongly gave the impression of being resigned to the ways of the industry, believing that improvements in labour relations would only come very slowly.

As a group, the forty-five shop stewards interviewed were very much younger and much more outspoken. Of this group, thirty-three had held office under the old company. These stewards felt that the previous management had little appreciation of the shop stewards' role and had certainly not attempted to make the job any easier.

The shop stewards were asked to indicate, from a given list of duties, how they ranked these duties in order of importance.

Table 5.1

Duties of a shop steward ranked in order of importance

To protect workers' rights	1
To keep workers informed	2
To work with management to improve labour relations	3
To encourage participation in union affairs	4
To recruit new members	5
To collect union dues	6

The view of the shop steward on the importance of encouraging participation in union affairs is perhaps a little ambiguous. Most men in the yard are members of a trade union, usually for reasons of self interest. The shop steward, when implementing the mandate given him by the men, can rely on their support and cooperation. In this sense, the workers are participating in union affairs. However, if this statement implies it is the duty of the shop steward to encourage participation in extra-yard activities, then it might have received a lower rating because of the reluctance (or apathy) of the average union member to participate at branch meetings and similar activities, and the view of many stewards that there is little point in trying to overcome this resistance.

The characteristics of the various unions in the yard are reflected by the different rankings given to the aspects of the shop steward's job.

Table 5.2

What function of the shop steward's job would your union list as being most important?

	ASB	NUGMW	AEU	OTHERS
To recruit new members	4	1	2	3
To collection of union dues	6	6	6	6
To encourage participation in union affairs	2	4	3	2
To keep workers informed	5	3	4	5
To protect workers' rights	1	2	1	1
To work with management to improve labour relations	3	5	5	4

The ASB shop stewards obviously believe that their main duties are to protect their members' rights and to encourage participation in union affairs. If a strong union can be obtained by these efforts, then it will be possible to negotiate with management to improve labour relations. The relatively low rating given to the need to keep workers informed is in part based on the stewards' belief that the men they represent should have confidence in them. There is also the effect of the traditional basis of organization in British shipbuilding, with a majority of issues being determined at work and often in branch meetings close to the yards, thus leaving little excuse for the failure of others to 'participate'.

The importance attached by the NUGMW stewards to the need to recruit new members was reflected in events in the yard. Increased membership will allow the union to give greater protection to workers' rights. By keeping members informed, it hoped to encourage participation in union affairs.

The AEU (now AEFU) shop stewards, the third largest group in the yard, followed a similar pattern to the NUGMW.

110

It is noticeable that both rated the need to recruit new members more highly than did the ASB shop stewards. It is interesting to note the low rating given by the NUGMW and the AEU shop stewards to the need to 'work with management to improve labour relations'. The two unions, in terms of philosophy and at national level, had a more pronounced bias towards cooperation than the ASB, whose militancy was frequently reflected in the attitude of top officials and policy-making bodies. This is probably a particular example of the gap which often exists between the thinking of trade-union leaders and other levels in the trade-union structure.

Two-thirds of the shop stewards did not think that they had been given sufficient opportunity to fulfil their roles as shop stewards by the old company. The following table gives some of the reasons, ranked in order of importance, why the shop stewards felt that they were not given sufficient opportunity to fulfil their duties.*

Table 5.3

Cause of difficulties in fulfilling the role of shop steward

	Ranked
Hostility of management	1
Difficulties in arranging meeting with management	2
Management had no appreciation of shop steward's job	3
Lack of adequate information on company policy	4
Union-management tension	5

The shop stewards were given no facilities for meetings and any discussion or contact with union officials had to be outside the yard. Communications between senior management and men were poor and tended to exacerbate tensions already existing. The shop stewards felt little or no allegiance to the firm. This was largely a reflection of their past experiences and

*An expanded account referring to shop stewards is included in an appendix.

a suspicion that they would be victimized by management if the opportunity arose. However, few of the shop stewards felt that they had been victimized, although all believed that such an event was possible. Their attitudes made employer-worker relations difficult, and the general tendency in the post-war period towards union militancy seems to have been stimulated by two major factors. First was the growth of trade-union organization and power within the industry, and second was the growth of job opportunities outside the industry. Combined, these factors gave an edge to the workers' traditional militancy and made an enlightened labour relations policy more than ever necessary.

Most of the workers at Fairfields had entered shipbuilding for no particular reasons: they had not been strongly attracted by shipyard work. The sample of long-service employees interviewed in July 1966 indicated that there was no agreement on why they had entered the industry. Some had followed relatives into the industry, others had no alternative job opportunities. Some of the men felt that in a period of job insecurity, an apprenticeship was something concrete upon which to base their working lives. However, one factor clearly emerged from the survey – once a man had entered the industry he tended to remain there, often in one yard if employment opportunities allowed.

The year 1966 was a time of managerial change. With the future of the new company uncertain it was not surprising to find the annual labour turnover rate was 95 per cent and the rate of voluntary turnover at 57·4 per cent. These figures for 1966 were inflated for two reasons. In July and August two ships were completed and this resulted in a large redundancy. Secondly, the finishing stages of a ship always precipitate a 'drift' of labour from the yards which inflate the 'voluntary' turnover figures. However, these figures were much higher than those of another declining industry, coal. In 1965–6 the Scottish Division had a total turnover of labour of 18·1 per cent of which 12·8 per cent left of their own accord.* In 1966–7 this division recorded a total turnover of manpower of 16·7 per

*Annual Reports of the National Coal Board.

cent with a voluntary content of 10·8 per cent. In Fairfields for 1967 the figures were 31·5 and 24·9 per cent respectively.

It is clear that in as much as Fairfields reflects the situation in shipbuilding, there is a high wastage of manpower between yards, but not necessarily from the industry.

Given the turbulence of the first six months of 1966, it is perhaps surprising to learn some of the reasons given by workers for staying with the company. The long-service employees gave their age as their chief reason for staying. Interviews with shop stewards in July 1966 gave different reasons.

Table 5.4

Shop stewards: Why did you remain with the company after October 1965?

	Ranked
Possibility of a new deal	1
Hope that yard would remain open	2
Loyalty to the company	3
Belief in future for the industry	4

Interviews held at that time indicated the strong loyalty of men to the industry – 'We disagree with the cynics who say that shipbuilding is finished on the Clyde'. Others saw the possibility through the creation of a proving ground of 'an industrial revolution taking place in shipbuilding'. It is against this background of challenge to secure their livelihoods that the workers' attitudes towards the proving ground should be considered.

The men through their shop stewards were inevitably suspicious of the new management. But they were in no doubt as to what they wanted from the proving ground – security of employment, improved pay and the provision of fringe benefits such as pension schemes, sick payment schemes, etc. The aims of the men were in many ways a reflection of the past inadequacy of the industry.

In knowing what they hoped to gain, the men also knew those areas where they thought the company would encounter the main difficulties. Asked to list, in order of importance, the main

113

difficulties facing the new company in July 1966 the shop
stewards listed the following:

Table 5.5

Shop stewards: What are the main difficulties
facing the new company?

	Ranked
Old traditions and practices	1
Wage differentials	2
Planning	3

The shop stewards felt that the old method of running the
company, and particularly matters affecting labour relations,
had engendered attitudes which would be difficult to overcome.
Despite this pessimistic outlook, in the first six months of the
company's existence the shop stewards had noted some
improvements.

Table 5.6

Shop stewards: What changes, if any, have you noticed
since the new company was formed?

	Ranked
Greater understanding between management and men	1
Greater cooperation between management and men	2
Improved communications	3

The mens' desire for future improvements, together with the
traumatic events of October 1965 had created an atmosphere
extremely favourable for management/employee cooperation.
Despite the improved atmosphere the turnover of labour in the
first year of the Company was high, primarily due to the building programme of the Company. In order to involve the workers
and management in the process of change, it was essential to
inform them of the reasons for change and explain the probable

consequences. This could be done only by improving communications within the yard between all levels of management and
men.

One of the main grievances of the workers under the old
Company was their lack of information about its policies and its
prospects. Workers felt remote from the Company and its
management. The new management introduced regular meetings with the shop stewards to discuss matters affecting the
Company and its employees. These meetings were necessary to
establish trust and to exchange views on problems. Shop
stewards were given information which had previously never
been disclosed to them – e.g. the state of the Company's order
book, future prospects, and the effect on labour loading. The
shop stewards reciprocated and aired problems, grievances, and
made known their views on a range of subjects. The educative
process was two-fold; the shop stewards began to see and to
some extent, appreciate management problems, whereas the
management were able to obtain at first hand the views, thinking, and fears of the workers.

Regular meetings between management and shop stewards
are commonplace in most industries, and in many shipyards. It
had never been so in the old Company. The required rapidity of
change at Fairfields made these meetings essential. The management was committed to a policy of full consultation with the
workers and their representatives. The latter required time and
facilities to discuss the often revolutionary proposals of management. To facilitate and expedite the discussions the management provided a meeting room for the shop stewards. It was
also decided that the convenor of shop stewards be on a full-
time basis. This was considered necessary by the general
manager because of his need to have quick access to the men
through a readily available spokesman, someone who would be
in a position to air potential grievances before they developed
into more serious issues.

Not all of the management or the trades unions were convinced of the need for a full-time convenor. However, such a
position was established and the convenor became an important link in the communications network in the yard.

The public relations officer was given the task of introducing and editing a company newspaper, the *Fairfield News*, which carried the usual items of news but was also used to convey policy items and general information to the yard workers. All major speeches, or important announcements were reprinted – e.g. the complete procedure agreement signed by all unions organizing in the yard. It played a very useful part in the efforts to provide as many people as possible with information on the company. The large circulation outside the yard did much to stimulate interest in the company and in the proving ground concept, and was an important explanation of the constant flow of visitors to the company.

Because of its proving ground status and the scepticism of the other yards on the Clyde, Fairfields was 'non-federated' and not a member of the Clyde Shipbuilders' Association (CSA). It had to negotiate with the thirteen unions organizing in the yard a procedure agreement to replace that operated by the Shipbuilding Employers' Federation and the Confederation of Shipbuilding and Engineering Unions.

These negotiations began in March 1966 and the agreement was signed on 2 June. Although the Fairfields agreement was very much in the spirit of the Geddes recommendations it was in draft and partly negotiated before the *Geddes Report* was published.

There are a number of differences between this procedure agreement and the agreement then in force in the shipbuilding industry.

The key body was the central joint council, chaired by the general manager and made up of four management representatives and representatives of the thirteen unions, each with executive authority. This CJC met monthly, and it was open to any member to suggest items for the agenda. The secretary was a senior trade-union official. As well as dealing with normal 'negotiation' issues the CJC frequently considered items on which management wished advice before formulating policy or making firm proposals. In addition, the chairman always reported on the present position in the yard and of the company generally. At the request of the shop stewards the practice grew up of the CJC meeting with the stewards after each CJC meeting, both to report on the meeting and to discuss items suggested by the stewards. With what was in effect a national negotiating and consultative body concerned with the problems of one yard there was an obvious need to prevent the thinking of the national body and of the yard stewards from getting seriously out of line. This problem of overlap occasionally led to competition between the two levels of union leadership for authority, with the executive members reasserting themselves successfully in the majority of cases. With a large number of unions involved it would not be practicable to expect bodies with executive authority to exercise close oversight in many yards or plants. The pressure of full diaries and scarce time was great even in this one case, and was overcome mainly because of the special feeling which the trade-union leaders concerned had for the Fairfields experiment. Even so it seems clear that any firm or plant which can secure such trade-union involvement at frequent and regular intervals and at executive level can derive great advantages. These advantages stem partly from narrowing the gap that too often exists between trade-union levels and partly from the educative effect that such contact has upon the management of a firm.

The most noteworthy part of the dispute procedure under the Fairfields procedure agreement was the Scottish Conference to which unresolved matters had to be referred. The findings of this conference were binding except in 'matters of grave importance'. The composition of the conference was usually four trade union officials and two management representatives. Although in each of its five meetings the union representation outnumbered the management representatives in eight of the nine cases considered the trade unions claim was rejected and the management view upheld. The main conclusion to be drawn from this is that rational argument rather than power considerations carries weight if given the opportunity to do so, particularly when there is an opportunity for involvement in the decision-making process. This result may also be taken as an indication that Fairfields management did not resist reasonable claims by fighting them through to the final stage of a Scottish

Conference. Rationality is strengthened by a readiness to compromise when the facts of a situation suggest that right is not
all on one side. Nevertheless, there was a pronounced tendency
for Fairfields management to resist all major claims that could
not be supported by changes in working practices leading to
increased efficiency. 'Nothing for nothing' was the management
slogan throughout most of this period. This makes the decisions
of the Scottish Conference all the more remarkable.

The procedure agreement contains an additional provision
encouraging rational negotiation and constraining any tendency
to coercive action. This is the provision that the payment of
agreed increases shall be back-dated to the commencement date
of a claim, always assuming that no strike or walk-out has
taken place during negotiations. In the event of any such
coercive action no retrospective payment can be made.

In considering 'the right to strike' at Fairfields it is necessary
to distinguish between (1) the formal contracts that bind the
company its employees and the signatory unions, and which
are embodied in the Procedure Agreements of 2 June and 1
September 1966; and (2) the 'pledges' which were passed
between Sir Iain Stewart and trade-union officials (at meetings
in London and Glasgow) and between Sir Iain and the employees of the old company (in the Lyceum Cinema, Govan) before
Fairfields (Glasgow) Ltd was established.

(This no-strike pledge was featured by Sir Iain at subsequent
meetings attended by all employees, when he asked those who
did not accept it to leave the employment of the company. The
pledge was thus kept alive and applicable to employees who
joined the company since the first Lyceum meeting in December
1965.)

THE FORMAL PROCEDURE AGREEMENT

1. No stoppage, overtime ban or other limitation on production was to take place until a decision of the Scottish Conference was made.

2. Normally the decision of the Scottish Conference was
final, that is, it had to be accepted and implemented by the

parties to the dispute. Thus no stoppage, etc., was possible if the union or its members were dissatisfied with a decision, any more than, say, a failure to pay up was open to the company if it did not like a decision. This position should be seen in the light of the nature of the arbitration process uniquely favourable to the unions in which it was recognized both in the agreement [7(b)iv] and in practice that the union members of the conference outnumbered the management members.

3. Reference is made to the possibility of a conference at which members of the Conciliation Branch of the Ministry of Labour could attend by invitation. Such a conference was to be called by the union (or unions) concerned in the dispute if the union was asked to do so and if it judge the matter to be one of grave importance. Either the management or the members of the union in dispute were free to ask the union to call such a conference. No definition was given of what was to be regarded as a 'matter of grave importance', judgement being left to the union, presumably at executive level.

After such a conference: 'Procedure at this point would be exhausted but no stoppage, overtime ban, or other limitation on production of work shall take place until this point has been reached.'

Thus the possibility of strike action, bans on overtime or other limitations on production only arose when the dispute had filtered through all the stages up to and including the special conference called on a matter of grave importance, and when this conference had failed to reach a decision satisfactory to the union. In such a case a union executive would presumably have given considerable weight to the earlier decision of the Scottish Conference and would be influenced by the views expressed by the Ministry of Labour conciliators. Even in normal circumstances one would expect that the number of strikes, etc., called through this procedure would be very few indeed.

The pledges to make Fairfields a no-strike yard during a 'proving period' were given freely to Sir Iain and used by him in negotiations with the government, and with trade union and private investors in his efforts to raise sufficient capital to keep the yard open. The pledges were also used by the new company when competing for contracts.

The management were well aware of how exceptional such a pledge by trade unionists was but even so probably under-estimated the difficulties on the trade-union side of making it completely effective. Such a pledge could only be effective if intelligent and responsible trade-union leaders at all levels strove to make it so. There is plenty of evidence that members of the CJC, district officials and executive members of the unions associated with Fairfields considered the industrial environment of Fairfields so favourable that they were willing to work with the management to establish a more mature and sensible way of resolving industrial differences of opinion. Although a number of strikes and threats of strike action did take place at Fairfields the 'pledge' did reduce the incidence of conflict in a period of imposed restraint and of rapid change. Paradoxically there was a negative effect: the existence of the pledge at times encouraged management to assume a permanency to the equable industrial relations of the early months of the new company, an assumption which could create friction rather than minimize it. All of the parties would probably agree, however, that such a pledge could only be effective for a short period, and that the strains and stresses that might otherwise have led to strike action could reappear in other forms.

In addition to the procedure agreement, the company also signed a demarcation procedure agreement with the thirteen trade unions organizing in the yard. This agreement was note-worthy in that the ASB agreed to take part in arbitration with the other trade unions concerned rather than insisting on exclusive meetings with management. This was a concession made by the ASB to the concept of a proving ground. The ASB was the largest single union in the yard, and was also the most powerful union in the industry. Traditionally militant, the Society had operated very much as a lone wolf. The circum-stances of Fairfields led the members of other unions in the yard to hope that their union could at least begin to share some of the power traditionally exercised by the Society, particularly because it was believed that the spirit of cooperation would blunt the traditional militancy of the Society and bring relative bargaining strength more into balance.

The ASB members were the highest paid men in the yard. This fact, together with their numerical supremacy in yard and industry made them very much leaders in the yards. Their clannishness and alleged belief in their superiority over other trade unionists, combined to make the Society as a whole feared and disliked. Their cooperation was vital to the progress of the firm – but many yard workers felt that this cooperation was equally necessary from other trades and grades, and accused management of favouring the opinions of, or succumbing to the threats of the ASB.

The position was that most ASB members were steelworkers, and these are concerned with the first stages of building the ships – they are very much pacemakers for the other processes in the yard. Management in their efforts to speed up production had to give prior attention to the steelworkers and therefore to the ASB. As the foremen felt neglected when attention was focused on shop stewards* so other unions' shop stewards felt neglected in comparison with the ASB. The increased status and attention given to trade unionism in the yard reinforced the organization, and stiffened the determination of the other shop stewards in the yard to get the best deal for their members. Two groups of shop stewards emerged; the ASB and the remainder of the unions' representatives. Within the latter group the NUGMW was the largest group, but it also included a number of craft unions.

The ill-feeling between the ASB and the other group is best illustrated in the circumstances surrounding the election of a full-time convenor. When the general manager indicated his support for a full-time convenor of shop stewards, the ASB was not enthusiastic, arguing that a shipyard contained too wide a range of diversified skills for one convenor effectively to represent all yard workers. The ASB believed that 'their business was only their business': they were not prepared to have a non-ASB member represent their interests under any circumstances. This was a principle. The ASB did not want a

* See Chapter 3 on Management.

full-time convenor, but if one had to be appointed, he should be an ASB member to reflect its predominant position in the yard. Previously the office of convenor had not been of such high importance. Now as a full-time position in the context of a proving ground, its status had changed greatly. The ASB was also concerned about the method of payment for the job, the determination of the rate and the extent and scope of the duties.

In May 1966 the management emphasized their belief in the need for a full-time convenor. The then incumbent in a part-time capacity had a long history of trade union work, and had been prominent in the campaign to keep open the yard during the period of foreclosure. A man of sound experience, popular and able, but as a semi-skilled man unacceptable to the ASB members.

To avoid the dangerous inter-union tensions which were developing in the yard at the time, the convenor's job specification was carefully drawn up to avoid direct conflict with ASB principles. A number of shop stewards meetings were held to discuss the issue, but the ASB stewards remained firm and unyielding. One potent issue of contention was the system of voting – should it be one vote per shop steward? Although having over one third of the total labour force as ASB members, ASB stewards represented under 30 per cent of the total votes. ASB workers elected two shop stewards per department, e.g. two shop stewards represented 175 men in the shipwrights sections. The Society complained that shop stewards representing perhaps less than ten men in other unions and trades had equal voting rights.

The issue came to a head on 6 June 1966. The position of full-time convenor had been endorsed by the union in the procedure agreement signed four days previously. At a meeting specifically called to elect a convenor, the ASB shop stewards refused to accept a majority vote. The meeting was abandoned. The non-ASB stewards felt that they could not allow the ASB representation on the yard committee when they were opposed to a majority decision. The shop stewards' committee was dissolved by a failure to reconvene it. For a week or so no formal system of shop-steward organization existed. However, the non-ASB stewards later formed their own yard committee, electing a convenor and other officers. The convenor was recognized by the management and eventually appointed full-time from 26 June 1966.

The ASB were not represented on the yard committee and remained unrepresented on the committee for some months afterwards. The ASB conducted their own business and had their own convenor (representing the trades within the Society) who eventually became full-time as part of a joint team set up to help implement a productivity agreement.

The feelings aroused by the issue of the convenorship illustrated the gulf between ASB members and the rest of the yard. The ASB jealously guarded their prerogatives and allowed their fear of losing a long-established and predominant position in the yard to cloud the realities of the situation. The job specification for the convenor had to be approved by the CJC which gave it careful and prolonged consideration. The agreed job specification did not infringe the prerogatives of the ASB and this was eventually recognized by the members of the Society in the yard, although they never gave up their belief that as the largest union in the yard they had the right to the convenorship.

The issue of the convenorship emphasized the tension between the ASB members and the other yard workers. The ASB shop stewards seemed to be demanding preferential treatment from management, while the other shop stewards were closely watching management to ensure that none was given. The delicate state of inter-union relations in the yard was clearly seen by management. Regular meetings with the shop stewards and the two-way flow of information which arose from these contacts helped them formulate strategy. In particular, the emphasis given to communications was one means of ensuring that minimum friction arose from misunderstandings. Policies were explained throughout the yard to avoid labour problems arising from misunderstanding of management policy.

The management were considerably helped in the field of labour relations by having access to and advice from the executive officers of the trades unions organizing in the yard. These contacts were usually made on the CJC but use was made of them in emergency situations, with consequences which were not always good for the company. Without doubt the company benefited considerably from its exceptionally close contacts with the trade unions. In the next chapter it will be seen how these contacts were used and developed in the every-day conduct of labour relations by the company.

CHAPTER 6

Labour Relations 2
The Beginning of Productivity Bargaining:
The ASB agreement

ON 2 June 1966 the company and the ASB signed an agreement for the relation of working practices (ROWP) between members of the Society. Although signed only six months after the formation of the company, it was substantially an agreement which earlier had been negotiated, but not finalized, between the Clyde Shipbuilders' Association and the ASB. The foreclosure of Fairfields in October 1965 had delayed completion of these negotiations. As a result of the Fairfields situation, the ASB and the other unions were fully occupied with efforts to keep the yard open, and negotiations on the flexibility proposals were suspended. The new Fairfields management were anxious to promote productivity agreements and the ASB felt that it could use the company as a test-bed for the proposals contained within the final agreement.

The proposals were initiated by the ASB which felt that its suggestions were likely to make drastic alterations to the existing working practices of the steelworkers and would give rise to increased productivity.

Before productivity bargaining could begin a number of conditions had to be met if the negotiations were to have any chance of success. First, there had to be mutual trust and desire for successful negotiations on the part of management and unions. During the course of discussions the management disclosed information not usually available to union representatives. Although very important as a basis for discussion, such information could have been used for narrow sectional advantage. This did not happen, largely as a result of the confidence and trust between management and trade union negotiators. The desire for a successful outcome to negotiations cannot always be assumed to enthuse both parties equally. It is not unknown for a negotiator to go through the procedure of negotiations without having any enthusiasm for, or intention of obtaining, a settlement. This was never the situation at Fairfields.

Given that mutual trust and desire to reach a satisfactory settlement exist, good communications between negotiators and the shop floor is the other necessary ingredient of the bargaining situation. The shop floor must be kept informed of the progress of the negotiations, because it is at that level that the agreements will operate. Without shop floor approval the agreements reached will be largely worthless.* At Fairfields, the senior shop stewards of the unions involved in bargaining were, whenever possible, included in the negotiations. Their presence was invaluable, not only as a source of information, but as a gauge of shop floor feeling. They acted as a channel of communication whereby some proposals of the negotiators could be tested in the workshop environment and reactions could filter back.

It is important to determine whether trade-union officials had the authority to negotiate. Where such authority is lacking, continued 'reference upwards' is time-wasting and a cause of frustration to management and to the other (if any) trade unions involved. In the negotiation of the outfit trades flexibility agreement eight trade unions were involved. The need for inter-union cooperation was evident, and they came to an arrangement by which one full-time official conducted the final negotiations for all eight unions. In this case, 'reference upwards' occurred only when the agreement was finalized and had to be referred to various unions' district committees for endorsement.

When all these conditions are present, the final prerequisite for a productivity bargaining environment is that management have available the means of costing the proposals. A bargain obviously cannot be productive without means of costing and measuring the effects of the agreement. At Fairfields this was done by the industrial engineering department. The task of this department in terms of productivity proposals was to assess the feasibility of the proposals and assess their value to the com-

*Research Paper 4, Royal Commission on Trade Union and Employers' Associations, Section E, H M S O, 1966, p. 10.

pany. In many areas, because of the nature of shipbuilding, calculations were less than precise. However, they did provide a basis for calculation which, together with data collected from work measurement, was invaluable for costing purposes. Without a work measurement staff it would be impossible to estimate the value of most productivity proposals.

The prerequisites for a productivity bargaining environment were present at Fairfields, and from this environment four productivity agreements emerged. In addition to the agreement with the ASB productivity deals were negotiated with the NUGMW (covering unskilled and semi-skilled workers) DATA (Drawing Office staff) and with the eight craft unions organizing the outfitting trades. In this chapter the ASB agreement is examined in some detail and the effects of the agreement on the rest of the yard analysed.

The corner-stone of the agreement and probably its fundamental weakness was that it permitted flexibility only where this would progress (the tradesman's) own work. It became an easy matter, particularly for the less craft-based trades, to ensure their future survival by 'protecting' their work. For a man of one craft to 'progress own work' it was necessary that no specialist service trade was readily available. After the implementation of the agreement some foremen complained that 'welders were refusing to allow other trades to weld for any length of time'. Eventually, the management was able to overcome such reservations by forming special service squads.

This agreement covered the largest trade union membership in the yard. In order to avoid the – 'infant mortality'* which such agreements face, the convenor of ASB members in the yard was employed full-time together with a manager to form a team to explain, discuss, and where necessary interpret the agreement in those areas covered by it. Discussions with foremen and shop stewards 'on the job' provided uniformity of interpretation and this helped to avoid any major problems arising from misuse of the agreement. The introduction of this 'trouble-shooting' team was a very successful innovation.

*G. Roberts, *Demarcation Rules in Shipbuilding and Shiprepairing*, Cambridge, 1967, p. 40.

There is no doubt that the ASB agreement had the potential to significantly affect productivity in the steelwork division. Unfortunately, at the time of signing, the management were not, for three major reasons, in a position to implement the agreement. The consolidation of wage rates had reduced incentive and effort in the steel trades as in the yard generally. The agreement could do little to affect the tempo of work because in the early months of the company the necessary control over production was lacking. No through-put could be sustained at a level to use fully the terms of the agreement. In this period of great change in the company, the productivity services organization was only beginning to develop and had limited effect on the pattern of work organization in the yard. The third barrier to implementation lay with the foremen. At this time morale was very low.*

They had little enthusiasm for the new changes and were generally apathetic towards the agreement and the company. In this situation it was difficult to obtain the main benefits of the agreement. As late as December 1967 a majority of a sample of steelwork foremen considered that they were obtaining less than 50 per cent of the potential benefits of the agreement.

Table 6.1

*Steelwork foremen: benefit derived from agreement
by December 1967, against potential benefits*

Percentage benefit derived	Number of foremen
Under 10	4
11–24	3
25–49	2
50–64	–
65+	2
Don't know	2

Given time, the majority of these foremen considered that they would obtain 'over 50 per cent of the potential benefits of the agreement'. This, of course, depended on the improve-

* See Chapter 3 on Management, p. 66.

ment in method and production control necessary for the improved utilization of manpower.

It will be noted that the agreement related only to working practices and made no mention of overtime working, production standards or manning arrangements. It was a bargain aimed at procuring a better utilization of labour through emphasis on flexibility of working practices. The men's reactions to the agreement varied. One shop steward felt that the training which the agreement stimulated broadened the horizons of the craftsmen and this 'tended to reduce tension between "touching trades"'. Another felt that the ability to 'progress own work' must have an effect on productivity by reducing waiting time for service trades. Some members were apprehensive about the possible effects of the agreement. One shop steward believed that retraining reduced the craft specialization on which his continued security of employment was based. Relaxation which allows encroachment into craft sections raises a certain amount of fear of an eventual loss of 'trade identity'. Whatever the apprehensions aroused by the agreement, the written guarantee of eighteen months' employment from the date of signing for all men covered by the agreement alleviated many anxieties. This was a guarantee believed to be unique in the industry, certainly on the Clyde, and did much to overcome the fears of workers in the yard.

When the productivity proposals were first brought to the management by the ASB they were evaluated by the shipyard manager. From his long experience of the industry, he considered that the proposals could increase productivity by 5–20 per cent. No one could be certain of the benefits to be gained from the proposals, and the management eventually agreed that a 12·5 per cent increase in productivity could be realistic. At this time the difference between the lowest and highest rates paid to Society members in the yard was 2s. 7d. per hour. The management decided to offer one-third of this difference as a payment for the proposals, and 9d. per hour became the bargaining basis. In addition, payment was to be made for the Society's acceptance of work study. Without work study the benefits of the proposals would be difficult to realize.

The evaluation of the proposals and the determination of a base were clearly less than scientific. The chief negotiator for the company was the general manager, who in the early months of the company had to rely heavily on the judgement of inherited management. However, the final payment of 9d. per hour for the agreement also reflected the fact that the ASB were in negotiation with the CSA and the general manager considered that, in the event of an agreement being reached between those parties, there would be a drain of steelworkers from Fairfields.

The major provocation to the other unions' members in the yard was the retrospective payment of 9d. per hour to all those ASB members on the company's books when negotiations began. Retrospective payment was a principle set out by the company in the procedure agreement – 'the settlement arrived at during such negotiations shall be back-dated to take effect from the first complete pay week after the date of the first meeting . . . '. There is some justifiable doubt surrounding the date when negotiations could properly be said to have begun. In addition, the procedure agreement which embodied the back-dating clause had come into force on the same day as the ROWP agreement was signed. It must be unique for a company to pay men retrospectively who were on the books at the outset of negotiations but who had subsequently left. The overall-result was a retrospective payment of approximately £30 to each ASB member. This cost the company £25,000 at a time when money was very tight. This figure, when it became known in the yard, caused great bitterness and added fuel to inter-union rivalries.

The ASB members were already the highest paid in the yard. The payment of 9d. per hour under the agreement further increased the differential between them and other workers in the yard. The lower paid workers were mainly organized by the NUGMW. The latter union had invested £50,000 in the Fairfield proving ground, and its members in the yard felt that this had been partly used to increase wage differentials and 'to line the pockets of the ASB who refused to invest in the yard'. Even without the payment of £30, retrospectively, the agreement would have provoked antagonism because of its effect of widening differentials. The situation in the yard in June 1966 was embittered and tense and with hindsight the general manager would not have made so generous a retrospective payment; there would have been more debate over the actual date of commencement of negotiations.

This agreement was subsequently adopted, with minor amendments by the CSA and the ASB and became common to the steelwork trades on the upper reaches. There were two important differences between the CSA agreement and that signed by Fairfields. The first was that the CSA paid an increase of 1s. per hour, which was staggered, i.e. 4d. for signing, 4d. on partial implementation, and 4d. on complete implementation.

This progressive payment certainly anticipated the incomes policy criteria of 'no payment on account'.* However, because the agreement had been paid for in one stage at Fairfields, considerable agitation from men and management developed in other yards. Eventually, the Ministry of Labour satisfied itself that the agreement was being implemented and sanctioned payment of the balance.

The other difference was that the total payment made by Fairfields included 4d. for trade-union acceptance of work study. No similar provision existed in the CSA agreement, and it is difficult to see how a productivity bargain could be unrelated to some form of measurement.

The ASB agreement was undoubtedly a major breakthrough for Fairfields. Yet it was to have consequences which were to remain with the management and affect labour relations until the merger. The immediate effect of the agreement was to increase the differentials between the higher and lower paid workers in the yard. Within days of the signing of the agreement the management received at least sixteen claims for wage increases based on grounds of 'parity' or 'preservation of differentials'. Within the Society, the apprentices and some semi-skilled men who had traditionally received a *pro rata* payment in relation to craftsmens' wage increases, were to be in

* *Prices and Incomes Standstill: Period of Severe Restraint*, Cmnd 3150, HMSO, p. 27.

dispute with the company. The management reiterated its policy of 'nothing for nothing'; wage increases could only be given in return for productivity-giving agreements. The workers, shop stewards, and full-time officials were encouraged to discuss possible productivity schemes. The ASB negotiations provided a stimulant for productivity bargaining in the company. In the next chapter we see how this stimulant resulted in protracted negotiations, disputes, and eventually agreements. In a later chapter the actual impact on productivity is assessed.

CHAPTER 7

Labour Relations 3
Disputes and Productivity Bargaining

THE agitation arising from the ASB agreement enabled the management to initiate discussions on productivity proposals with various sections in the yard. One of the main pressure groups, and probably the most vociferous in its condemnation of the ASB agreement's effect on differentials, was the cranemen. This group walked out from the yard on 10 June 1966 (four days after the signing of the ASB agreement) to signify their 'general discontent with the wages structure' and also to discuss the possibility of combining the members of the NUGMW in Fairfields into one branch.

The cranemen's claim for an increase in wages was taken up by the rest of the NUGMW's members in the yard, and the claim became a general one. The NUGMW claim and the eventual agreement is a good example of the process of productivity bargaining at Fairfields – a process which was new to the men and also to some union negotiators. The NUGMW agreement had its origins in the claim brought to the Scottish conference on 18 September 1966, on behalf of the unions' unskilled and semi-skilled workers.

The claim was for a general increase in wages 'because of the increase in differential between the ASB and our members as a consequence of the recent award made by the company arising from the agreement on the relaxation of working practices'.

The claim was based on the traditional grounds of 'comparability and the preservation of differentials'. The union negotiators wanted an increase comparable to that given to the ASB – 9d. per hour; in return they were prepared to offer various 'flexibility' concessions. The Scottish conference rejected the claim in the following terms – 'the committee having examined all aspects of the case, find that they reject the claim for a general increase, but will examine all details of any flexibility offered and suggest that this be done as speedily as possible'. The union submitted to management their flexibility proposals on 3 October. On 24 October the management met the union and said that the industrial engineering department was examining the proposals and would explore in detail the suggested areas of flexibility.

The men were not happy with the pace of the negotiations. This was their first experience of productivity bargaining and they were impatient about the time taken to evaluate the proposals. On 8 December the shop stewards approached management for a progress report on the evaluation. The results of the evaluation were reported back to a Scottish conference held on 9 January 1967 at a meeting which became important in the subsequent negotiations because of a mis-understanding between management and men regarding what was actually said. The management reported on their evaluation of the flexibility proposals and outlined a possible productivity scheme whereby the flexibility proposals could be combined with a rundown in the union's labour force in the yard by means of natural wastage. The scheme was based on proven trends in labour turnover, and the rundown, which was to account for approximately a hundred men, was to be back-dated to begin from 24 October 1966 (the date on which the union's flexibility proposals were first put to the Scottish conference). No redundancies were anticipated, but any occurring would be included in the rundown total.

The source of confusion was an example written on a black-board to show how the scheme could operate. A figure was used to 'approximate' to the numbers employed in the yard who would be affected by the scheme. The figure given in this example was that which the shop stewards believed was their total union strength in the yard as at 24 October; the actual figure was, in fact, considerably higher. The personnel services manager stressed that his illustration was only an example and made clear that he was not making any propositions, 'I am merely reporting back to the conference'. It was anticipated that the operation of the scheme would allow an increase in the region of 6d. per hour to be paid to all N U G M W members, unskilled and semi-skilled, male and female.

On 11 January, the productivity services director, together with the local official of the union, addressed a meeting of the workers in the canteen. The principles of the scheme were explained and questions invited; the meeting gave approval to the scheme and agreed that the company and the union would work out detailed proposals and would then discuss these with the shop stewards. These proposals were drawn up, discussed with and approved by the shop stewards by 3 February. The necessary supporting documents and calculations were made, and the proposals placed in the context of the criteria set out by the Prices and Incomes Board for productivity bargains. The claim was presented to the Ministry of Labour on 8 March.

In its submission to the Ministry the management justified the proposed agreement by estimating that it would cost the company £25,000 per annum, but would provide an overall saving in labour costs of £91,500 per annum. The main savings were expected from the rundown in the labour force through the process of natural wastage; as employees left, they would not be replaced. The labour requisition system ensured that only necessary labour was taken on. The authorization of the productivity services director was required before labour could be engaged. The other benefits would be obtained from the interchangeability and flexibility proposals which the agreement proposed. A study of these proposals made by the industrial engineering department stated that 'with respect to flexibility only 13 per cent of the membership would be affected, but with respect to interchangeability, approximately 96 per cent of the N U G M W members would be affected'.

The company proposed 6d. per hour as the price of these proposals. One senior manager explained the basis for the calculation. The deal could not, for political reasons, exceed the 9d. per hour paid to the A S B members. He considered that the A S B agreement was valuable to the company in proportions of 50 per cent flexibility and 50 per cent interchangeability. The N U G M W proposals on a comparative basis were worth approximately 100 per cent for interchangeability, but only

135

10 per cent for flexibility. Therefore the interchangeability was worth 4½d. (equal to the ASB proportion) and 1½d. for flexibility (approximately 10 per cent of ASB award).

At this point it is interesting to note the attitudes of the parties. The union representative and the shop stewards were enthusiastic and 'confident' that the agreement would be approved, but some senior managers did not share this confidence.

On 21 March the Ministry wrote to the company saying that they approved of the agreement in principle, but asked that further consideration be given to the rate of payment – 'we suggest that it would be more consistent with government policy if the payment of increased wages were to be more closely related to the running down of the labour force, and the increase in productivity this is intended to give rise to, so that, as far as possible, there is no increase in labour costs'. The Ministry also asked to be informed before the agreement was implemented. Most unfortunately this letter became lost in the company and, although dated 21 March, did not arrive on the personnel services manager's desk until 17 April. This delay was never satisfactorily explained, but it did seem to be the result of error and not duplicity – although naturally enough this suspicion further clouded relationships.

The Ministry's decision was given to the union, and a meeting was held with the full-time official and shop stewards on 21 April. At this meeting the management said that in view of the letter they could now only offer 2d. per hour with the balance of 4d. per hour when the prospective rundown in the labour force occurred. The men rejected this offer. A counter-proposal from the union negotiator of 3d. per hour (back-dated to 1 January 1967) and 3d. per hour related to future rundown was accepted by the management subject to Ministry approval. Later in the day, the company were informed that the proposal was not acceptable to the men, and the offer was withdrawn.

On 24 April, discussions were held between the personnel services manager and the shop stewards. The shop stewards wanted 4d. per hour paid immediately (and retrospectively to 1 January), and 2d. per hour on rundown. The negotiations were adjourned to permit the personnel services manager to consult with the productivity services director – who would not accept the proposals as he considered them 'inconsistent with the Ministry's letter'. The productivity services director was engaged in a series of explanatory talks with other yard workers on the MDS and was not prepared to break off these important discussions to see the NUGMW shop stewards. He offered to hold discussions with the stewards in two days' time, when that union was due to discuss the MDS proposals. The PSM appealed to the stewards for a seventy-two-hour adjournment to 'allow management to consider the proposals'. This request was taken by the shop stewards back to the various departments, where it was rejected. A mass meeting of the workers concerned was held later in the afternoon at which a unanimous decision in favour of strike action was taken; in all, 540 workers were involved.

The men were very angry at the alleged procrastination of the management, 'this has been dragging on for seven months'. Relations between senior shop stewards and some managers seriously deteriorated, the wider issues involved being tainted by personal animosities. This affected not only the shop stewards, but also their full-time official who said that he had been 'greatly offended by some remarks made to him', and consequently vowed never to 'treat employers here any differently from elsewhere'. This was the low point in relations between the shop stewards, full-time officials and the management.

The company took expert opinion on the proposed agreement and were strengthened in their belief that only 2d. per hour could be paid immediately. In order to get the men back to work the company contacted national executive officials of the union and telegrams sent out in the name of the union and ordering a return to work were despatched that afternoon. The men returned to work, most reluctantly, on 26 April. Meetings continued with management throughout the morning. The management gave the following written declaration to the shop stewards: 'the company is prepared, and always has been, to honour the terms of the interchangeability and flexibility agreement in full. This, the Government has not allowed. The company will pay any amount within the terms of the agreement, back-dated to any date the Government will accept.'

The company, with the approval of the district secretary of the NUGMW, invoked clause 5 of the procedure agreement and called a meeting of all NUGMW members for 3.00 p.m. in the canteen.

The men believed that the company was not prepared to honour the flexibility agreement. Argument centred on the interpretation of the Ministry's letter. The management offered to send a deputation – including shop stewards – to the Ministry to seek an interpretation of the letter. The shop stewards refused this offer as they anticipated Ministry firmness – 'we know the answer!' The shop stewards' reaction to this offer is some indication of their attitude towards management at that time. There was not only a lack of faith with management, but also often distrust of their intentions.

After a morning of inconclusive discussions, the stewards reported 'lack of progress' to a mass meeting held at lunchtime. The company's statement about payment of the terms of the agreement was read out. This did not affect the vote of the meeting to take immediate strike action.

On 27 April the company again approached executive members of the union to obtain a return to work. Top-level consultations took place in the yard while the men were on strike. The action of the company in approaching the executive officers of the union and by-passing local officials soured the opinion and hardened the attitudes of the shop stewards and some full-time officials. There were strong rumours of disciplinary action being taken by the union against the shop stewards. These rumours appeared to be given some substance when the shop stewards concerned had to appear before the district committee of their union – thus promoting the reaction that 'Fairfields management is now running our union'. There was an obvious relationship between the attitude of the men and the fact that the union concerned was one of those which had invested capital in the company.

On 28 April another mass meeting was addressed by the full-time official who had helped negotiate the agreement. He informed the meeting that their union was instructing them to return to work. 'Now that management is offering to take the letter back to the Ministry, your quarrel is now with the Government. We cannot fight the Government.' The meeting was unruly and chaotic, and the official's case was not clearly understood because of the absence of a microphone. Despite the eloquent pleading by the official a decisive vote was taken to continue strike action.

Later in the afternoon a secret, unofficial exchange of views took place between the shop stewards and the general manager, who had, until that time, not been involved in the dispute. The meeting was useful as an airing of views and of grievances and brought home to the general manager some of the difficulties inherent in the manner labour relations policy was administered in the company, of which he had been previously unaware.

On 1 May the Scottish district secretary of the NUGMW addressed a meeting of the strikers. The meeting was again noisy and antagonistic towards the officials. The district secretary pleaded a strong and realistic case. His main contentions were that the Fairfield management 'had no authority to interpret the Ministry's letter – this can only be done by the Ministry'. He also pointed out that negotiations were currently being held at the highest level – he had been instructed by his executive to negotiate on behalf of the union while Fairfields board had empowered the general manager to take over negotiations. Negotiations at this high level could continue, but only if the men returned to work. The meeting discussed this proposition and eventually, after much bitter discussion, decided by a vote of 185 to 135 to return to work.

Immediately after this decision was taken the full-time officials and shop stewards met the management to discuss the deputation to meet the Ministry officials. The general manager proposed that the company's delegation should be headed by the productivity services director, who had carried out most of the negotiations. The latter objected '. . . we have other important discussions taking place which must not be interfered with. There is more than one union in this yard.' He was referring to the discussions on the MDS which were currently taking place. This objection, however valid, further increased the tension between the productivity services director and the shop stewards.

On 2 May the men returned to work; next day the deputation went to the Ministry of Labour in London. On 5 May the chairman of the company met with all of the stewards in an attempt to restore relations in the yard. A summary of the exchanges at this meeting is appended to this chapter. This brings out very clearly the strong degree of involvement in the affairs of the company which the stewards felt. On 8 May a mass meeting was held to inform the men that the Ministry had authorized full payment of the agreement as from 1 May. Nine months of agitation, frustration and hard bargaining had eventually proved successful.

One of the main stumbling blocks impeding the payment of the agreement was that the necessary rundown in the labour force had not occurred. On 24 October 1966, the date on which the rundown was to be based, the company had 538 NUGMW members on its payroll. By 9 January 1967, when a possible scheme was outlined to the shop stewards, the slowing trend of rundown should have cautioned management. By 1 May the rundown had totalled only twenty-four men, the number on the books being 514.* The company felt that full payment of the terms of the agreement in the light of the Ministry's letter would be in contradiction of incomes policy. The men did not understand why a rundown had not occurred. The shop stewards believed that the scheme would be based on the figures illustrating the scheme when it was outlined to them on 9 January. Although the management had clearly indicated that these figures were only illustrative, the men were convinced that they were fact, and this became a contentious point.

The company could have avoided much of this acrimony if it had fully warned the men of the consequences of a slowing down in natural wastage of the labour force. It had always been made clear that any agreement had to be acceptable to the

* These figures became available only in 1968. In May 1967 it was believed that the 'number on books' figure was 536, thus showing a rundown of only two men.

Ministry – but it ought to have been made clear that this might mean partial implementation to avoid 'payment on account'. This was never done, despite expert advice on the need for a contingency plan in case of Ministry restriction.

The slow progress of negotiations was regarded by the men as indicative of the apathy of management towards the agreement. In fact, the agreement was being negotiated at a time when the MDS was being drawn up and explained to the men. There was a very heavy pressure on management and this was one factor affecting the progress of negotiations.

The negotiations had created great tension in labour management relations, particularly between NUGMW shop stewards and the productivity services director. Much of the antagonism resulted from clashes of personality rather than from the objective issues in dispute. Within management, the consequences of the negotiations and the lessons learned from it should have led to administrative changes, but such changes were never made. Despite the problems arising from the agreement, it turned out to be very successful. It was calculated that twenty-eight men would have to leave the company in order to meet the costs involved. By the end of 1967, the actual reduction was from 740 to 611, that is 129 (these larger figures include all workers covered by the agreement). Not only were labour costs being reduced to offset the cost of the agreement, but full interchangeability and flexibility of labour, which were a valuable acquisition in the drive for increased productivity, were also conceded.

The outfit trades flexibility agreement also had its origins in a 'straight' wage claim. On 10 May 1966, a productivity agreement had been signed with the maintenance department employees. These employees were members of the AEU. One of the shop stewards was keen to employ productivity bargaining as a means of improving his pay, and that of his colleagues. He began, on his own initiative, to sound out opinion in 'touching trades' about the possibility of them agreeing on various flexibility proposals. Soon electricians and joiners were declaring an interest although progress was slow. The shop stewards agreed various proposals amongst themselves, and

141

eventually brought them to management, who saw the possibilities in the proposals and hoped to develop them on a wider basis, covering all the outfitting trades. Such an agreement had already been signed for the shipyards on the east coast of Scotland.

Management wanted an agreement based on principles, a 'comprehensive' rather than a 'specific' agreement of the ASB type, arguing that specific agreements, i.e. those agreements which emphasized and itemized what could and could not be done, were likely to create as many barriers as they surmounted. Furthermore, disputes arising from the agreements turn on the letter rather than the spirit of the agreement.

On 24 May 1967, the AEU members in the MID lodged a claim for a wage increase with the departmental manager. The claim was based on comparability and the contention of the men that productivity had increased because fewer men were now manning jobs. At this preliminary meeting the stewards indicated their disapproval of the management's intention to negotiate a comprehensive agreement to cover all outfit trades. This proposal was considered by the shop stewards to be dangerously unspecific.

On 1 June, the shop stewards submitted a written request for an increase in wages and a local conference was held on 15 June, when the claim was rejected. The union delegate would not accept reference to the next stage in procedure, a Scottish conference; he advised the company that the men would be giving twenty-one days' notice of their intention to strike, this to expire on 7 July. The refusal of the full-time official to take the claim to the next stage in procedure was unconstitutional. He justified his decision by stating that the company had failed to keep a promise relating to wage increases made by the management in November 1966. The officials and shop stewards claimed that they withdrew their twenty-one-day strike notice (in support of a wage claim) in November when the management had promised to increase the members' wages by 2s. per hour by February 1967. The management certainly conferred with the union officials at that time but no minute of the discussion was made. The management believed that the members' expectations arose from a misunderstanding – 'I can only assume that reference to the two shillings per hour increase is the company's indication that this would be the maximum amount which would be paid under our measured daywork scheme.' It was this misunderstanding which lay behind the union official's action, hardening the men's intention to strike action if their demands were not met.

On 20 June the men held a meeting to discuss their attitude to the strike. Opinion was very much in favour of strike action – 'We believe this management understands muscle.' By 5 July, the situation seemed to have reached impasse. The management felt that the company could not give any concessions to the men without infringing the Fairfields' principle of 'nothing for nothing'. The general manager contacted an executive official of the AEU and asked his help to break the deadlock. This action stiffened the resolve of the men, and offended the local officials with whom the management would have to negotiate.

On 6 July another meeting was held with the shop stewards and their local official. The PSM made three main points. That the rates paid at the yard were higher than at any other yard on the River; that the company had money to settle the claim only if the reward was related to a settlement giving rise to productivity through flexibility and interchangeability of labour; that the company's proposals were essentially those already accepted by the union in the agreement with the shipyards on the east coast of Scotland.

The management considered the proposals as they stood to be worth about 5d. per hour; with the proposed amendments they could be worth 9d. per hour or more. The intention was to refer the proposals to the CJC for inspection – in particular, advice would be taken on the clause which placed a time limit on the period which a craftsman could be interchanged with another job (the clause proposed a maximum period of forty-two days in any one year). The men were not impressed by these arguments. They saw their action at Fairfields as similar to general wage pressure being exerted on other yard managements: 'where wages are concerned, we are tired of being second-class citizens'. The men also exhibited their fear for the company's future – 'like it or not, Fairfields will soon become part of a merger and we will be dealing with reactionary employers: we must take our money now'. The meeting was obviously dead-locked and the participants moved to the general manager's office.

The general manager outlined the state of the company: the precarious cash-flow position; the critical effect of any strike particularly on possible contracts. He emphasized that the company would be happy to sign an agreement as they had done with the A S B. The men reiterated their readiness only to accept 'fringe' flexibility. The meeting was adjourned and re-convened in the PS M's office. After further discussions the company made an offer – 'to pay the men 4½d. back-dated to 3 July when an agreement is signed. Any later monies to be paid for interchangeability and flexibility to be paid from the date of the signing of the agreement. Payment of all monies is depend-ent on the ultimate agreement being acceptable to all unions'. The meeting was adjourned, the union official strongly recom-mended that his members accept the proposal – 'the 4½d. you get for absolutely nothing'. The meeting was noisy and seemed still to be strongly inclined to strike action. The shop stewards refused to commit themselves to support of the proposal. The theme of the meeting was clearly expressed by one man – 'we've waited long enough, why wait any longer?' The pro-posal was rejected. Hectic discussions between management and shop stewards took place all through the afternoon. During these discussions the management persuaded the shop stewards that an agreement covering the outfit trades could be concluded by mid-September. The personnel services manager said that he was taking the principles of the agreement to the CJC. If these principles were not accepted, he pointed out that the men's tactical advantage of delaying engine installation on a bulk carrier would not be reduced. In this situation the PS M was recognizing a factor in the negotiations – that the men did have the power to delay installation and any reference of the claim might have been construed by some as a delaying action aimed at reducing the men's tactical position.

Next morning, 7 July, a mass meeting of the A E U was

addressed by shop stewards who recommended acceptance of the management's proposal, which was accepted by fifty votes to forty-four. The senior shop steward asked for this to be made unanimous, but this the meeting refused to do and the meeting was adjourned.

The senior steward feared the effect of the sharp division within the department on the capacity of his members to take effective, united action in the future. When negotiations were reopened in the afternoon the following written proposal was obtained from the company – 'The management has agreed that an interchangeability and flexibility agreement must be signed by the AEU and one other union by 8 September 1967. A payment of $4\frac{1}{2}$d. for members of unions who accept the principles of flexibility and interchangeability prior to 8 September 1967.'

The shop stewards had every reason to be happy with this written proposal. The management had guaranteed to negotiate the agreement within a set time and had accepted the onus of getting one other union to sign. The proposal had enabled the shop stewards to extract themselves from the dangerous predicament to which the negotiations had brought them. They were delighted that the management had agreed to take the responsibility, and consequences, of any failure to get another union to sign before 8 September. This new proposal was put to the men, but even then it took an hour's persuasion by the senior shop steward before it was accepted.

Discussion on the proposed agreement continued throughout August with the eight unions involved. At the meeting of 29 August, the unions were expecting management to 'talk money'. Disagreement between senior managers on the nature of the claim and its potential value caused delay. Discussion centred on the limits to be imposed on flexibility, and the time period involved. One union said it was prepared to accept that 20 per cent of its departmental strength be interchangeable at one time, for a period no longer than twenty-one days. The meeting was adjourned to allow the PSM to consult with the PSD. An offer of 6d. per hour was made by the management. The unions regarded this as 'insulting' and the meeting broke up. Next day a further meeting was held, this time chaired by the PSD.

The PSD spoke of the effect of restrictions on the proposals – 'without these the agreement would be worth 9d. per hour'. Further discussion took place around the limitations set to interchangeability and an adjournment took place. After the resumption the unions accepted 9d. per hour for the deal with the proviso that there be no overtime working in the department if redundancy threatened; that the unions agreed to accept that a maximum of forty men, or 20 per cent of a department's strength, whichever was the higher, could be transferred to another department; that a four week period for such flexibility was adequate, and in certain circumstances this period could be extended after consultation. The conditions were then embodied in an agreement which was referred to the Ministry of Labour, where it was delayed (partly because of the withdrawal from it of one of the unions party to the negotiations). Payment under the agreement was finally made in mid-October.

The fourth major productivity bargain covered the drawing offices and was negotiated with DATA. This agreement was no easier than the other to negotiate and was largely based on flexibility proposals which would allow the greater use of manpower.

The experience at Fairfields has been that productivity agreements are not easily or quickly negotiated; although pressures from workers to be paid money without very much in return was steadfastly resisted, more flexibility was paid for than was achieved in practice. This was the case with the ASB agreement and also with the outfit trades agreement. Two months after the signing of that agreement, the whole sample of outfitting foremen interviewed had not used any of its provisions. In one department implementation had not been possible because men were being redeployed due to lack of work, but in other areas opportunities of implementation were being missed. Management was paying for the right to use certain reserve powers, perhaps in an emergency situation, rather than for powers to be used in the course of normal working.

When implementation is delayed, the possibilities of 'infant mortality' increase. Impetus for change, engendered by negotiations, diminishes with the passage of time, and inertia takes over. Not all of the problems affecting negotiations are internal to the company. During the outfit trades negotiations another yard on the Clyde paid a group of workers an increase in wages for what the union representative later described as 'nothing'. The unions' members at Fairfields then wanted this extra payment on the basic rate before accepting the provisions of the outfit trades agreement.

At Fairfields productivity bargaining centred on the flexibility of labour. In the case of the unskilled man, attention was given to interchangeability. Craftsmen are wary of flexibility deals because they erode the boundaries of the craft and weaken a previously undisputed claim to a job. Fear of unemployment, not pride in craft, is the prime motive. Acceptance of the agreements at Fairfields reflects a growing realization that rigidity and stratification of a labour force at certain times can be a cause of unemployment.* The existence of some degree of flexibility provides management with scope to avoid the worst fluctuations. Yet flexibility is not enough – the long-term goal must be full interchangeability of workers through training.

These productivity agreements brought benefits to men, company and trade unions. The men enjoyed increased earnings which, as they were paid on basic rates, also increased holiday entitlements. One agreement provided a guarantee of employment never available before. Management acquired the ability to deploy the labour force in a way that encouraged stability, minimized friction and avoided uneconomic redundancies, all of which contribute to cost reduction. Labour loading became central to the manpower policy of the company. The trade unions gained a certain degree of prestige from the agreements, which indicated their willingness to discuss proposals leading to increased efficiency, and secured considerable wage increases for their members.

Perhaps the most important by-product of the negotiations

* One yard on the Clyde provides an example. To avoid redundancy it was proposed that some shipwrights be transferred to the plating department. This was rejected by the platers who belong to the same union as the shipwrights.

was the rapport which, despite setbacks and periods of high tension, developed between management and trade unions. The long and detailed negotiations had educated both sides in the understanding of each other's viewpoints, and greatly increased the willingness to 'give and take'. These changes in attitudes allowed a unique exercise involving demarcation to take place. The company was building a 'lead' ship where most of the outfitting work was done in metal rather than in traditional woodwork. The woodworkers rapidly became aware of the threat to their employment. The company noted the areas which would most probably be in dispute and initiated discussions with the unions involved before the work took place. Of the nine jobs in dispute, only one had to be referred to arbitration.

The productivity bargains with the outfit trades and with the NUGMW were initiated basically by the reaction to the ASB agreement. This agreement also gave rise to one of the more serious disputes in the first year of the company – the ASB apprentices dispute. The dispute really centred on the boys' claim to a traditional form of payment which the management believed undesirable. After the ASB agreement had been signed the executive officers again raised the question of apprentice payment, which they had raised in earlier discussions. The general manager is alleged to have replied that 'the boys will be taken care of'. It is the different interpretation given to these words by management and ASB officials which explain the dispute.

During the negotiations on the agreement the officials had resisted every pressure by the apprentices to include them in the agreement – 'when the journeymen have been settled, the apprentices will be given every consideration'. After the signing of the agreement the union officials interpreted the general manager's remarks to mean that the apprentices would be paid their traditional *pro rata* proportion of the journeymen's increase in wages, and also a *pro rata* award to cover the retro-spective payments made to the journeymen. There is no doubt that the general manager's words were interpreted unanimously by the ASB in this way. Historical precedent was strong; one negotiator said at a much later stage in the dispute, 'We never anticipated any trouble over this matter.'

The management viewpoint was that they were intending to examine the payment and training of all apprentices in the yard. In future, payment to apprentices was to be geared to training and not production work. The company reiterated its policy of 'nothing for nothing'. Any *pro rata* payment to apprentices would not give rise to increased productivity. The company's intention was to revise the apprentices' wages structure on the basis of training needs which would give the apprentices 'considerably more money than any *pro rata* payment'. The ASB officials regarded the claim for a *pro rata* payment for their apprentices as a separate issue from the negotiations on the proposed apprentices' charter. They considered the *pro rata* payment claim as attaching to the ROWP agreement. They wanted to reach settlement on this claim before giving attention to the charter. The management felt that the ASB apprentices should not be treated differently from the proposals for all apprentices set out in the draft charter.

Negotiations on this claim were interrupted by five walk-outs by the apprentices, the first taking place on 6 June 1966 and the fifth on 17 November. The officials could exert only limited control over the apprentices who had come to believe that 'militancy pays'. Three walk-outs occurred even after the apprentices had witnessed their officials pledging 'no further strike action'.

During the long negotiations attaching to this claim, numerous drafts of the apprentices charter were made. One proposal contained in the charter related to the grading of apprentices. The management regarded this as a necessary adjunct to training – the union officials felt it to have discriminating possibilities and wanted the company to drop the idea. By 23 August, at the seventh meeting between the management and union representatives, the union officials were prepared to accept an hourly *pro rata* increase for their apprentices at the rate of 2d., 4d., 6d. and 8d. (according to year of apprenticeship, the fifth year apprentice to gain journeyman status) provided the company dropped its proposed grading system. This proposal was rejected by the company, as it was by a Scottish Conference convened on 16 September.

The situation rapidly deteriorated and a crucial meeting was held on 16 November between the company and union officials. The union again reiterated their claim for a *pro rata* payment, also pointing out that there was 'deep anxiety about this matter in the Society – it's a matter of principle'.

The company felt that the ASB was avaricious in demanding the *pro rata* payments as well as the proposed charter payments. The ASB regarded the issues as being separate – and were not prepared to sign the charter until the *pro rata* issue had been resolved. At this point the issue was deadlocked with management and union taking stands on grounds of principle. The tension was increased on the same day when a mass meeting of ASB journeymen agreed to hold a one-day token strike in support of the apprentices. The men were already making a financial contribution to the boys who were on strike.

On 17 November the issue was raised as a 'matter of concern' by a member at the CJC. A discussion on the matter illustrated the concern of other CJC members for their workers in the yard. The CJC proposed that if the ASB officials could call off the one-day token strike, it would convene a special meeting, chaired by Sir Iain Stewart, to try to resolve the issue. After a brief adjournment, this proposal was accepted.

On 21 November a special CJC was convened with Sir Iain Stewart in the chair. He outlined his involvement in the yard and reiterated his belief in the 'no strike' pledge. The meeting lasted throughout the day and included three adjournments. Eventually an ingenious compromise was reached, largely through the efforts of one experienced ASB negotiator who had more than the usual amount of flair and talent. It was agreed that *pro rata* payments would be made to each apprentice in the employ of the company before 2 June 1966, increases not to be paid retrospectively but from the date the apprentices returned to work, 28 November. The apprentices would get the *pro rata* payments in addition to the charter increases for age payment,* from the implementation of the charter up to 1 June 1967.

* See Chapter 9, on training.

From that date forward each 'rate for age' charter increase would progressively absorb the individual *pro rata* payments until they were eliminated from each boy. The solution was agreed, and both parties approached the Ministry of Labour to seek approval for the charter's implementation.

This was a difficult dispute to concede because it arose from a genuine misunderstanding and developed into an issue of principle. Two factors made the company's approach particularly difficult. Other yards on the Clyde had paid their apprentices their *pro rata* money when their agreement with the ASB had been signed. Although events in other yards had no binding force on Fairfields, it was difficult to resist certain comparisons. But the greatest danger was that any compromise which hinted at surrender to ASB militancy would have further inflamed yard feelings. The CJC were sympathetic to both parties and helped to pave the way for a solution to the dispute by allowing the ASB to negotiate individually with the management. Previous discussions on the charter had been collective, i.e. all of the unions represented on the CJC with management.

The main disadvantage of the strikes was the bad publicity which they brought to Fairfields. One shipowner froze an instalment payment of £124,000 due on a ship being constructed until he was assured that the strike action would not affect delivery date. It is certain that international reporting of the incident did much to jeopardize discussions with possible customers. In all, the ASB apprentices dispute lost 22,006 hours of work, 84 per cent of all hours lost in 1966.

Some of the difficulties encountered by the company would have been eased if there had been a clear management structure for the administration of labour relations. In the first eight months of the company the general manager and productivity services director shared responsibility for labour relations, with day-to-day negotiations being delegated to the PSD. A personnel specialist was not recruited until September 1966. On appointment he was made responsible to the PSD. This was an unusual placement judged against the typical organization structure. It allowed the PSM to work under the auspices of the PSD to acquire a 'feel' for labour relations in the yard, and to get to know the various trade-union officials involved. This subordination of personnel to productivity services emphasized the company's intention to cost all labour agreement and to insist that cost consciousness dominate management thinking in negotiations. The difficult task of convincing the unions and yard workers that the company intended to implement its 'nothing for nothing' policy was the task of the PSD. This policy was difficult and unpopular but it was advocated with great vigour and considerable skill by the PSD.

Towards the end of 1966, once the PSM had had time to 'learn the ropes' and had proved his ability, full responsibility for labour negotiations should have been transferred gradually but progressively to him. This was never done, and unfortunately this failure to transfer authority created a major weakness in the administration of labour relations in the company. This weakness stemmed from three sources.

The PSM could only conduct negotiations of limited scope, and even his freedom of decision was firmly constrained. In cases of doubt or dispute he was obliged to refer to higher authority, which had the effect of undermining his own position with the workers and unions, who preferred to take their grievances to a level with the authority to deal with them. Some officials believed that reference to the PSM was a delaying tactic on the part of management. The frequent need of the PSM to refer to the PSD was the cause of some delay. The PSD was heavily involved in general administration in addition to his overall responsibilities for productivity improvement. Often time was not available to deal with emergency labour issues which required immediate evaluation of the productivity implications for the company.

The PSD had inevitably become unpopular as a result of his advocacy of a 'nothing for nothing' policy. This, together with his tough negotiating attitude, upset many shop stewards and trade-union officials and at times produced a high degree of tension between them and the PSD. The good relationship between shop stewards and PSM inevitably suffered whenever reference upwards took place. Although this situation led to a serious deterioration of relationships within the company, the PSD eventually gained the respect of a large number of shop stewards and full-time officials as a tough and skilful negotiator.

The PSD kept the general manager informed on the progress of labour relations. In some cases, e.g. the NUGMW dispute, the general manager personally conducted final negotiations. On matters of payment the authorization of the general manager was usually final, but occasionally he referred matters to the board. This structure often made coordination of labour policy difficult. In some cases the PSM received conflicting instructions from his superiors. In the case of the NUGMW dispute the PSM could probably have averted the strike at the 24 April meeting when his need to refer to the PSD encountered the latter's refusal to leave another important meeting. In emergency situations this trinity of labour negotiators became an obstacle to effective labour policy.

One situation probably crystallizes these difficulties more clearly than any other. A disciplinary procedure had been negotiated between the company and the shop stewards. It was based on a system of three written warnings on breaches of discipline or rules before dismissal could take place. This system was undoubtedly fair to the worker. The day after the procedure had been approved it was used by a manager to discipline a worker for lateness. Immediately the shop stewards in the section threatened to call a walk-out. Using a 'crash procedure' under which the general manager was prepared to meet the shop stewards on matters of extreme urgency, the shop stewards stated their case, succeeded in having the disciplinary measure revoked, and secured agreement that the system would be examined by a committee of managers and shop stewards.

In this situation the general manager took the action he thought best. Unfortunately in doing so he acted without consulting his two subordinates involved in labour relations, and by implication withdrew support from his line manager. This further reinforced opinion among shop stewards that 'pressure pays' when dealing with what some considered to be a weak management. The shop stewards were not slow to realize the implications of the 'crash procedure' and sometimes used this to by-pass the usual chain of command.

In some respects the weakness in the administration of labour policy was a reflection of the concern of the general manager to be as fair as possible to the yard worker. His sincerity and integrity were never doubted by management or workers, but unfortunately this concern for labour relations was interpreted by some shop stewards as weakness. The unwillingness to resolve these administrative problems also contributed to the managerial tension in the yard which is referred to elsewhere. The confusion was entirely structural. Labour policy was perfectly clear – to secure the most efficient use of manpower through productivity bargains to allow the company to employ a stabilized labour force.

Labour Relations 3: Appendix

Notes of a meeting between all shop stewards and the chairman (5 May 1967)

CHAIRMAN: The company is now moving into a critical period. I am very unhappy about recent events. Therefore I have called this meeting to find out what exactly is going on. I intend to hold another Lyceum meeting, and therefore want to be better informed than I am. It is important that we stress the principles upon which Fairfields was founded. Unless we can contain our disagreements within the company we are finished. There is no purpose in taking the dispute into the Govan Road. I ask you what we can do to put this right. The first two disputes may be regarded as skirmishes. The recent dispute has become much more serious.

The chairman then invited questions from the assembled stewards.

CONVENOR: The Fairfields negotiation structure is responsible for the disputes. We went right through procedure. Originally our claim was submitted on a departmental basis. However, on the advice of management we consolidated departmental claims into a total NUGMW claim. This then became subject to prices and incomes regulations. Because of our frustration at the slowness of management we decided to bring this dispute into the open.

CHAIRMAN: If we allow these disputes to come into the open we are sunk. Fairfields is based on a list of priorities, and national interests have a greater priority than company policy. This project is one of three years' duration, to put shipbuilding back on its feet. It is not a short term project.

STEWARD A: There is a credibility gap in the yard. We accuse the management of deliberately lying. I choose this word with care. I agree it is not always a good policy to wash dirty linen in public. However, in certain situations we have to do so.

CHAIRMAN: I have no reason to question the integrity of the

155

management of this company. There is great pressure on the management. If I thought that they were lying they would go. What we must stress is the fundamental belief that the aims of men and management are similar.

CONVENOR: In addition to management deceit there have also been threats made against shop stewards.

STEWARD M: We agree with the concepts of Fairfields but feel frustrated by the group within the organization which causes delay. This appears to be the fault of individuals.

CHAIRMAN: There is a need for a long term view. We expected troubles in the future but want to avoid irresponsible action. I as chairman of the company am interested in strategy. Tactics are the responsibility of management. The next six to nine months are critical. We should meet more often.

STEWARD A: Who is irresponsible?

CHAIRMAN: Strike action is irresponsible. We must take the heat out of the situation and review tactics.

CONVENOR: We asked to meet you and to exclude the management who are likely to inhibit the free flow of discussion.

STEWARD C: You are too divorced from the men. What has happened to your pledge to report back to us?

CHAIRMAN: My object was to try and establish a climate within which management can operate. I am not the manager. Managers were introduced to the company on the understanding that they would have freedom of operation. I cannot come closer to the yard without undermining the management.

STEWARD N: We require more information from the central joint council. Men do not seem to be getting information from this body. Management seem to be missing out the district officials. The central joint council need to meet the stewards to iron out these problems.

CHAIRMAN: I will check this with them.

STEWARD H: Basic unrest is caused by wage structure. The priorities seem to be wrong. The level of productivity in the yard is low. Yet the firm continue to spend money on offices and other accommodation.

CHAIRMAN: We have established a list of priorities. These we think to be in the best interests of the company. If we had failed to invest in the future we would go bankrupt in three years time. We now expect to be profitable in 1968–9.

STEWARD F: There is a great need for a monthly meeting between yourself and the shop stewards. You will get the truth from us. Otherwise you will only receive the polished board-room version. I refer you to the plight of the non-craftsmen in the yard. The B M S agreement has increased tension. Some-thing must be done now for the unskilled and semi-skilled men. Trouble will continue if this is not examined.

CHAIRMAN: Sure. But I must emphasize the question of priorities. There are limitations to our actions because of the amount of money we have available. Give us productivity and we will achieve all that we have set out to do. If these disputes and situations are to continue then my position will become untenable. I do not want to give up and I am far from this point at present.

STEWARD A: Are you asking or are you telling us that you are quitting ship?

CHAIRMAN: I am only telling you what may occur.

STEWARD G: We will provide productivity and cooperation provided the management cooperates with us. The Lyceum meetings take up twenty thousand man-hours of potential production time. It would be better to meet the shop stewards once a month rather than continue these cinema meetings.

STEWARD A: I agree. There is a crisis of confidence in the yard and therefore you should meet the shop stewards regularly.

CHAIRMAN: I will do what you suggest.

STEWARD M: The boilermakers have never had any difficulty in arranging meetings with management. We hope that these informal meetings will continue.

CONVENOR: Brother M has touched on one of the major difficulties of the yard. That is, the boilermakers continue to sectionalize the yard.

CHAIRMAN: From this meeting I can see that our com-munications are still bad.

STEWARD A: We must improve communications in the yard to help remove this crisis of confidence. We take it that the management does inform you of what goes on?

(*At this stage the convenor put a motion to the meeting regarding future meetings with the chairman. It was agreed that the chairman, together with senior management, would meet the stewards once a month. In the future Lyceum meetings would be held only with the agreement of that meeting.*)

CHAIRMAN: (*summing up*)

* 1. If the yard continues to go off the rails as it has done in recent labour disputes, my position would be untenable.

2. I promised to meet the shop stewards more regularly but could not become more closely involved in the yard without interfering with the functions of management.

3. These meetings are safety valves and from them any decision to hold future cinema meetings will come.

4. I appreciate the unrest caused by differentials, but restate that elimination will depend on productivity and priorities.

At this stage three members of executive management were admitted.

STEWARD A: It is important to have the management's intentions towards the workers declared.

PRODUCTIVITY SERVICES MANAGER: Our intentions have always been firm. We have never broken any pledges. However you have often done this. I am not going into the dock at the Lyceum. As far as I am concerned the pledges are not one way. If you criticize us I want to see the evidence where management have broken the pledges or walked out on the men.

CONVENOR: If you want to hold a mud-slinging match then you can have it.

Meeting adjourned.

CHAPTER 8

Labour Relations 4
Job evaluation: Progress towards stability:
Overall assessment

INSECURITY of employment, fostering a sectional approach to job-protection, has been a major cause of friction between trades and grades of labour in shipbuilding. Even when the general level of employment on an estuary is high, job insecurity persists because of imbalance in the demand for labour which the shipbuilding process creates, an imbalance which shifts its emphasis from one period to another, and can force the individual worker to shift his place of work in pursuit of continuing employment. This, too, accentuates schisms between trades and their unions, as well as weakening the shipbuilding worker's remarkably strong feeling of attachment to his industry. The migrant in shipbuilding will try to leave a job 'before it folds', not in pursuit of higher earnings but to get ahead in the next job queue. Earnings opportunities in shipbuilding can vary from yard to yard and are affected by the bargaining pressures created by the nature of the building process. A management desperate to achieve a delivery date, for example to avoid incurring heavy losses as a result of a penalty clause, can face escalating wage demands as the deadline draws near. It is quite usual for a management to offer a 'finishing bonus', with the intention of at least minimizing the tendency to draw out a job once it has been agreed to pay higher rates. Despite such opportunities for individual short-term gains over and above the wage levels generally available to a trade, certain shipbuilding trades have a very strong sense of identity, expressed in an attachment to wage differentials favourable to themselves. The steelworking trades represented by the Amalgamated Society offer the clearest example of such a sense of identity. In fact a number of related trades and 'identities' are involved, but there is a unifying element amongst steelworking trades, strengthened by the amalgamation process which had produced the Society.

There is an apparent contradiction between the wage advantage enjoyed by the steelworking trades and the weaker demand by other industries for steelworking labour relative, say, to the alternative demands outside shipbuilding for engineers, woodworkers, painters and electricians. One trade-union official expressed the contradiction in this way: 'They get more out of the industry than any of us, threaten its very future and yet – if the yards do have to close – they have nowhere else to go'. The emphasis on the absence of alternative job opportunities is exaggerated, but none the less reflects the situation. What it misses is the influence of tradition, organizational cohesion and militancy on wage structures. The strong ties of steelworkers and their Society to shipbuilding has encouraged them to fight tenaciously for the retention of the advantageous position they have in the industry. The result may be taken both as a tribute to the Society's effectiveness and as an illustration of how institutional factors can outweigh economic ones in the determination of bargaining power, at least for a time.

Against such a background it is to be expected that the Amalgamated Society would be against a 'job evaluated' approach to wage determination in shipbuilding. Firstly the logic of job evaluation is that the negotiating autonomy of separate unions is translated into a negotiating process in which all unions participate together, and secondly those who enjoy favourable differentials will naturally fear that job evaluation could reduce or remove these. If a union believes that it has already maximized its bargaining position it will be chary of changing the structure or the basis of bargaining. The attitude of the major precursor of the Society prior to the amalgamation was clearly stated at an ILO conference on job evaluation.

'The United Kingdom Workers' member said that neither the United Society of Boilermakers, Shipbuilders and Structural Workers of which he was a representative, nor other metal trades workers' unions in the United Kingdom, had any intention of accepting job evaluation. It did not seem that the employers' members accepted the principle of collective bargaining on job evaluation. This attitude could not be reconciled with the view that job evaluation should lead to increased benefits to the workers. Job evaluation was, in his opinion, one of the means for breaking down the skills and consequently it was aimed against craft unions. It should, however, be remembered that craft unions were of great importance for the metal trades.'*

Despite this, when the issue of job evaluation was raised at Fairfields neither the steel workers and their stewards in the yard nor their representatives on the CJC opposed the development. When a job evaluation exercise was launched a full-time official of the Society was on the working party in charge of the exercise and in the yard there was full participation by Society members in the studies involved. This was one of the more obvious and remarkable of the examples of cooperation given by the unions to the Fairfields experiment.

The *Geddes Report* recognized the unsatisfactory character of the then existing wages structure in the industry† and proposed a new wages structure that 'should have as one of its main objectives securing some consistency of rates within each of the two groups' – metal trades and outfit trades – 'and within the various grades of ancillary and other workers. It should also seek to avoid random differences of earnings between workers of equivalent degrees of skill'. It was also recommended that the period between the publication of the *Report* (March 1966) and the terminal date of the then current national agreement at the end of 1967 'should be used by the parties to make progress towards a new wages structure' (paragraphs 422 and 423).

At Fairfields there had been recognition that the wages structure in the yard bore little relationship to the need for either incentives and efficient operation or a sense of justice. The chairman had described the wages structure as a 'dog's dinner' and this description had become part of common usage

* *Job Evaluation*, International Labour Office, p. 120.
† As did J. R. Parkinson; see *The Economics of Shipbuilding in the United Kingdom*, pp. 171 – 81.

amongst both managers and workers in the yard. There was a general impression that a more rational structure would be one in which differentials were narrower – but this was not set out clearly, and it was a view which would have faced some spirited opposition had it been made explicit.

No approach to the revision of the wages structure was possible at Fairfields until a unified negotiating machinery was established. Once the Central Joint Council had become established a paper was presented to it (in October 1966) by management proposing that a start be made. It was argued that:

'The existing wage structure at Fairfields is a potent cause of discontent. Additionally it will impose constraints upon attempts to relate wages to productivity. There would be strong support from workers in the yard for the examination and revision of the wage structure.'

'Any such exercise would be seen as essentially one for *negotiation*. Necessary parts of the exercise would be: (1) "fact-finding" on existing wage rates and earnings and (2) job evaluation. However, the likelihood of general agreement on a revised structure would be greatly increased if such information were "fed" to a small negotiating committee which would then have an opportunity of digesting the information, exchanging views on it and reaching agreement.

'Probably the best approach would be to establish a small wage structure revision committee on the same basis as the standing sub-committee of the CJC.'

This procedure was adopted. The shop stewards had already been informed of the proposal and given it their support. At this meeting strong feelings were expressed against the recent increases paid to members of the Amalgamated Society of Boilermakers. Management was asked 'why the lower paid men were being left behind' and 'whether in the light of this unilateral settlement Fairfields workers were wise to continue to trust their management'. Although the management had explanations to offer for the widening of differentials brought about by the ASB's settlement, these were not acceptable to the other workers in the yard and the revision of the wages structure began against a background of increasing resentment, pressure for an upward adjustment of other wages and of a narrowing of the differential between the ASB members and the rest. Thus the approach to job evaluation was in part to be seen as an attempt to reduce inter-employee and inter-union tensions in the yard.

The first meeting of the sub-committee appointed by the CJC was held in mid-November. It was pointed out by management that the examination of the wages structure would throw up anomalies which could be taken and used for sectional advantage. This attitude, if adopted, would frustrate the work of the sub-committee. It was resolved that no use would be made by any side, for the purpose of negotiation, of any information disclosed to the sub-committee. Such information would be held in abeyance for consideration at the completion of the exercise. It was agreed that a personal 'no worsening' clause be part of the wage revision procedure.

There was some discussion about how best to carry through the job evaluation exercise. The trade-union side was firmly of the opinion that outside consultants would be in a better position to divorce the evaluation process from contemporary management – worker concerns in the yard and to establish that their criteria were strictly 'objective'. This proposal was accepted and a firm of consultants suggested by a trade-union member was invited to propose a procedure.

A feature of the working of this sub-committee was that it was understood and accepted that each member would have open access to the consultants carrying out the exercise and that the overall exercise would remain under the joint supervision and control of the sub-committee. The work of the sub-committee was given up when it became clear that Fairfields was to merge with the other yards in the Upper Clyde. It was accepted that no major revision could or should take place in the wage structure of one yard when it was shortly to be merged.

The job evaluation exercise began on 12 December 1966, and was programmed for completion by the end of April 1967. In the event this terminal date was put back to 9 June, when the first stage of the exercise was completed. Initially a pilot survey was carried out, covering twenty-two jobs in the yard. Statistical analysis of the results of this pilot evaluation suggested that there was considerable overlap between some of the thirty-two factors to which worth points were being assigned. On this basis alone it was thought reasonable to cut out eleven factors. A further four were eliminated on other grounds, mainly the difficulty of establishing clear verbal distinctions between them and other factors. All of this was argued out on the wages revision sub-committee, after the union representatives and the management had had repeated meetings with the consultant. This joint committee had the full programme for the exercise, and drafts of the documents including the job questionnaire, presented to it for final decision. The terms of reference of the various committees which were to carry through the job analysis and evaluations were set out. In addition to the sub-committee and a technical reference committee, with overall responsibility, committees were established for the metal trades, wood and paint trades, plant machinery and services and for drawing office, administration and clerical. Each committee had foremen, shop stewards and workers' representatives, and an industrial engineer from productivity services. Each such committee had responsible to it a number of trade group working parties which interviewed operatives and foremen and completed a job questionnaire and job data sheet in connexion with each job, and used this information to prepare job specifications. These working parties had to agree on the worth points-rating of each factor. If unanimous agreement was not reached the responsibility for decision was to be referred to the chairman of the appropriate job evaluation committee for his guidance.

Participation in these committees and working parties requires considerable intelligence and certain numerical skills, and because of this nominees for the committees went through a standard selection procedure including two basic intelligence and aptitude tests. Eighty-one employees took part in the evaluating process as members of a committee or working party. At the peak of activity fifteen teams were at work, evaluating forty jobs in a day. As a result of the pilot survey and of an examination of management data concerning the yard it was estimated that there were 352 specific jobs within the range apprentice to foreman. In the event, this proved very close to the actual number of jobs in the range which were distinguished during the exercise. Because of the addition of design and clerical staff, the extension of the range to include professional staff and the inclusion of women workers the total number of jobs evaluated was 553. In a total labour force of around 2,400 this indicates a very high degree of job differentiation.

For the 352 jobs estimated to be within the range from apprentice to foreman there were fifty-one basic rates and 306 gross hourly rates, after allowing for the various extra 'plus rates'. Differences in gross hourly rates occurred *within* jobs as well as between jobs, and it will be seen that these differences between jobs provide the major obstacle to wage structure rationalization.

The pattern of wage rates is illustrated by Table 8.1.

Table 8.1

*Range of male manual operatives' basic
and hourly rates (March 1967)*

Rates, in pence per hour	Number of basic rates	Number of gross hourly rates
19–37	8	27
38–55	8	29
56–73	17	56
74–91	15	70
92–109	3	30
110–27	0	70
128–45+	0	24
	51	306

The final report on the job-evaluation exercise suggested grouping the 553 jobs into ten groups, seven of which applied to manual trades. The method of evaluation was essentially

165

one of applying the judgement of men experienced in the industry to particular jobs, having equipped them with precise scales against which to assess the points to be allocated under each factor heading. It is no criticism of such a method to describe it as an attempt to introduce objective criteria into the making of judgements from which the subjective cannot be completely excluded. There is, of course, a very wide choice of methods of job evaluation available, some of which rely less on human judgement and more on the application of formulae. Within the methods that rely on judgement a wide choice of approach is also possible. The Fairfields exercise is, therefore, no more than an illustration of how the shipbuilding industry might try to find a basis for a more rational wage structure. Before any industry-wide exercise is begun a thorough exploration of alternative approaches should be carried out. A detailed study and assessment of the Fairfields exercise should play a useful part in that exploration.

It is interesting to assess the method of the job evaluation adopted at Fairfields against the controls designed to minimize bias and errors of judgement suggested by a recent comprehensive review of the subject.*

Of the seven controls five were fully met. The raters were chosen by a process of selection and training, and were drawn from all areas of employment containing jobs to be evaluated. The jobs rated provided a cross section of the whole range and comparison with 'anchorages' distant in value from the jobs rated were avoided. The job descriptions used were fairly uniform in length, avoiding this common cause of bias. The numbers involved in rating were much higher than the fifteen suggested by Thomason, though the interlocking structure of the review machinery and the vast range of jobs to be evalued probably justified this. The one control which was not clearly imposed was the need to make raters aware of the effects that differential status can have on the process of reaching consensus and the check which simple averaging as opposed to a discussion of differences can have on such a bias. This probably

* *Guide to Job Evaluation*, George F. Thomason, Institute of Personnel Management, 1968.

meant that the views of the chief consultant engaged for the exercise exerted a strong influence on the ultimate ratings reported by the committees and embodied in the first report.

In the two years of the company's existence 48,301 man-hours were lost due to stoppages of work – this figure included approximately 5,000 man-hours sanctioned by management for meetings to discuss 'union business'. In all, 1966–8 produced a reduction of 22 per cent in man-hours lost due to disputes compared with 1964–6. In the context of a proving ground with all its necessary radical changes, this reduction in man-hours lost was a very considerable achievement for both management and men.

In these two years, a great deal was achieved in the field of labour relations. Perhaps the most important gain was the cooperation trade unions and men were prepared to give the management. This notion of cooperation was the corner stone upon which Fairfields was built; without it, the company would not have survived. Trade unions and men cooperated when they saw it in their interests to do so; motivation was practical, not altruistic. The management was trusted, and there was confidence in its ability to evolve policies and practices in shipbuilding which would bring considerable benefits to employees.

Nevertheless, on a number of occasions groups of workers threatened strike action, or took strike action in an attempt to strengthen their bargaining positions. This traditional bargaining tactic was pursued for two main reasons. First, because the shop stewards felt that in some situations they were dealing with a weak management. This was largely the explanation of the threatened strike by the AEU members in the MID in July 1967, which forced management to finalize a protracted negotiation by a deadline set by the engineers. The men thus placed management in a defensive and dangerous position. Second, a manifestation of militancy was thought necessary to convince management of the relevance and urgency of various grievances. The strike of the NUGMW members, after seven months of patient negotiations, was a particular example. As one shop steward put it – 'The meek will not inherit the earth!'

167

There is little doubt that the men realized the importance of the proving ground, as did their union officials. At a time of tension during a negotiation one official reflected this distinction when he threatened 'not to treat Fairfields management any different from other employers in the future'. Although prepared to cooperate with management, the trade unions were loath to concede certain major changes. The attempt by management to introduce double-day-shift working was completely unsuccessful. These negotiations took place with the ASB but feelings in the yard at the time indicated that little support was available for shift work amongst workers. Some union officials accepted that double-day-shift working would probably have to be introduced in the future and could bring considerable benefits to the men, but the majority of men regarded the proposals as regressive, and a serious threat to their established pattern of social activities. This clash of aims crystallized the situation at Fairfields; a dynamic, progressive and sometimes incautious management trying to move a number of trade unions who wanted slow but definite progress. The difference was partly one of time-scale and partly of width of responsibility. The management wanted speedy changes which would benefit the company and its employees, the unions also wanted changes, but had to consider their implications in a wider context, and this introduced caution and a desire to make progress more slowly.

The willingness of the unions to accept change is seen in their acceptance of productivity bargaining. It was a process which was new to most of them, but when it became clear that no other means of increasing wages was available they wholeheartedly entered negotiations. The first agreement, with the ASB, was 'specific' in nature, i.e. the details of the agreement were clearly itemized. The other agreements were much more 'comprehensive' in the sense that no detail was listed, but only principles for operation. The management prefer this latter type of agreement, as easier to operate, involving consultation with employees covered by the agreement, and turning on the spirit rather than on the letter of the agreement. The agreement with the NUGMW was a straightforward cost-reduction scheme, depending for its success on a willingness of workers to perform a wide range of duties or, in some cases, simply to work more intensively, and on a firm control by top management of foremen's desire to replace men lost by 'natural wastage'. Its simplicity must take some credit for its success.

There was no conscious attempt by management to bring together the extensive process of consultation and communication built up and the process of productivity bargaining. Although the concept of 'single-channel' bargaining was only just coming into use, it was considered by top management at Fairfields and rejected. The reason for this rejection seemed to be based more on entrenched commitment to the two-channel approach reached in different circumstances than on an assessment of what would be most effective in the Fairfields situation. Management attitudes can also be slow to change, even in a 'proving ground' milieu.

Something of the anxiety of trade-union officials to improve industrial relations in shipbuilding is illustrated in the appendix to this chapter, a minute of a meeting between full-time officials and shop stewards called to explore the cause of stoppages in the yard. The approach was remarkable in shipbuilding, with members of several unions discussing the 'internal affairs' of particular unions. This, and the general tenor of the meeting with the obvious desire to minimize unnecessary strife, may be taken as a reflection of the success of the new attitudes and new, CJC, machinery built up around Fairfields. That this particular meeting took place several weeks after Fairfields had been merged in Upper Clyde Shipbuilders Ltd indicates that the progress made can be built on and improved on.

Labour Relations 4: Appendix

1. Summary of proceedings at a meeting between the trade-union members of Fairfields (Glasgow) Ltd, the Central Joint Council and shop stewards, held on Monday 18 March, at 10 a.m. in the yard.

2. PRESENT: Shop stewards and seven trade-union officials.

3. CHAIR: Mr A (a trade-union official) outlined the purpose of the meeting and reminded the meeting of the CJC decision to investigate breaches and/or alleged breaches of procedure and stated that the first attempt at investigation had been abortive when shop stewards refused to cooperate. Management had placed two items on the agenda of the last meeting of the CJC and the trade-union members had decided that it would be useful to meet the shop stewards to consider these two references and the general question of procedure in the yard.

4. CORRESPONDENCE: (a) The secretary read a letter from management, dated 24 January 1968, in the following terms: 'At 10.30 a.m. on Wednesday, 24 January 1968, we were informed by the platers' shop stewards, a group organized by the Amalgamated Society of Boilermakers, Shipwrights, Blacksmiths and Structural Workers, that their members who had been out of the yard at a meeting would not be at work during the day and their members on night-shift would not come into work. We were informed that the reason for the men not coming in was line management's refusal to discuss the arrangement for the transfer of men from shop working to shed working. During the course of the discussion, it was agreed that both men and management's interpretation of these arrangements was the same. It is difficult, therefore, to understand what the stoppage of work is about.

'We were informed that the men would be returning to work

at the normal starting time on 25 January and it is appreciated that in these circumstances it is not possible for you to contribute to expediting the return to work.

'As you know, there is a well established "crash" procedure; if it appears that a stoppage of work may occur whereby shop stewards have a direct approach to the personnel.line of management so that the issue may be considered at an appropriate level: this procedure was not evoked.

'I wrote to you informing you of this situation as required by decision of the Central Joint Council.'

(b) The Secretary also read the relevant letter of two dated 29 January 1968, in the following terms:

'At 10.10 a.m. on the morning of 29 January 1968 I was informed by the production manager, pipework, that your members employed in the pipe shop were threatening to go on strike unless the company ceased to use a caulking tool in the company's re-training section which is incorporated in the pipework department.

'I met your shop stewards, together with those of the other union involved, at 10.30 a.m. that morning, and informed them that it was essential that a caulking tool was used for the work going on in the re-training section at that time. I was, however, prepared to do three things:

(i) introduce a noise level recorder to the department, and if the noise level was such that it was injurious to health, caulking work would stop immediately.

(ii) by changing various techniques in use, we would reduce the amount of caulking required to be done to one-eighth of the existing level, and

(iii) we would continue our investigations into eliminating the use of the caulking tools for the job completely.

'This was unacceptable to the men. They left the yard at 12.15 p.m. saying that they would return to work at the normal time tomorrow morning. The numbers involved in the stoppage are:

Journeymen   77
Helpers   46

These numbers include people employed in parts of the shop

where the noise cannot be heard, but we have been informed that they went out "in sympathy".

'I would be grateful if, as a matter of urgency, you would investigate the cause of this breach of procedure.'

This letter had been addressed by Management to the PTU and a letter in similar terms had been sent to the SMW.

5. DISCUSSION: (a) Letter of 24 January.

A shop steward stated that the third paragraph of this letter inferred that there had been no problem to resolve, when in fact management had 'somersaulted' after one hour's discussion and thus brought themselves into line with the shop steward's interpretation. A hostile atmosphere, it was claimed, had been provoked unnecessarily by management.

(b) In connexion with the second letter, a shop steward stated that although management had offered to introduce a noise level recorder to the department, they were not prepared to give a date when this would be done. Prompt action was obtained only when the men stopped work. The shop steward was of the opinion that the situation leading up to sanctions being applied could have been avoided by management adopting a more flexible attitude.

(c) In general discussion, views were expressed about management attitudes to vacancies, transfer of shop stewards, excluding one man from overtime, consultation between shop stewards and men. Several stewards, evidently with the concurrence of everyone present, expressed the view that some line managers appeared not to have assimilated the philosophy of Fairfields and were rigid in their attitudes, failing to understand that the spirit of agreements was of consequence when observing the purpose of the agreement. Instances of line managers refusing to meet stewards 'because the interpretation was clear' provoked reactions; situations did not just happen but were built up on a series of minor matters culminating in situations which exploded. An attitude which appeared to be universally accepted by all the stewards was that they were firmly of the opinion (and it was their desire) that procedures should be observed, but so long as line management were apparently unaware that a certain resilience was needed when dealing with

172

industrial relationships, adopted a hostile attitude at the inception of any question arising or issue being taken up, and only
responded when the men 'rattled the ṣabre', then breaches of
procedure were inevitable. One question was asked and emphasized, viz: 'What is a breach of procedure?' If men have
to be consulted when a question, issue or claim is under discussion, shop stewards require facilities, and when management
refuse to cooperate or offer facilities then the men must stop
for a meeting (this being particularly acute when line management actually refuse to talk with shop stewards). A problem
that was highlighted was an apparent desire among some foremen not to have shop stewards in their squads as the time shop
stewards needed to deal with problems was regarded as non-
productive time. Running through the discussion there were
references to issues on which it was felt progress might have
been made if there had been a manager with executive authority
responsible for industrial relations available with power to
make decisions, instead of which irresolution and delay aggra-
vated situations and led to stoppages.

6. During the discussion the chairman made several observations and corrections and clarified several points. He made it
clear that crash procedure should always be invoked if line
managers refused to talk with stewards. He would not accept
that disciplinary procedure was within the competence of
the CJC as this was a function of management. He agreed
that line managers had real responsibility in developing
and preserving a spirit of amity within negotiating procedures. He asked the meeting to agree that the CJC
should discuss the matters raised and also asked the meeting to
agree:

(a) that the stewards would make every attempt to operate
crash procedure,

(b) that the CJC members might propose that the personnel
services managers should be responsible for giving answers
on urgent issues or, if unable to exercise this authority, should
be responsible for arranging a meeting with an executive
manager as a matter of urgency,

(c) that the shop stewards agree that cases of alleged breaches of procedure should be investigated by the CJC and that they would cooperate, and

(d) that there should be discussion within the CJC about the role and authority of the personnel services manager in accordance with modern management techniques.

7. The meeting concurred with these proposals.

CHAPTER 9

Training

FAIRFIELDS, like many other shipyards and establishments in
other industries, suffered from over-manning and low productivity. The management inherited a situation in which the
labour force was estimated as 40–50 per cent greater than required to run a yard of that size efficiently. The under-utilization of labour was a major barrier to increasing productivity
levels. Management had to reduce the labour force to a size
more in keeping with the needs of the yard. This inevitably
raised the question of redundancy.

Traditionally, trade unions have resisted any measures leading
to redundancies; they have, for example, adhered to demarcation rules, followed policies of short-time working, restricted
overtime working. There is little doubt that the trade-union
attitude to redundancy is one of the factors inhibiting industrial efficiency. The new management hoped to persuade
the unions that some redundancy was an essential part of
industrial change by introducing training facilities which
would allow the redundant worker to acquire new skills
and be redeployed to other work. Training was to become a
central feature of the Fairfields proving ground, and a means
whereby unemployment was no longer the consequence of
redundancy.

Sir Iain Stewart had long campaigned for a new approach
to the problem of redundancy. Although well aware of the
limitations of one shipyard, albeit a proving ground, for re-
training purposes, Sir Iain believed that an example of the
positive aspects of a redundancy policy could be displayed at
Fairfields. To provide such an example, he believed, was central
to the operation of a proving ground; ' . . . the Fairfields
experiment will establish an indisputable argument for the
Government to establish national facilities for re-training and
planned re-employment, which of course is, and has always

175

been as far as I am concerned, the main object in setting up the Fairfields platform'.*

Sir Iain felt that it was the positive aspects of redundancy that should be stressed and not the 'ineffective measures of redundancy payments, higher unemployment benefits, selective employment taxes and regional employment premiums'.

The management accepted the Chairman's ideas on retraining. Very quickly they recognized the low standard of apprenticeship 'training' and the consequent variable standard of work produced by the time-served men in the yard. Management believed that the future of the yard, and in the long run of the industry, could only be secured by greater emphasis on work pace and quality. Although money was tight at Fairfields, one of the earliest decisions made was to build an apprentices' training centre where the boys coming to the company could be properly taught and supervised.

The object of the company was to train each apprentice in as wide a range of shipyard skills as possible. This wide-based training would allow the eventual craftsman to have a greater ability to redeploy to other jobs if, and when, his own specialist skill is not in demand. The building of a training centre and the opening of negotiations with the trade unions on the training of apprentices was the company's two-pronged attack on this problem. The training centre was begun in May 1966, ready for use in August and officially opened in September of that year.

The centre incorporated a large, well-equipped lecture theatre and provided training facilities for the range of shipbuilding skills. The approximate cost of building and equipping the centre was £35,000. This expenditure was a considerable gesture by the company of its faith in ultimate trade-union cooperation with its new training proposals, and its belief that the company would be in business long enough to obtain benefit from the improvements.

The initial development of the training centre, the selection of training staff and their training in the technique of instruc-

* Speech given at the 'New Thinking' luncheon sponsored by the Industrial Society, 20 June 1967.

tion, was entrusted to a consultant. The vacancies for training supervisors were advertised within and outside of the company, in accordance with its policy on these matters. By 1 August 1966 the consultant had selected and appointed ten training supervisors. Of these appointments, nine men were from within the company, and the other man was a former Fairfield employee. The appointments were the responsibility of the consultant who screened the applicants by means of interviews and the usual tests. The selected men were given two weeks' intensive tuition by the consultant on methods of teaching and were then allocated to their various sections. This staff of ten training supervisors was headed by a training manager, recruited from a major motor vehicle manufacturer, who took up his duties on 1 August 1966.

In addition to setting up the training organization, the consultant advised management on the reorganization of the apprenticeship system in the yard. Management wanted radical changes from the situation they inherited and began to negotiate with the trade unions a document which became known as the apprentices' charter. This document governed the training of apprentices in the company, and was unique in the shipbuilding industry.

The charter referred to the training and payment of apprentices in the company. The charter was negotiated with the trade unions over a period of two months, and was finally approved by the central joint council in July 1966. During negotiations careful attention was given to the views of unions such as the ASB and DATA which had gathered considerable experience of apprentice training in other industries. In addition, the recommendations of the Shipbuilding Industry Training Board and of the consultant retained by the company were given careful attention. The aims of the company in apprentice training were clearly set out in the preamble to the charter – 'the aim throughout is now to establish a sound foundation on which the training of young men in the next decade may be based. A rigid structure will not survive on the shifting sands of technological and social changes and it is intended to provide an inbuilt flexibility in all training programmes and facilities'.

However, before these principles could be implemented negotiations had to resolve the existing situation in the company. The apprentices were formally indentured to the company but were 'trained' in only a rudimentary way. The apprentice was brought into the company and seconded to a tradesman. The apprentice 'served his time' by learning what he could from the tradesmen. He was expected to attend day-release classes for further education, but attendance at these classes was not rigorously enforced. The apprentice's progress was largely dependent upon his own initiative and the interest taken in him by the tradesman. The latter was very much a variable interest, and the foreman often regarded the apprentice as a cheap addition to the labour force in his section. Such conditions were not peculiar to Fairfields, but were general in the industry.

As a result of this on-the-job training, a series of anomalies developed between wages of apprentices in different trades. The company had to rationalize the apprentice payments structure before it could have a sound basis for apprentices' incentive payments. The company set out a number of principles regarding the payment of apprentices. It believed that it was beneficial to the apprentice and to the company that there should be incentive payments to an apprentice. However, it was considered that for the first three years of his training, emphasis should be laid on training and not on the short-run contribution to production. The apprentice was not to be used as a cheap supplement to the labour force.

In parallel, the management sought to persuade the unions to relax the restrictions around apprenticeships, particularly those relating to the length of apprenticeships. The duration of apprenticeship was five years. The boy was usually indentured between the ages of sixteen and seventeen. The company felt that, using modern methods and techniques, it was possible to train an apprentice to journeyman standard within three years. The company's demand for a lower period of apprenticeship posed both a dilemma and challenge to the unions, which were aware of the archaic methods of apprentice training, and of the frequent irrelevance of training to the needs of the apprentice and the industry. While recognizing these defects the unions realized that they could not sanction too radical a departure from existing arrangements – even in a proving ground – without Fairfields getting too far out of alignment with the rest of the industry. A compromise was effected.

Recognizing that changes in the training of apprentices were long overdue and were perhaps imminent,* the unions on the central joint council agreed to a reduction in the period of apprenticeship at Fairfields from five to four years. This was a major step forward and gave Fairfields a unique position in apprentice training in Britain. The reduction was, above all, a trade-union reaction to positive management recognized as aiming for all-round benefits for the company and its employees.

Not all of the company's proposals were acceptable to the unions. It was not conceded that the period of apprenticeship begin before the age of sixteen. To avoid a wasted pre-apprenticeship year, the company inducted him into the training centre where he followed a normal first year course of training. It had been usual in the company to employ pre-apprenticeship boys as messengers and general factotums, a wasteful and very often demoralizing practice.

The company also wanted to reserve the option of granting an apprenticeship to a boy over seventeen years of age and to 'adults, who for some good reason, had missed their opportunity to determine their vocation'. It was on issues such as these that the limitations of Fairfields as a proving ground were exposed. The unions had clearly defined rules relating to apprenticeships. They regarded the reduction in the period of apprentice training as a major concession to Fairfields. To go beyond this, particularly into the field of adult apprenticeships was considered too big a step to take. They were concerned about the acceptability of such training to the tradesman they represented. This was an important caution, given that men completing courses at government training centres have had difficulty in finding employment in shipbuilding which would allow them to use their new skills.

* The Shipbuilding Industry Training Board was established in November 1964.

When the main provision of the charter had been agreed, the problems of apprentices' payment were examined. It was agreed that the company would pay the apprentice a 'rate for age' irrespective of the year of apprenticeship. An agreed consolidated rate was paid to apprentices by age and in addition there was a training bonus. The training bonus depended on the half-yearly grading of the apprentice by his manager, foreman and training supervisor, compiled by ranking his performance under defined headings against other apprentices. The training bonus was introduced to encourage the apprentice to apply himself to his training – and as a means of rewarding apprentices for their performances on training tasks rather than on production results.

Those apprentices who were over twenty years of age or in their fifth year were given journeyman status by the company after an intensive training course, and recognized as such by the unions. The intake of apprentices in August 1966 was the first to be trained in the new methods. The first year of training is off-the-job training. The company adopted this procedure before it was made compulsory by the Shipbuilding Industry Training Board (SITB). In his first year the apprentice is given an appreciation of the wide range of skills in the industry. He is not allocated to a particular trade although his preferences are noted. In his first three months of training the apprentice is taught basic skills and how to use the tools of various trades. The apprentices are sent to the nine trade sections for two-week periods to acquire this familiarity with the various trades. Following this period the boys are put into trade groups where they are trained in a range of skills. Those boys who are placed in the steelwork group are taught the whole range of skills before specializing in one trade. The specialist training for the chosen trade takes place in the last three months of the first year.

Throughout his apprenticeship, the boy must spend one day per week at a selected college. Before the end of the first year, the apprentice, his parents or guardian, and the company decide what trade he is most suited to. One important consequence of the broad first-year training is that it enables the company and the apprentice to assess his suitability for various trades.

The remaining three years of training are devoted to acquiring 'planned experience', that is, gaining experience of the chosen trade in a production area. It is important to note that these production areas are separate from the general production activities. The boys remain under the control of the training manager, and their progress is carefully recorded. In the third year the boy will be entrusted to a selected craftsman to do certain production work. The boy is still the responsibility of the training manager, and his progress is as carefully recorded as in past years. The emphasis is continually on the training of apprentices, and the on-the-job aspects of training are closely recorded and periodically these records are scrutinized by SITB training officers.

The detailed and careful recording of progress is an essential part of the system of training. These records provide the basis for a twice-yearly assessment of apprentices. The assessment form is compiled from reports by training supervisors, foremen, colleges and others who have been in contact with the apprentice. The assessments of all apprentices are compared and each boy is given a grade which determines his training bonus for the next six months. When the assessment is made, it is discussed and agreed by a committee made up by the training manager, training supervisor, trade shop stewards and relevant managers. The training manager or his representative personally tells each apprentice the grade he has been assessed at.

As part of the assessment process, the apprentice is given a form on which he assesses himself. This is then entered on the main assessment form. One of the major difficulties is the amount of subjectivity involved. Factors such as conduct, appearance, contribution to group effort, etc., are open to wide interpretation. Shop stewards have been unhappy with some aspects of the assessment because they see in it a means of 'rewarding blue eyes'. The stewards feel it their responsibility to fight for the highest grade for the apprentice, yet they may have no information on the trade potential of the boy, and are themselves arguing on subjective grounds.

Despite these problems, few arguments arose from the grading of apprentices. This is surprising because grading was one of the aspects of the training proposals most strongly contested by the unions. Some improved form of assessment, including the weighting of factors, was introduced latterly. However, the most important aspect of the assessment is the awareness by the apprentice that his work is constantly being monitored. This new approach to apprenticeship training has certainly interested more boys than ever before in the possibilities of an apprenticeship at Fairfields. The following Tables show the increase in interest and in numbers trained.

Table 9.1

Apprentices

	August 1966	August 1967
Enquiries	40	700
Applications received	32	210
Apprenticeships awarded	23	78

Physical limitations at the training centre impose restrictions on the numbers of boys accepted. In February 1968 there were 213 apprentices training in the company. The process of selection is more careful than it was. The old system was for a relative or friend to bring the boy into the yard for interview by the foreman, or at best by the personnel officer. If the interviews were successful and the boy was taken on, he began 'training' in the usual way – secondment to a tradesman.

There is now one intake of apprentices in August of each year. From the application forms the boys submit, a screening process is begun, when all applicants are interviewed by the training supervisors and are given aptitude and intelligence tests. If these tests and the initial interview prove satisfactory, the boys are then interviewed by the training manager whose final decision it is to admit a boy to an apprenticeship. The boy then begins his apprenticeship in August, the first year of his training being a probationary year.

In addition to his work as an apprentice, the boy is encouraged to widen his hobbies and recreational activities. The younger apprentices are given a limited amount of physical exercise and training each morning, and all apprentices are given swimming lessons at the local swimming baths. On two evenings a week the training centre is used for handicrafts and recreation for the boys.

The time and money given to apprentice training was essentially a long-term investment, but the establishment of a training centre and the recruitment of a training staff provided the company with the means of undertaking adult training. In June – July 1966 the company had to pay off approximately 600 men because of the completion of two ships which had required a large number of outfit workers. In this instance the management successfully followed a policy of redeploying workers within the company to avoid redundancy. This policy required a large amount of training for those men who were to be moved to other work, the majority of workers concerned being in the steelworking trades and members of the ASB.

In June 1966 the company and the ASB had signed an agreement on the relaxation of working practices. In order to maximize the benefit from this agreement the management had to ensure that the workman was able to do the jobs necessary to 'progress [his] own work' when a specialist tradesman was not available. The training manager in conjunction with senior management devised training courses where basic skills could be taught, e.g. a shipwright to learn the principles and techniques of welding.

The courses are run by training staff in satellite training centres located in production areas. The steelwork production planning unit allocates a certain number of men for retraining each week. The numbers vary according to courses and availability of places – e.g. up to sixteen men can be taken on the welding course, but only eight for burning, and two for air-arc gauging. In some areas lack of equipment is the limiting factor. In addition to the men selected for training the training staff have organized courses for men who have been declared 'work unavailable', a euphemistic expression for temporary redundancy. Between 2 June 1966 and 7 February 1968 the company had trained 1048 men.

It was usual for a course of training to last for five days. This was not only a convenient work unit but usually provided the worker with enough time to absorb and implement what he was taught. In the unusual case where a man failed to attain the acquired course standard, if it was judged that he could attain the standard within a further two days, he was brought back to the course. In cases where men reached the standard in less than five days, they were returned to their work immediately. The content of the course was limited by restrictions in the agreement. Trade shop stewards could at all times inspect the training process and would complain if they considered the practice exceeded what they considered necessary to 'progress own work'.

An example from the programme to train a shipwright to weld illustrates the type of activity covered: (1) basic manipulation of the equipment – e.g. electricity, choke, etc., (2) safety factors: ray burns, wearing of glasses, etc., (3) simple bead welding on flat surface or in down-hand position, control of arc, (4) simple fillets in down-hand position, (5) vertical fillet welding, (6) overhead fillet welding.

Training groups are from 'touching trades', i.e. from trades where skills are likely to overlap. In most steel trades the ability to tack weld was most important because this was simple work and usually caused some delay on ships particularly when a man had to wait for a service welder. However, the shop stewards were always anxious to protect any encroachment on 'their' trades and did their utmost to preserve the mystique of the craft from interlopers.

These training schemes could undoubtedly have been more comprehensive had the agreement permitted. But they were well received by the men, who entered into the training with enthusiasm. Many of them welcomed the opportunity to secure a better understanding of other steelwork trades, and thus a start was made among adult tradesmen to achieve a common approach to steelworking.

In addition to apprentice and adult training the company had undertaken a certain amount of training in other fields.

For all foremen, the company organized a full-time, one-week course on work study appreciation. This was essential as part of the company's introduction to the ETPS, and to emphasize the importance of the foreman's role in the successful implementation of the scheme. In addition to this course, forty foremen attended a full-time in-plant course on management and technical skills.

One interesting exercise in foreman training which also involved higher management was later to be termed the 'vertical approach to management training'. This experiment was conducted in the pipework department. The foremen were asked to analyse their jobs and to prepare a job specification and an eventual man specification as if for recruiting purposes. The departmental managers were asked to assess their foremen against the man specification. The purpose of this assessment was to indicate any weaknesses in the foremen so that suitable training needs could be identified.

When these areas of weakness had been identified, the departmental managers were given a topic which broadly covered the weak areas. This topic they researched, wrote up, and then presented to the foremen as a discussion topic. The whole theme of this training was self-help. This brought all levels of management together around the notion that training was by the department for the department. Because of their involvement in the preparation of the course, the departmental managers were obviously very concerned that the foremen should apply their training on the job. This experiment was regarded as being very successful and was to be repeated in other departments.

Senior management training was very much on an *ad hoc* basis. An intensive in-plant course was organized by the company to cover a wide range of management skills. Individual managers were sent on selected courses. Generally the scope of senior management education was limited by pressure on the managers' time. In a yard dedicated to change it was not always easy to ensure the availability of managers even in the evenings when the courses were held.

The importance of the training achievement at Fairfields is that it was accomplished in an industry noted for its backwardness in training and general management skills. Fairfields has demonstrated the scope for training in an industry which is notoriously craft-conscious and prone to demarcation. Within the two years of its operation it is probable that Fairfields' training activities allows it to be compared favourably with any other company in British industry.

The concept of a shipbuilding tradesman should be neither ludicrous nor terrifying, even to the most craft-conscious traditionalists. Fairfields, like all other shipyards and general industry, depends on the specialist worker. What is needed and what the new system will provide, is a specialism based on a broad range of skills which allows labour to be fully utilized on the job and to be redeployed as and when this becomes necessary. The link between broad-based training and redundancy policy has already been noted. One shipyard was far too small a platform to provide anything but an example of what could be done, given initiative, cooperation and enthusiasm. The limits of size, of money, and equipment were severe but did not seriously restrict the joint efforts of company and unions to open out new training and redeployment opportunities at Govan.

Perhaps the most important aspect of training at Fairfields was that much of the achievement was the result of its own initiative before the inception of the SITB. The latter attached three of its training officers to the training centre to observe and learn. Much of what has been done at Fairfields will be used in the new group and probably by other groups in the industry. Undoubtedly there is a great deal left to be done in the field of training in shipbuilding, but Fairfields have provided an example of how progress can be obtained in a limited time over a fairly wide range of skills and topics.

CHAPTER 10

Productivity

FROM the outset management had realized that a substantial increase in productivity was the most important of the several improvements necessary to make the yard viable and profitable. Preliminary investigations in the yard indicated a need for some type of management services to be introduced. Few of the usual quantitative controls were used: production-control was loose and in some areas, non-existent. A system of network analysis had been introduced and was being developed. There was little data available on work measurement. Two years before the formation of the new company, a firm of consultants had been retained to introduce a system of work measurement for steel-workers, but it was eventually abandoned as impractical. Little systematic attention was given to labour loading or to machine utilization rates. The existing payment-by-results scheme was inefficient, unrealistic, and applied to only some sections of the yard. In effect, much of the planning and control of production was undertaken on an *ad hoc* basis, with great reliance placed on the considerable experience and traditional methods of individual managers.

The broad sequence of production was laid down but there was no developed information 'feed-back' which would allow a production control system to operate. Productivity, although notoriously difficult to assess in a shipyard, was estimated from activity sampling tests to be 'very low'. In the period March–April 1966 these activity samples indicated a yard work pace of approximately twenty to thirty.* Clearly, the task of raising productivity in the yard was formidable.

Three main reasons were advanced in support of work measurement. First, such a system would facilitate the planning of production. Second, the system would provide a work

* That is, the men were performing at only 20 or 30 per cent of the standard pace accepted for industry generally.

discipline which created more organization of and control over work effort. Third, the system would provide a convenient basis for payment.

The initial intention of management was to introduce a measured day-work scheme into some areas of the yard by December 1966. Difficulties of staff recruitment, the need to train people for new jobs, and the complexities of the task forced an extended time scale on the management. The process of introducing a work measurement scheme was to have two phases. The first phase was to introduce a transitional scheme, the estimated target payment scheme (ETPS). This transitional scheme was based on estimated times for various jobs or activities. These times were analytically derived and validated wherever possible. As the bank of data increased and was refined it would then be possible to move from the transitional scheme to a full measured target payment scheme (MTPS), under which the times would be derived from work studies and validated estimates.

Studies, data collection and some training in work measurement techniques began in March 1966 and culminated in the introduction of the ETPS on 15 June 1967. The introduction of the MTPS was expected to take place twelve months later.

Before the transitional scheme could be introduced, personnel had to be trained in work study methods and this responsibility devolved upon the embryonic productivity services organization. Few people combined both a knowledge of the shipbuilding industry and work study methods. Some people combining these attributes were recruited from the north-east coast of England where a few yards employed some work study methods. In all, twenty senior managers were recruited for the industrial engineering section from outside the company. One of the first jobs of these men was to recruit and train people as industrial engineers and analytical estimators.

Recruitment of these trainees was from within the yard. Notification of the vacancies was posted in the yard, and all applicants were screened by means of intelligence and aptitude tests to establish their suitability for training. Training was given by the company's own staff with occasional guest lecturers discussing special topics. Training lasted for ten weeks, the last two weeks being concerned with on-the-job exercises. In all, seventy-two men were recruited from within the company and trained as industrial engineers or analytical estimators.

An important consideration arising from the application of work study is the probability of disputes between management and men concerning time allowed for jobs. In most situations, the shop stewards represent the interests of the men. However, most shop stewards in shipbuilding have little knowledge of work study techniques and would be at a serious disadvantage when discussing disputed time studies. To minimize this disadvantage the company offered to train one in twenty of the work force as workers' representatives. The trainees would come from each department and were nominated by the men in conjunction with the shop stewards. The nominees were trained subject to their suitability being established after aptitude tests. The company saw the role of workers' representatives as ' . . . [to] participate in the investigation and setting-up arrangements, and to give assurance to those whom he represents as to the authenticity of the techniques being used. Further, during the operation of the measured daywork scheme to act as a "consultant" to the shop steward should a dispute arise in respect of a standard time'.

In addition to training personnel, the company had to familiarize the rest of the yard with work study. Work study appreciation courses were held for foremen and shop stewards. All the foremen attended a one-week full-time appreciation course on work study at Strathclyde University. Three one-week appreciation courses were held for shop stewards at the Electrical Trade Union's training college at Esher. These courses were given by the company's managers, by consultants and by guest lecturers. In all 110 shop stewards, deputies and full-time trade-union officials participated in the courses. These courses were very useful in stimulating discussions on work study and particularly regarding its introduction to a shipyard.

The company began to make studies and to introduce the documentation necessary to support a system of work measurement. The recruitment and training of staff, the compilation of systems and documentation, and technical investigation studies were taking place on a continuous basis. When the first training course was completed, on 1 August 1966, twenty-seven industrial engineers and analytical estimators began to make studies in the yard. On 22 August, another seventeen joined this work.

From technical investigations made at that time, it was noted that there was no standard sequence of work method, there was a high percentage of non-productive time (60 per cent) and that approximately 10–20 per cent was 'abortive'.* It was apparent that production difficulties in the yard resulted from bad work methods as much as from the low pace of work. However, because of the need to establish priorities, a 'conscious decision was made to ignore method study, but to accept current methods of production and to concentrate on work planning, measurements and estimating for the purpose of introducing a measured day-work scheme'. The first phase of the scheme was concerned with the collection of data for the proposed ETPS.

It was the accumulation of work study data and the increasing accuracy of the process planning and estimating sections which enabled the company to introduce the ETPS. This transitional scheme provided a much needed measure of control over work and production and provided an incentive for the worker.

The ETPS was based on work measurement and the estimation of job times. The component parts of a job were studied and given a time and the process was continued until a total time for each job was built up. Much of the data compiled in one study was synthesized for use in other studies. Whenever possible these estimates were validated by time studies – 'a validated estimate is obtained by taking work studies of operations or jobs and comparing the total results with the estimate for the job, and adjusting all estimates for similar operations or jobs accordingly'. Such a process allows for the synthesizing of times.

* Abortive work is modification and/or rectification work which does not add to the value of work done.

The scheme was applied to all workers in the yard. The indirect and service workers were included in the scheme by 'association' with the group of workers they serviced. For example, cranemen servicing production workers in the shed are, for purposes of payment, attached to the group which they service. The application of the scheme is based on the concept of a production group, or team. The basis for payment is the number of standard hours which the group produce per hour of work. The standard hour is defined as 'the amount of work which an experienced trained worker shall produce in one hour when using the specified method, tools and materials, taking the necessary rest, and is motivated to work at a 100 rating'.

Payment is made weekly but calculated over a four-week period. The basis for calculation is:

$$\frac{\text{total standard hours earned by group for four-week period}}{\text{total attendance hours of group for four-week period}} \times 100$$

Payment is made at the rate of 1d. per point from a scale of 70 to 74, and at a rate of 0·5d. per point from 74 to 94, i.e. the total production payment earned by a man working at a rate of 94 would be 1s. 2d. per hour (4d. + 10d.).

The first 4d. payment was made to those departments which agreed to allow work studies to be taken. The management had originally envisaged a payment of 1d. per point all along the scale. However, the inadequacy of the collected data ensured that subsequent 'tightening' of times would be necessary as more studies were taken. The management believed that the workers would expect monetary compensations for any tightening of times for a particular operation or job. By introducing an intermediate scheme based on estimated times, future studies which resulted in tighter times (and therefore demanding increased effort) could be compensated by an increase in payments from 0·5d. per point to a rate of 1d. per point. Until the data was good enough to permit this tightening, payment in excess of a performance of 74 and to a maximum of 94 was set by management for convenience of calculation. It was originally envisaged that the overall productivity payment would be 1s. per hour, (i.e. 94 — 70 = 24 × 1d.), and that the 'ceiling' could be raised when circumstances made it necessary.

The basic consolidated rate is the 'fall-back' rate which approximates to a 70 performance to which is added the same payment per point which all groups receive. Payment increases when the four-week average performance is higher than that for the previous period. Increased payment begins in the first week of the subsequent period. In the case of reduced performance, payment is reduced only after three consecutive four-weekly period performances show a decrease compared with performances in the previous three consecutive four-week periods. In short, it takes one month for increased performance to be rewarded and three months for reduced effort to be penalized. Diagram 10.1 illustrates the working of the scheme.

Indirect workers and service workers are paid by their association with a group, being paid the average performance rate for the group. The scheme can be terminated by either party on receipt of written notice two months prior to withdrawal.

Three major areas of difficulty could have jeopardized the operation of the productivity scheme. First, the problem of collecting data within the proposed time scale. Second, the problem of production control. Third, the problem of supervision.

The time scale within which the scheme was to be introduced was very important. Government restrictions on wage awards, other than productivity bargains, together with the inherited discontent caused by wage anomalies and differentials within the yard caused great pressure on management to introduce the scheme. It was one means available to workers to obtain a substantial increase in wages. The problem for management was to collect sufficient data to introduce the scheme and to allow its further refinement. Time was of the essence because the productivity bargain with the ASB, in June 1966, had accentuated feelings on wage differentials, and the lower-paid workers were demanding an opportunity to increase their wages. Under these circumstances and in this environment the scheme which was to be introduced had to cover as many of the yard workers as possible. In the time available only an

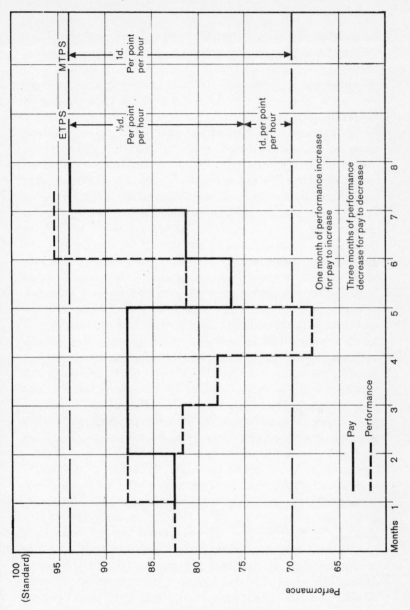

Diagram 10.1 *Measured daywork scheme*

intermediate scheme could be introduced on a comprehensive basis. However, this transitional scheme was needed for two reasons other than the requirement to provide worker incentive. First was the need to provide a more formal control over production and second was the need to raise production from the low level to which it had fallen after the consolidation of wages in April–June 1966.

The existence of a payment-by-results scheme in some sections of the yard together with the historical distortion of wages, allowances, and bonuses had resulted in a very confused wages structure. For example, in the sheet iron shop there were approximately seventeen different wage rates for 170 men. This was by no means an uncharacteristic example. It was intended to pay any productivity bonus arising from the scheme on basic rates. As one means of simplifying the calculation (and of bringing some order to the wages structure) the management decided to consolidate the wages of the workers in the yard. Existing incentive schemes were abolished. A reference period (from four to thirteen weeks) was chosen for each group of workers in consultation with trade-union officials. A calculation was made of workers' earnings over that period, excluding overtime and allowances. The resulting average hourly rate was agreed with the men and the trade unions and was known as the consolidated rate. It was on this rate that any productivity payment was made. One effect of the consolidation of rates was to remove the incentive to work harder – an earnings level equivalent to at least the best results obtained during the reference period was guaranteed by the consolidation process. The decrease in worker effort after consolidation was considerable. On 27 February 1967 the productivity services director met all the steelwork division's shop stewards, telling them that there was 'a problem in steelwork – productivity is not rising but the situation is not yet desperate'. On average, there was a delay on unit construction of approximately six days in the shed and eleven days on the berth. Within this pattern some delays were longer and some shorter. The meeting was called to present the facts to the shop stewards and to ask their help in pin-pointing the problems. The company's tender for a contract had been based on anticipated productivity increases. It was essential to improve productivity to meet cost targets and ensure the future of the company.

The shop stewards agreed that there were problems in their division. One steward said that there were still serious deficiencies in planning: 'One unit has been on the floor so long that it's regarded as a monument'. Another steward felt that management changes which had removed the head foreman position had done much to dissipate the team spirit that was engendered in small groups. The major cause of slackness in production was the consolidation of wages: 'There is no incentive for the worker to increase effort'. All stewards were agreed on this point. Later, at an informal meeting, a welder told how his average output on piece-work rates was 26–8 feet per hour. The average was now about 50 per cent below this figure, and he knew one welder producing an average of only 9 feet per hour. The need for some reintroduction of incentive payment was clear, particularly in the steelwork division where throughput determined the over-all output and efficiency of the yard.

It was in the steelwork division that the scheme was expected to have most effect. The flow process of production allowed studies to be made more easily than on the berth. However, despite the extensive modernization between 1960 and 1969, the fabrication shed remained badly designed. Production bottlenecks were caused by the smallness of the pre-fabrication bays relative to facilities of the rest of the shed. This was a situation which management could do little about. Redesigning and modifying the facilities was financially prohibitive. The pattern of work flow could only be modified within the confines of the existing facilities. Without a production control unit it would be difficult to ensure a work flow continuous enough to support the productivity scheme and to reduce the amount of non-productive time. The reduction of non-productive time to the expected level of 15 per cent was most important, because non-productive time, for example, 'waiting for work', was paid at the performance rate.

Most measured work schemes are introduced into situations where a production control system is operating. No such system operated at Fairfields, and such a control unit could only be developed after the scheme was introduced. Some work scheduling was done by the process planning section, but it was insufficient to provide a sustained work flow. These difficulties were apparent in the early days after the scheme had been introduced. The development of a production control department did not gain impetus until September 1967.

The problems of time scale and production control were added to by the shortage of work study staff. The collection of data fully occupied the available manpower. The study coverage in the steelwork division was a particular problem. The management wanted to transfer industrial engineers from other sections to assist with steelwork studies. The steelworkers, who were mostly members of the ASB, refused to be time studied by industrial engineers who were not Society members. This refusal to concede flexibility seriously retarded the collection of work study data and directly contributed to the low coverage of steelwork shown in Table 10.4. This ban on flexibility was still in force in February 1968. In addition to these difficulties in setting up the scheme, there was considerable anxiety about the ability and competence of the foremen to supervise and operate the scheme.

The introduction of the scheme would make new and considerable demands on foremen whose morale was to be a continual source of worry to management. Foremen were given an appreciation course on work study and were fully briefed on the operation of the scheme. Most production areas had industrial engineers attached to them to give assistance to the foremen. The introduction of job cards into some areas in December 1966, helped to familiarize foremen and workers with some aspects of the scheme. Initially these cards were of more use in familiarizing people with the scheme than as a means of providing management information, but this became increasingly effective as the scheme developed. The introduction of job cards did not take place smoothly. The foremen and workers were unfamiliar with the cards, and with the necessity of accurately recording job times. To some degree the confusion engendered resulted from the inadequacies in the job card system. For some weeks the introduction of job cards caused a considerable strain in the traditional system of labour control.

PRODUCTIVITY TARGETS

The new management's initial thinking was that the 'experiment' would cover a period of five years from January 1966. The publication of the *Geddes Report* two months later made it clear that rationalization of the industry was the price for governmental financial support. The *Geddes Report* and other indications of future rationalization persuaded the company that their time scale for the experiment should be reduced from five to three years. The reduction in time scale did not alter the management's resolution to build for the future. This is the reason why the period from January 1966 to June 1967 (pre-ETPS) may be regarded as a time given to the building of a managerial infra-structure. The immediate short-term gains which might have been achieved were deliberately sacrificed so that future expansion would provide even larger, and sustained, benefits.

It was inevitable that this pre-ETPS period should have an appreciable dampening effect on productivity in the yard. The reduction in productivity was a burden that the company had to bear – part of the price of change. The company had a two-phase target to meet. First, there was the task of recovering the productivity it had lost in the pre-ETPS period, and second, it had to further increase productivity above that level to meet the best British and eventually, foreign competitors. Productivity targets had to be flexible to allow for the uncertainty of potential productivity improvements. A major problem was the determination of a base point against which trends could be measured. Some managers thought this base point should be 1 January 1966; others thought that consideration should be given to the development of the management infra-structure in the first year of the company, and advocated 1 January 1967 as the base. The selection of a base point was never authoritatively decided, and caused considerable controversy whenever productivity was discussed.

In April 1967 the company submitted the ETPS to the

197

Ministry of Labour for its approval. The documents supporting the presentation contained forecasts of potential productivity gains in various divisions. These forecasts seriously under-estimated the problems of raising productivity in the yard. In September 1967 the management were able on the evidence of measurement, to revise the forecasts. In particular the steel-work division had fallen below expectation and a considerable revision was made.

Table 10.1

Anticipated divisional productivity improvement for
year ending 31 December 1967
Base – 1 January 1967

	Forecast percentage		
	A	B	C
Steelwork	40	15	7·5
Pipeshop	35	17	6·7
Machinery installation	20	16	10
Hull outfit*			
Joiners	60	26	20
Electricians	35	23	20
Painters	40	43	40
Sheet-iron workers	35	21	15

A – forecast as at April 1967
B – forecast as at September 1967
* – trades selected to allow comparison.

The figures shown in column C are those agreed by the divisional managers as representing a realistic assessment of productivity gains from 1 January 1967. This assessment was endorsed by the divisional managers on 27 September 1967. These figures of achieved improvements are considerably less than those shown in Column A, and are indicative of forecast-ing hazards in a situation of rapid industrial change. However, there was still considerable discussion among management about the validity of these forecasts and the controversy was to continue throughout the existence of the company.

ASSESSMENT OF PRODUCTIVITY

In the analysis of productivity trends in Fairfields we are concerned with the period January 1966 to December 1967. From late November 1967 the imminence of the proposed merger had a dampening effect on morale and productivity. The failure of the company to negotiate a double-day-shift working arrangement with the ASB members further dampened productivity potential at a time when the fabrication shed was becoming overloaded with work.

1. *Steelwork Division.* To attain a basis for comparison in shipbuilding productivity, the British Ship Research Association devised an index which attempts to weight the complexities of building different types of ships. The basis for comparison is an equivalent ton, a standard unit of measurement in terms of work content for shipyard steelwork production which, assuming a constant productivity level, should require the same expenditure of man hours on its production.

There is not available a building figure for January 1966. The basis for comparison is the figure for October 1965 when the previous company was building at a rate of 76·6 man-hours per equivalent ton. At the end of the pre-ETPS period in July 1967 the new company was building at a rate of 84·3 man-hours per equivalent ton – a productivity decrease of 9·1 per cent.

This decrease was not peculiar to Fairfields. In 1965–6 there was a decrease in steelwork productivity in British shipbuilding of approximately 4 per cent. This trend continued into 1967 and was not, in total, very dissimilar from the reduction experienced by Fairfields. On the Clyde, several other yards were in a much worse position, two of them experiencing a decrease of 22 per cent in productivity between 1965–6, with the trend continuing into 1967. From the available information, it does not appear that Fairfields in the pre-ETPS period was significantly less efficient in the use of labour than the average shipbuilder in the UK.

The ETPS was introduced in June 1967 and from that date

199

until the end of December 1967 the Fairfields company obtained a remarkable 25 per cent increase in productivity. Taking the July 1967 figure of 84·3 man-hours per equivalent ton as a base, the rate of production at the end of December 1967 was 63 man-hours per equivalent ton; a productivity increase of 25 per cent.

Therefore, taking account of the loss of production in the pre-ETPS period, the overall increase in productivity from October 1965 to December 1967 was 15·9 per cent, which fulfilled the target mentioned previously.

The increase in productivity resulting from the introduction of the ETPS gave a production rate at the end of December 1967 (63) slightly better than the best ever performance of the old company (63·6) achieved in July 1964.

At the building rate of 63 man-hours per equivalent ton, Fairfields was below the average figure for the shipbuilding industry in the UK, but still approximately double that for the Swedish and Japanese industries. This position is illustrated in Diagram 10.2

2. *Outfitting Division.* The information available for this division is less specific than for steelwork, but evidence is available to indicate improvements in productivity. On bulk-carrier work, using as a base one of the six bulk-carriers built by the company in the last four years, with corrections in the figures for changes in specification and size, performance against standard was as follows:

Table 10.2

Date of delivery	Productivity performance
October 1964	100
January 1965	101
June 1965	91
March 1966	91
April 1967	92
October 1967	105

Steelwork productivity comparison based on bulk-carrier construction

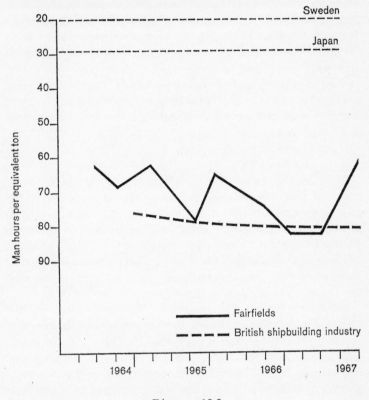

Diagram·10.2

This index of performance conceals some very major productivity achievements. In the electrical outfitting department a comparison between the outfitting of two sister ships, for the same level of completion, shows a reduction of 47 per cent in man hours used. Comparisons on completed sister ships show reductions in man hours used for blacksmith, joinery and paintwork of 23, 31 and 16 per cent respectively. Some reduction in man hours used on a 'sister ship' would occur as a result of the 'learning process' but the improvements recorded were well above those which could be attributed to this cause.

201

3. *Machinery Installation Department*. This department was created in July 1966 to take over the installation of main engines and other machinery after the closure of Fairfield-Rowan. The lack of historical data makes it impossible to compare with previous work done in these sectors. Indications that a high pace was being maintained in the machine shop were verified by a considerable amount of work measurement. On board ship, there were considerable improvements in productivity in some areas – for example, a 27·9 per cent reduction in the total man-hours required to fit out the inside machinery spaces of two sister ships.

4. *Pipework Division*. The available evidence for this division indicates that productivity had not increased in the lifetime of the new company. However, because of the company policy of accepting sub-contract work for this division, most of its outside contract work proved profitable.

There are many difficulties which prevent an accurate assessment of productivity in a shipyard. Amongst these difficulties the major ones arise from the size and widely ranging composition of what is being produced at different times, and the extent to which shipbuilding is a process in which labour effort is not amenable to close supervision. In addition there is the influence of weather. The concept of steadily increasing (or decreasing) trends in shipyard productivity is unrealistic. There can be substantial fluctuations, sometimes affecting most of the yard but more usually distributed unevenly between the different production areas. It is possible, with hindsight and time for dispassionate analysis, to see these as 'fluctuations around a trend', but the level of measurement and control of labour effectiveness necessary for management to be able to have such hindsight in time for it to be operationally significant was only being achieved at Fairfields towards the end of 1967.

At Fairfields the problems were greater than in most yards because in the building programme were two ships of a type never before built in the UK. These were allocated 'weights' to allow productivity calculations to be made, but it is not known how accurate the weighting is in relation to final man-hour expenditure. However, on the best available information there was a productivity increase of 16 per cent in the steelwork division and 14 per cent in the outfit division. It has not been possible to assess the impact of productivity improvement in the MID because of the lack of comparative information relative to the period before the formation of the department. In the context of bulk-carrier building on which the above assessments were made, MID is accountable for approximately 10 per cent of total man-hours, and therefore even significant improvements in productivity are likely to have only a marginal effect on overall productivity and costs. Because of merger there was not sufficient time available for these improvements to be monitored over the required period and this made evaluation of achievement difficult. The effects of the merger have been referred to elsewhere, but not least among these was the effect on morale transmitted through to production.

THE COST OF PRODUCTIVITY

The increases in productivity at Fairfields were obtained after a large investment in manpower and methods. The productivity services organization was the result of a considerable investment, which was made on the assumption that only with such an organization could the required productivity increase be achieved. It is difficult to distinguish unique 'added costs' for the new company for two reasons. First, some of the costs of the new company were difficult to separate from inherited costs. Second, comparative figures of the costs of the old company ignore the radical changes in aims and philosophy. However, it is possible to arrive at some estimate of the increase in overhead cost.

The amount of £183,000 set against revenue investment takes account of the build up of services and systems other than those mainly concerned with labour productivity, which will bring future benefits. The establishment of purchasing, quality control, and value engineering departments had already resulted in a contribution to savings of approximately £89,000 by the end of 1967. Without these additional overheads it would

Table 10.3

Comparison of overhead costs between old and new companies

	£ millions	
	1967	*1966*
Budget for year to June 1966 (old company)		1·315
Budget to December 1967 (new company)	2·19	
Less development expenditure	0·32	
	1·87	
New company's increase in overhead costs	0·555	
Less:		
Revenue investment	0·183	
Buying and value engineering	0·29	
Contribution from quality control	0·60	0·272
Adjusted increase in overheads		0·283

This is equal to an amount of –

$$\frac{283}{1870} = 10s.\ 3d.^* \times 1s.\ 6d. \quad \begin{array}{l}\text{additional overhead}\\ \text{costs per hour}\end{array}$$

* Average hourly earnings in yard for four weeks ended 8 December 1967.

have been difficult to have increased productivity as was done in the post ETPS period.

In January 1966, the average hourly earnings in the yard were 8s. 5d. per hour. This figure had increased to 10s. 3d. by the end of 1967. This increased payment of 1s. 10d. breaks down into a payment of 4d. per hour to all those sections accepting work study, a maximum bonus of 10d. per hour earnable where the ETPS was introduced, and 8d. per hour as an average cost of the three productivity bargains covering all parts of the yard.

The rise of 1s. 10d. per hour in wage rates was necessary to achieve productivity. Without the initial payment of 4d. per hour, no work studies could be done, and consequently no productivity scheme could have been introduced. This payment was regarded as part of the earnable productivity bonus and was not an *ex gratia* payment. It was this payment which allowed the formulation of the ETPS to be laid down, and which distinguished Fairfields from other yards on the River. The average payment of 8d. per hour was slightly higher than that paid by the other yards on the River – but Fairfields' payment covered three agreements* to most yards' single agreement. It is valueless to attempt to distinguish any part of the increase of 1s. 10d. per hour as 'unique' to Fairfields. Without these payments Fairfields would not have obtained the increases in productivity in the post-ETPS period.

The total increase in labour and overhead costs for the new company was 3s. 4d. per hour.

Labour cost	1s. 10d.
Overhead cost	1s. 6d.
	3s. 4d.

If it was assumed that the new company was expecting a 100 per cent recovery on the extra costs incurred, the hourly costs excluding the new developments would have been:

20s. 6d. − 3s. 4d. = 17s. 2d.

On a strict 100 per cent recovery on labour costs the situation would have been:

20s. 6d. − 3s. 8d. = 16s. 10d.

Taking the overall increase in yard productivity during the period of the new company to be approximately 15 per cent, the overall cost assuming 100 per cent recovery calculated on a base of 17s. 2d. is:

$$\frac{15}{100} \times 17s.\ 2d. = 2s.\ 7d.$$

To achieve this 3s. 4d. was spent to leave a deficit of 9d.:

3s. 4d. − 2s. 7d. = 9d. per hour.

These figures show that despite the overall improvement in productivity there was still some way to go before the break-even point was reached. Break-even between the cost of obtaining

* Agreements with the ASB, NUGMW, and Outfit Trades. See Chapter 7.

productivity and the resultant improvements will not necessarily make a company profitable if the overall relationship between cost and productivity is out of balance. A large proportion of the cost of a ship is bought out, giving an area of cost over which the company has only limited control. Improvements in yard efficiency may be reduced or even off-set by external factors.

Some caution must be observed in assessing yard productivity trends. Although there was undoubtedly an underlying trend towards increasing productivity, some aspects of the ETPS makes calculation of productivity gains hazardous. Tables 10.4 and 10.5 show for each department, by ship (and shop where applicable) the percentage measurement and working performance recorded for certain weeks. The weeks were selected to illustrate the position of each department at the end of each month between August 1967 and December 1967.

Table 10.4

*Percentage of measured work in total hours
worked by division for selected weeks, and working performance*

Division	SHOP Week Number									
	34		39		43		47		52	
	%	WP	%	WP	%	WP	%	WP	%	WP
Steelwork	17	76	16	75	22	86	30	91	30	96
Pipework	40	98	27	97	38	99	40	96	52	94
M.I.D.	43	96	54	96	46	98	36	96	53	97
Outfit	25	90	29	94	25	96	21	96	22	94

The percentage measured work refers to the work actually measured (productive and abortive) out of the total clock hours recorded in the division for the particular week. The work performance (WP) is the pay performance, i.e. for week 52 in the steelwork division, the worker was paid a maximum bonus although 30 per cent of the work was measured in that week. What is clearly illustrated by this table is the low level of measurement relative to the number of hours booked against the divisions. This is particularly so in the case of steelwork and for pipework done on board ship.

Table 10.5

Percentage of measured work in total hours worked by division for selected weeks, and working performance

Division	SHIP Week Number									
	34		*39*		*43*		*47*		*52*	
	%	WP	%	WP	%	WP	%	WP	%	WP
Pipework	13	96	23	82	13	98	9	98	18	96
Machinery installation	42	99	45	99	44	96	52	96	55	98

These figures indicate that there is a serious danger of cost 'leakage' when maximum bonus can be earned for only a limited degree of measurement. The tables are also indicative of the extent to which productivity services had to stretch their resources to introduce a comprehensive work measurement scheme. Some people familiar with work study techniques and measured daywork schemes felt that the productivity services organization's resources need not have been stretched. One person considered that there were 'at least a 100 work study engineers too many in the company'. In addition to the low degree of measurement the scheme introduced had other weaknesses. First of these was the system of payment for 'allocated work'.

The management tried to overcome the limitations of measurement by 'allocating' certain work to sections, and assuming that the work was done at the same performance rate as was the actual measured work. This assumption can push up cost per unit of output considerably. Much of the allocated work is not measurable or is not worth measuring. Quite clearly there are areas of work in a shipyard where it is too costly or too difficult to determine measured standards. One priority of the company should have been to identify these areas and to either detach them from the scheme – or more probably – introduce a graded incentive scheme to cover such areas.

Another major risk in the scheme arises from the fact that non-productive time is paid for at the rate earned for working performance. In the case of the worker 'waiting for work', his waiting time is paid for at his working performance. This aspect of the scheme places great importance on the management ensuring that a continuous flow of work operates. This they were not always able to do. The foremen are responsible for signing the workman's job card but there can be some doubt whether the times filled-in by the workman are always verified. Also, because it takes three months for decreasing performance to result in a drop in pay, there is considerable scope for the worker to maintain a less than optimum performance. The scheme could be improved if there were some incentive placed on workers and supervisors to decrease the amount of non-productive time. Clearly this is primarily a management function, but in a complex industry like shipbuilding there is a case for sharing responsibility for it and focusing this shared responsibility on an incentive. Even where, as at Fairfields, a very high performance was being given by workers when they were occupied, all of the benefit can be lost by excessive non-productive time. Thus the rates of pay need to be more clearly and closely related to fluctuations in work performed and not only to performance rates.

Despite these defects, the productivity scheme introduced at Fairfields in June 1967 produced remarkable results in the first six months of its operation. The gains noted in this chapter are only minimum achievements in the sense that these can be determined with a fair degree of accuracy. It is not unlikely, given the limitations of shipyard productivity indices, that the productivity increases were higher. However, unless action is taken to reduce the comprehensiveness of the scheme, more closely relate payment with performance, and increase the degree of work measurement, the savings suggested in previous calculations cannot be regarded as permanent. The battle for increased productivity in shipbuilding is not a once-for-all skirmish, but must be continuous.

CHAPTER 11

Evaluating the Experiment

ANY assessment of 'the Fairfields experiment' faces two great difficulties. The first is that the aims of the experiment were never set out clearly and comprehensively, so that the criteria against which success or failure are to be judged are themselves in doubt and may be disputed. The second difficulty is that the life of the experiment was foreshortened by the merger with other yards on the Upper Clyde, so that tentative judgements of trends rather than firm recording of objective results is all that is possible. Firms must be judged against a number of performance standards, and at any one moment of time it is possible to dispute the weight being attached to such standards (e.g. trends in costs per unit of output as against trends in productivity per man-hour). This difficulty is enhanced in an 'experimental' situation in which commonly accepted weightings may not apply, and further accentuated if the objectives of the experiment are not defined unambiguously.

Rather loosely expressed the aims of the experiment have been stated as: the improvement of industrial relations by the provision of high and stable earnings, these to be achieved by a combination of modern management techniques and the full use of channels of communication, better utilization of labour, manpower planning, the extensive use of retraining, the erosion of restrictive practices and the voluntary abandonment of the strike weapon. Remarkable successes were achieved in most of these areas. The speed with which modern techniques were introduced almost across the entire range of management inevitably created new problems. The process of absorbing change is more difficult than that of initiating it, particularly when the scope is all but universal and a high proportion of the management concerned had become set in the traditional attitudes of shipbuilding. Nevertheless the initiation and absorption of change was effectively carried through. From an initial attitude of reserve and suspicion the majority of managers in the yard came to accept and even endorse the new approach. There was an atmosphere of striving in the yard – striving to learn, to apply, to improve – which was commented upon by many widely experienced observers. There were considerable fluctuations in yard morale – both amongst managers and amongst workers – but the underlying support for change and improvement remained a constant.

Manpower planning was restricted by the size of the yard and by the inherited building programme. The desire to reduce fluctuations in the demand for labour played an important part in determining the build-up of the order-book under the new management, decisions being taken in the light of careful forecasts of the future shifts in manpower requirements involved in alternative building programmes. Manpower forecasts were complicated by the need to build in to them the sizeable increases in productivity which were to follow upon the changes in management techniques and methods of payment, and such forecasts had to be revised in the light of experience. Fairfields could not lay claim to having achieved the objective of greatly reducing fluctuations in the demand for labour, but had evolved methods for approaching this problem and had begun to give it serious attention in top-level decision taking. Even with these techniques a company controlling more berths and able to re-deploy within a larger building programme would be necessary if a high degree of security of employment *within* ship-building were to be provided. Such an attempt should be combined with a policy of stabilizing earnings, retraining and re-deployment between industries, a policy which requires governmental as well as managerial attention.

Restrictive practices were reduced substantially at Fairfields, as a result of changing attitudes and productivity bargains. There was evidence that not all of the changes that would have been acceptable to workers in the yard were in fact introduced, partly due to the problems of management absorbing rapid and extensive changes within a fairly short period of time. The voluntary abandonment of the strike weapon was not achieved, although the incidence of strikes was reduced in a period of rapid and fundamental change affecting workers, and this is an indication that the pledge given by employees at the formation of the new company was not an empty one. The target of 'no strikes' was an unrealistic one, certainly for the short run, against the background of the industry's labour relations and in the face of the extensive changes which were to be made. Nevertheless its very substantial effect could not have been made in any other way. A pledge to 'reduce strikes' would have been more realistic but less effective, because lacking in dramatic effect.

Improvements in industrial relations were a major aim of the new management at Fairfields, and in this area success was considerable, both at the institutional and the personal levels. The creation of a joint council embracing management and all of the unions, meeting regularly and considering all major developments within the company, was of importance not only for the company but for the industry. From within that council evolved machinery for resolving disputes and for developing effective communications between trade unions and shop stewards on matters affecting employees of the company. To some extent deficiencies in trade-union communications were remedied through joint-trade-union efforts, this having the effect of reducing inter-union and inter-employee friction and increasing the sense of cohesion and solidarity amongst shipyard workers. In an industry in which inter-union frictions contribute so substantially to disruption and conflict the achievement of joint machinery, the blurring of some of the sharpest lines of demarcation, the establishment of an approach to training and apprenticeship which accentuated the notion of 'a shipyard worker' and the development of new channels of communication operated jointly by all of the unions concerned all reflect the very substantial headway made in the industrial relations field at Fairfields.

The efforts of both management and union representatives to involve workers in the affairs of the company had only limited success, though measured against the rest of the industry the positive response to the policies advanced by management and unions was very impressive. There was none of the resistance managements have frequently encountered in attempts to interest and involve employees in the position of the company.* The extent of participation was limited. The yard was not the locale of an experiment in 'workers' control' and the extent of industrial democracy was not very great. Participation by shop stewards in the meetings of the executive managers' committee was an interesting but limited experiment. The main extension of industrial democracy came with the increase in the availability of information about the company's affairs, the considerable improvement in communications and a willingness to discuss all relevant aspects of how the yard was run without recourse to entrenched and defensive positions of 'managerial prerogative'. The line between consultation and joint control was firmly drawn by management, however. There was none of the 'mock democracy' which Jacques commented upon in some of the committee work at Glacier Metal.† Nevertheless there were opportunities for increased participation in and influence over the affairs of the company which union representatives did not exploit. This inhibition was partly due to a rational calculation of the desirable limits of participation, and the dangers thought to be involved for the independence required for effective trade-union action if shop stewards became very closely involved in management decision-taking. Such inhibitions were occasionally expressed, and obviously played some part in restraining processes for extending worker participation, but they were not a dominant feature. There was, in addition, a lack of initiative on the part of shop stewards to explore the potentialities of the new situation. The management at Fairfields would have been extremely receptive to constructive suggestions for extending the consultative and participative processes. Experimentation in industrial democracy – for example in single-channel bargaining – would probably have been attempted had there been any groundswell indicating a desire for it, but no such rank-and-file or shop

---

* See for example, 'Understanding human behaviour in organization: one viewpoint', C. Argyris in *Modern Organization Theory*, (ed.) M. Haire, Wiley, New York, 1959.

† Jacques, E, *The Changing Culture of a Factory,*

steward interest was expressed. Trade-union initiatives within the shipyard were primarily directed towards traditional objectives, mainly wage increases, and there was very little attempt to extend the areas of interest about which joint negotiations could take place. Given that shipbuilding is a work-process and combination of technologies in which ship-yard workers have been in a position to exercise considerable control over the pace and even the ordering of production, it was rather surprising that the move by management towards a modified measured day-work system did not induce either resistance or an attempt to substitute alternative controls to those which work-people would lose as a result of the new methods. Trade unionists have frequently expressed opposition to such systems of payment and work-measurement on the grounds that they reduce the influence of shop stewards and of militant policies over the determination of wage rates, but in shipbuilding the matter goes much deeper as the nature of the productive process and in particular the difficulties in the way of supervision have often allowed workers on fixed rates of wages to decide their own pace of work. Shop stewards and trade-union representatives were involved in the process of work-measurement and of agreeing performance, but there was no attempt to build up a control structure independent of management. It is not easy to decide whether this was due to trust or to lack of understanding or of initiative. Our estimate would place considerable emphasis on the atmosphere of trust and the desire for improvement which had built up in the yard. This trust was far from unqualified, but it was there and kept in being by the range of opportunities to question and have doubts resolved which the many channels of communication provided. Certainly a lack of understanding amongst shop stewards of the significance of changes in train was not of importance; the stewards had a very precise understanding both of the implications of the extant arrangements and of the proposed changes for their bargaining power within the yard.

New management techniques and problems of industrial relations impinged upon each other with greatest force around this area of productivity bargaining. The introduction of work study techniques as a tool for shipyard management was a major break-through for the industry, demanding careful preparatory work with management, foremen, and workers. If work study is to contribute seriously to the improvement of productivity, relations between the management and workers must be reasonably good before an attempt is made to introduce it and the workers must have confidence in the sincerity of the management towards them, otherwise they will regard it as another trick to try and get more work out of them without any benefits for themselves.*

The emphasis on consultation was clearly illustrated by the long and careful preparations which were made to introduce the ETPS. The cost in time was amply repaid by the absence of labour troubles arising from the operation of the scheme. Management showed that it was possible to use work study in many areas of shipyard production. What it failed to do was to identify those areas where it was uneconomic to introduce work study and then to devise a means of grading this non-measurable work for payment purposes. The ETPS recognized that some work was uneconomic to measure by 'allocating' a performance rate to it. Analysis has shown that in many areas, e.g. steelwork on board ship, the amount of measured work was only small in proportion to the total hours recorded in the area. Payment was made at the performance rate for the measured work, and this pattern provided areas of potential cost 'leakages'. In these areas where the ratio of allocated to measured work was high, it would have been wise to detach them from the scheme.

For effective contribution to company profitability, any work study based incentive scheme must be adapted to meet the particular production characteristics of the plant. Care should be taken to ensure that payment levels closely correspond to sustained performance. At Fairfields the performance-payment gap was too far apart and allowed for production 'slackness' after a performance peak had been reached – i.e. once a performance rate had been achieved it was maintained

*I.L.O. *Work Study*, 1967, p. 46.

as a payment rate for the next two months irrespective of subsequent performance. In their concern to be fair to the workers, the management had introduced a scheme where in the long run the productivity increases could be out-weighed by cost leakages. One consequence of the merger was that the management team which had introduced the new payment scheme was not able to monitor its progress beyond a few months or to introduce changes the need for which would have been suggested by experience.

The progress towards a jointly-agreed job-evaluated wages structure was one of the clearest signs that attitudes between workers and unions were changing, as well as attitudes between workers and management. It was also an illustration of how, in a process of rapid change, some aspects of which were introduced in response to the pressures of particular subsections, there is always the danger of getting the different parts of a total change out of phase with each other. The need to introduce the new payment scheme before the firm foundation of a job-evaluated rate structure had been created could have made further problems for the productivity scheme. These dangers were avoided, largely as a result of the intensive process of explanation and consultation which preceded the introduction of the ETPS, but it is possible that the scheme itself would have had to be adapted once the pattern of job evaluation rates had been agreed.

A feature of institutional industrial relations at Fairfields was the extent to which trade-union officials carrying the authority and power of decision-taking of their executive councils were directly involved in the affairs of one company and place of employment. This level of contact and involvement allowed speedy decisions to be taken and on occasion the saving of time made a considerable contribution to good industrial relations and operational efficiency. This experience indicates the benefits which could flow from higher staff to member ratios within trade unions, especially when combined with a delegation of authority to take decisions to a lower level within the hierarchy of full-time officials. At Fairfields this top-level involvement was combined with a high degree of involvement from yard representatives and the evolution of an effective channel of communication between the executive level and shop steward level of trade-union representatives. These structural aspects of trade-union involvement made a considerable contribution to the achievement of improved industrial relations at Fairfields.

One measure of the support amongst trade-union officials for the Fairfields approach was the letter sent out by the trade-union side of the central joint council to the Prime Minister arguing that the Fairfields management and philosophy be given a central place in the merger then under negotiation. There were several such clear indications of the 'special relationship' which many trade-union leaders and activists felt there to be with the new Fairfields. The aim of improving industrial relations and attitudes was certainly achieved.

Turning to the introduction of new management techniques in shipbuilding, the first aspect of note was the difficulty of establishing a structure of control capable both of effecting the changes and of running the yard as efficiently as possible during the upheaval. Given the task they had been recruited to perform it was natural that the interest of top management should be primarily long-range, the achievement of major changes in the company over an extended period (originally seen as five years). The company was only of medium-size, however, and therefore the new top management had to become involved in lower levels of management decision-taking. This was accentuated by the importance attached by the new top management to inter-personal leadership, which also involved them intimately in medium and lower-level decision taking. The rather delicate shift of emphasis required from managers and supervisors necessitated the attention of top management. Supervisors in shipbuilding had been production-centred in the narrowest sense, and it was obviously desirable to inject them with concern for employee-relations, yet without making them exclusively employee-centred, which could have been seriously damaging to productive efficiency in the short run. This shift of emphasis required more attention from top management than it received, yet it received more attention than the management structure was designed to give it, with consequent loss of attention to other vital problems.

The over-centralized control structure was inherited and persisted with because it was seen as appropriate to the rapid introduction of extensive change, to some extent against the grain of the middle managers who would have to be the vehicles of the changes. However the interpersonal style of the new top management and the pressure of events, accentuated by the characteristics of shipbuilding processes, kept pulling them away from long-run and towards short-run problems. There was a failure to devolve authority quickly and widely enough, and to clearly delineate the work roles necessary if the company was to achieve optimum efficiency.

The organization structure introduced in June 1966 did not solve these problems. The structure was functional, and like most functional structures tended to force the decision-making process to the top. This continued the excessive tendency towards centralization with its attendant burden on the general manager. The organization included no 'screening' device to save the general manager from the trivia of much of day-to-day operation. Important matters were easily overlooked in the mass of information which had to move upwards, and delays caused confusion and frustration. The general manager instead of being involved in the initiation and concluding stages of policy became too close to everyday affairs. His direct span of supervision was thirteen managers, too many for efficient operation. The factors affecting limitation of supervision are the abilities of the person supervising, the structure of the organization, and the quality of subordinate management. A very important factor is the nature of the work to be supervised. Shipbuilding is a varied and complex operation, not suitable for such a large span of control.

The situation at Fairfields required a hierarchical organization structure with relatively small spans of supervision at the top. This was particularly so because of senior management's lack of shipbuilding experience. In a highly centralized organization it is necessary for the top echelon of management to have considerable experience of the range of technical and commercial problems associated with the industry concerned. This is important not only because without it the efficiency of decision-taking can be impaired, but because effective authority in part derives from technical know-how.

One consequence of the over-centralized management structure was a failure to use the full capabilities of the subordinate managers, resulting in some disillusionment and frustration amongst them. They felt isolated from the major decision-making function and the breadth of the second-level echelon made this group too large to provide motivation. There was some fragmentation amongst top management, and the formation of distinct and to some extent rival groups within the overall structure. Coordination became difficult because of the insularity of each particular function, each identified with its own contribution to the overall product, jealous of its own prerogatives, and not primarily concerned with the overall position of the yard.

The changes made in April 1967 remedied some of the weaknesses of the previous structure. The general manager's direct span of supervision was reduced from thirteen to eight. He also divested himself of responsibility (but not, of course, accountability) for production and sought to make clear the role of the productivity services organization. This was necessary because the head of the organization, as a result of his main board membership, gave to the organization a status not normally enjoyed by service divisions. The situation was further complicated by general recognition within the company that the productivity services director was *de facto* deputy general manager. In this situation the line managers were not always sure whether a course of action was being recommended to them or ordered.

The changes made were not effective. The newly elected members to the management company were not convinced that it would involve them more closely in the major areas of policy formulation; credibility in management is as relevant as in other spheres of activity. In late 1967 the problem facing the company was not primarily one of organizational balance but one of managerial confidence. The position was such that strong action was required, action which could only come from the board. Unfortunately preoccupation with the merger situation meant that this situation was not fully appreciated and therefore never resolved.

A question raised by the experience of Fairfields is the extent to which there is a place for acknowledged experimentation in particular industrial situations. It may be argued that even the most 'scientific' of managements must proceed by trial and error to some extent, and that in a period of evolving managerial techniques all managements are involved in a process of experiment. The distinction to be made, however, is between experiment recognized as such and subject to assessment and review, and experiment as an inevitable part of dynamic management. The advantage of recognized experiment is that it may make possible changes which would meet opposition if they could be used as an argument for comparable changes right across the board.

Cases of firms which have had to choose between introducing changes they favoured in industrial relations and parting company with the employers' association appropriate to their industry have been fairly common, and the decision has often come down against change. Similarly, trade unions have sometimes resisted proposals from particular managements more because of a fear of the precedents which would be established than from a doubt or distrust regarding the consequences of the specific change being proposed by the particular management. The creation of an isolated experiment leaving the remainder of the industry immune from the danger of immediate contagion can overcome some of the external opposition to change.

Ideally such an experiment should be conducted with the support of the rest of the industry. This was the aim of the proposals advanced for experiments in workers' participation and single-channel bargaining at the Prime Minister's conference on productivity in September 1966. Such agreed experiment makes it possible for managements and trade unionists in the industry to observe the experiment, receive reports on its progress and to decide the extent to which they would wish to apply its methods more widely.

When the new company was formed to run Fairfields Sir Iain Stewart hoped that the shipbuilding industry would endorse his 'proving ground' approach in this way. The trade unions did, although there was no formal undertaking as to how fears of establishing precedents would be set aside. The shipbuilders refused any part in the experiment, even avoiding a general declaration of support for its aims or good wishes for its success. A more open-minded approach could have contributed to the content and the success of the experiment, and would have avoided many of the difficulties which arose around the position of Fairfields both in the formulation of broad policy for the industry and in the merger movement on the Upper Clyde.

A willingness to consider the proving ground approach at that early stage would have involved formulating the means and ends of the experiment more precisely, and this would have been of value in itself. There is no doubt that such willingness would have been welcomed and would have exerted some influence over developments at Fairfields. There may have been some loss to the experiment through attempts to limit its scope and slow down its pace, but given the limited aims of the experiment this seems unlikely. Problems could have arisen had employees at Fairfields shown enthusiasm to expand their positive participation in management decision-taking. Whereas management at Fairfields probably would have yielded to pressure for greater participation – and some would have welcomed it – the involvement of the rest of industry as observers of the experiment would have created pressures against any basic shift in the locus of decision-taking.

The establishment of proving-grounds would not, of course, remove all such pressures and enable those directly involved in experiments to operate in an industrial vacuum. It could create opportunities for exploring new aproaches to industrial problems which otherwise would remain unexplored because of timidity, the heavy hand of tradition or the hidden hand of external counter-pressures.

Given the need for change and the resistance to it in British industry there does seem a case for exploring the possibility of establishing proving grounds within which ideas which have not yet received widespread acceptance may be tried out, monitored, conclusions drawn, and the results applied more widely. Ideas for improvement abound in government and trade-union reports, and in management and academic literature. There is no shortage of men anxious to speed up the process of change. The difficulty is that such men are denied the opportunity, usually because the power to decide – or to block decision – lies elsewhere. It was the eminence and energy of Sir Iain Stewart and his ability to see and grasp the opportunity, that made the proving ground at Fairfields possible. The juncture of man and opportunity is too rare if the idea of managerial experiment is to be adopted and given practical expression. Could the 'little neddies' explore the possibilities of such experiment?

Academics could play a useful part in such experiments, both in the design of them and in monitoring results. Experience at Fairfields suggests that academics given the opportunity of observing the day-to-day life of a company face a difficulty arising out of the involvement: the effect which personal relationships can have on their ability to form objective judgements and having formed them to express them. We confess that our affection, admiration and respect for various of the Fairfields *personae* may have affected our judgement. Being able to cross-check our individual assessments with each other, we hope we have avoided this danger. We recognized it from the outset, although its potential was not fully appreciated until we had become closely involved with the people concerned and their problems. There is the alternative risk that having recognized the danger of bias favouring our associates we over-corrected for it, 'leant over backwards', and have been more sharply critical at points than the circumstances warrant. We are sure that we will be judged by different individuals to have made both types of error. The one fault we know we cannot be charged with is of having reached a firm conclusion and of then omitting to publish it.

APPENDIX 1

Shop Stewards

MUCH of the material used in this appendix was collected by means of a questionnaire survey of shop stewards made in June 1966. This basic material has been supplemented by interviews and discussions with shop stewards and by 'participant observation' during the research project. The main aim of the shop steward enquiry was to provide a better insight into the background of the shop steward, to learn something of his views on his role in the yard, and particularly to ascertain his opinion on the proving ground. In short, we were concerned not with the role of the shop steward in general industry, but specifically in Fairfields.

The shop stewards were elected by the members of each department or sub-department in the yard. Nominations were made from the members of each department and a show of hands determined the election. This information was then passed to the trade union concerned who accredited the shop steward, and notified the management of the appointment. It is usual for most stewards to seek re-election every twelve months, although on issues of confidence or in case of resignations, elections are held immediately unless a deputy is elected *pro tem.*

In the Fairfields procedure agreement the procedure for accrediting shop stewards and for notifying resignations is laid down. The company also recognized the needs of the steward in pursuit of his duties: 'The shop steward shall be able to leave his department to deal with relevant matters or at the request of the district official of his union or the convenor but he shall inform his foreman/departmental head before leaving and return to work as quickly as reasonable.' In this clause the management were clearly recognizing the breach that can arise between foreman and shop steward when the latter constantly absents himself from the department without informing the

222

foreman. It is a very difficult task to know when the steward's absence is in fact necessary 'to deal with relevant matters . . .'. Some stewards at Fairfields were virtually full-time stewards in the sense that they were hardly ever at their work. However, the majority of stewards were able to attain an acceptable balance between work and duties.

The shop stewards' organization at Fairfields, as in most shipyards, was two-tiered. The ASB elected their own convenor to preside over the coordinate meetings of the trades within the Society. Each trade elected two shop stewards who were responsible for their trade's interests in the yard. They liaised with similar trades in other yards and formed unofficial trade committees. Within the Society each trade retained a fierce independence but cooperated with other trades in the Society to form a powerful group.

The other unions in the yard elected their own shop stewards and, from amongst these, a convenor was appointed. These unions also acted with great independence, but were united in their dislike of the ASB group of stewards. This dislike was to a large degree based on their contempt for past management who had given in to the ASB militancy, for the ASB for employing – and succeeding – in these tactics, and in part on the ASB's belief in their superiority over other workers. The ASB is the largest union in the industry and has demanded and received special negotiating rights from management. Under the concept of a proving ground, the other unions' stewards in the yard wanted these rights equalized.

The attitudes of both sides were made clear in the issue of the full-time convenorship of shop stewards.* The eventual outcome of this issue was for the Society's shop stewards to propose and have accepted by the other stewards a revised voting system. The original system was for each steward to have one vote (two stewards per department). Although having the largest membership in the yard, the ASB stewards were outvoted when the other stewards combined – as they often did – to vote against them. The new system suggested by the ASB stewards was aimed at recognizing their dominance, in

* See Chapter 5, on labour relations, pp. 121–3.

terms of numbers in the yard and industry. Each steward was to retain his vote, and be given one vote for every fifty members – 'or part thereof' – in his department, for example: forty-nine men in department – one vote, 105 men, three votes, etc.

In June 1966 there were forty-eight shop stewards at Fairfields. There was insufficient time to interview each steward individually so a questionnaire was issued to and completed by each steward in the presence of a research worker. Because of illness, and in one case promotion, only forty-five questionnaires were completed. The largest group of stewards were members of the ASB.

Table I.1

Number of shop stewards per union

	Number
ASB	16
NUGMW	11
AEU	10
Other unions	8

Of these stewards, thirty-one were skilled men. The majority of the stewards were over forty years of age.

Table I.2

Shop stewards: age distribution

Age	Number
20–29	7
30–39	9
40–49	20
50+	9

Over half of the stewards had been in the continuous employment of one of the Fairfields companies (i.e. Fairfields (Glasgow) Ltd, Fairfield Shipbuilding and Engineering Ltd, or Fairfield-Rowan Ltd.

Table I.3

Shop stewards: continuous employment at Fairfields

Service	Number
Under 3 years	15
3–5 years	17
6–10 years	3
11 +	10

One of the shop stewards had only been elected to his office two weeks before the survey was held; another steward had held office for eighteen years. Just under half of the stewards had held similar positions in other shipyards (eleven), and in other industries (nine). The pay-offs endemic to the industry had made many of these men mobile between the yards on the River, and in some trades, e.g. electrician, joiner, between industries. This mobility brought the steward into contact with many different employment situations, and gave them some experience of wages and conditions of work in other yards and industries which was useful to the steward in negotiations with management.

An attempt was made to obtain an assessment of the relative importance of the various functions of the shop stewards. A list of probable shop stewards' duties was given and each man asked to rate them according to the importance attached to them by himself, the workers he represented, his union, and by management.

Table I.4

Of the following list of duties, which do you consider to be the most important task of the shop steward?

	Ranked
To protect workers' rights	1
To encourage participation in union affairs	2
To work with management to improve labour relations	3
To keep workers informed	4
To recruit more members	5
To collect union dues	6

That the stewards placed 'need to work with management to improve labour relations' before the need to 'keep workers informed' is perhaps not surprising when related to the idea of Fairfields as a proving ground. The pattern evolving in the yard in June 1966 was one whereby the idea of a partnership between management and men necessitated the free flow of information to shop stewards and to the yard worker level. In a situation other than that existing at Fairfields, it is un-likely that the need to 'keep workers informed' would rate so high in the list. In fact, the rating given to it might be interpre-ted as a sign of the shop steward's approval of the manage-ment's efforts to improve communications.

The stewards were asked to rate the duties according to the importance attached to them by the workers they represented. In this rating, the shop steward clearly saw himself as a source of information for the yard worker.

Table I.5

Of the following duties of a shop steward, in which order of importance would the yard worker place them?

	Ranked
To protect workers' rights	1
To keep workers informed	2
To work with management to improve labour relations	3
To encourage participation in union affairs	4
To recruit more members	5
To collect union dues	6

The importance attached by shop stewards to the need to encourage participation in union affairs is surrounded by a certain ambiguity. Most men employed in the shipyard are members of a trade union. The shop steward, when imple-menting the mandate given him by the men, can rely on their support and cooperation. In this sense, the workers are par-ticipating in union affairs. However, if this statement implies that it is the duty of the steward to encourage participation in extra-yard activities, then it might have received a lower rating because of the reluctance (perhaps due to apathy) of the average union member to participate in branch meetings and similar activities.

When asked to indicate what they considered to be their union's interpretation of a shop steward's duties, the rating did show more deviations from the two previous tables.

Table I.6

What functions would your union list as being the most important job of the shop steward?

	Ranked
To protect workers' rights	1
To encourage participation in union affairs	2
To collect union dues	3
To keep workers informed	4
To recruit new members	5
To work with management to improve labour relations	6

The stewards believed that the unions placed more emphasis on recruitment and participation in union affairs than they themselves did. The 'collection of union dues' was also rated quite highly. The low rating given to the 'need to work with management to improve labour relations' might well have been their interpretation of the unions' attitude before the proving-ground concept was introduced. The following table is based on a breakdown of the data of Table I.4 and suggests how the characteristics of the various unions are reflected in the rating given to the duties by the stewards themselves.

The ASB stewards clearly believe that their main duties are to protect their workers' rights and encourage participation in union affairs. If a strong union can be obtained by these efforts, then it will be possible to negotiate with management to improve labour relations. The relatively low rating given to the need to keep workers informed is in part based on the belief of the stewards that the men they represent should have

Table I.7

Functions of the shop steward classified by union

	ASB	NUGMW	AEU	Others
To recruit new members	4	1	2	3
To collect union dues	6	6	6	6
To encourage participation in union affairs	2	4	3	2
To keep workers informed	5	3	4	5
To protect workers' rights	1	2	1	1
To work with management to improve labour relations	3	5	5	4

confidence in them. There is also the effect of the traditional basis of British shipbuilding trade unions, with a majority of issues being determined at the place of work or at branch meetings close to the yard, thus leaving little excuse for the failure of others to participate.

The importance attached by the NUGMW stewards to the need to recruit new members was a reflection of events in the yard during June 1966. An increased membership would enable the union to be in a stronger position to protect workers' rights. By keeping members informed they hoped to encourage participation in union affairs.

The AEU stewards followed much the same pattern as the NUGMW. It is noticeable that both rated the need to recruit members more highly than did the ASB stewards. All stewards gave a low rating to the need to collect union dues.

It is interesting to note the low rating given by the NUGMW and the AEU stewards to the need to cooperate with management to improve labour relations. The two unions in terms of philosophy and at a national level had a more pronounced bias in favour of such cooperation. This is probably an example of the gap which often exists between the thinking of trade-union leaders and other levels in the union structure.

It is interesting to note the rating of the duties as the shop stewards considered management would like to see them.

Table I.8

*Of the following list of duties, which do you consider
that management feel to be the most important?*

	Rated
To work with management to improve labour relations	1
To protect workers' rights	2
To keep workers informed	3
To encourage participation in union affairs	4
To recruit more members	5
To collect union dues	6

The table shows that the stewards believed that management considered them to be part of the lines of communication in addition to their roles as peace-keepers and protectors of workers' rights.

The previous tables have provided some general indication of the shop steward's understanding of his role. To support this general understanding the men were asked what they considered to be the three most important qualities of the shop steward. The answers were varied. Some respondents indicated the three most important functions of the shop steward rather than the qualities. However, the next table illustrates their contentions.

Table I.9

*What do you consider to be the three most important
qualities of a good shop steward?*

	Ranked
Integrity	1
Being a good organizer	2
Ability to negotiate	3

The above opinions were supplemented by one steward who said that the steward needed to be 'a good speaker'. Another warned that a steward 'must not try to force his opinion on to the men'. This opinion was not shared by the management at Fairfields who regarded the shop stewards as leaders of men, rather than merely reflection of attitudes in the yard. This function of leadership was accepted by some shop stewards, e.g. the forceful and eloquent pleading of the senior steward which succeeded, very much against the initial feelings of the meeting, in getting the AEU members to call off their proposed strike in July 1967. A combination of all three qualities, together with the required militancy when the occasion demanded, seemed to be regarded by the respondents as necessary qualities for a 'good shop steward'.

It is perhaps surprising that the shop stewards' relations with foremen – their most frequent and direct contact with management – were good.

Table I.10

*How do you consider your relationship
with your foremen?*

	Number
Good	27
Average	18
Bad	—

Perhaps these favourable conclusions were reached because the majority of the men believed that foremen understood the role of the shop steward in the yard. Only nine stewards considered that their foremen did not have an understanding of their position. Moreover, only two stewards felt that their foreman did not assist them fulfil their jobs as stewards. To illustrate the majority opinion one steward told how, when he had been elected as a shop steward his foreman had transferred him from work on board ship to the shop in order to be more easily available, and accessible to his members.

The stewards were largely of the opinion that it was their task to keep the men informed of company policy.

Table I.11

Who should keep the men informed of company policy?

	Number
Foremen	10
Shop stewards	29
Both jointly	6

To some extent the management recognized the feelings of the stewards on this matter, and the convenor of shop stewards and two senior colleagues were usually invited to management briefing groups and participated in the executive management committee. This participation ensured that the stewards were fully briefed on the company situations and were able to communicate news and views to the men. Communications were given great emphasis by the management, as reflected in the following table.

Table I.12

In which way has your position as a shop steward been made easier by the management?

	Ranked
Introduction of meeting room facilities	1
Better relations with the management	2
More information	3

The provision of meeting room facilities eased the steward's job. With the many ramifications of the proposals for a proving ground to be discussed, it was essential that the stewards be given facilities to meet regularly, and in relatively comfortable surroundings and without loss of earnings. In June 1966 the reaction of the stewards to the changes were put by one man as follows: 'We were suspicious at first, but now seem to be moving towards a position of mutual trust'.

One of the most interesting reflections of change was the growing appreciation of management problems gained by some stewards: 'We are now better informed and are able to see and appreciate the problems of management.' This theme of improved management-worker cooperation is clearly expressed in the following table.

Table I.13

What changes, if any, have you noticed since the company was formed?

	Ranked
Greater understanding between management and men	1
Better cooperation between management and unions	2
Improved communications	3

That these changes had been noticed in the first six months of the company says much for the enthusiasm and intent of the management to offer conditions which the stewards could positively react to. There was frequent contact between management and shop stewards and this enabled the stewards to have direct access to management with the problems of the men. Most of these problems centred on the steward's intepretation of his duty to 'protect workers' rights'. One of his main duties in this area lay in bargaining with management over wages and other financial problems.

The shop steward took wage claims to the management on behalf of the men. The usual basis for a claim was 'comparability'. The yard workers always regarded their wages in relation to other trades, e.g. a welder had an established differential over, say, a plater. Most claims are therefore based on movement in wage rates in other trades or in other yards. The informal network of contacts between yards – reinforced by the movement of workers among yards – provides the stewards with a fund of knowledge of wage rates and conditions of work. The claims are based on this knowledge and until the proving-ground concept was introduced – with the 'nothing for nothing' policy – claims were likely to include reference to existing differentials, parity with other trades, or the existence of a *pro rata* payment tradition.

At Fairfields the traditional basis for wage increases was not recognized by management. Claims had to be based on some proposal giving rise to a 'demonstrable increase in productivity'.* The management's strict adherence to this principle was necessary to safeguard the future of the company, but this in fact did not always convince all shop stewards of the necessity of such rigidity. In a resort to the old methods of bargaining, some shop stewards introduced workshop sanctions in an attempt to 'reinforce' their bargaining positions, e.g. bans on overtime working, unofficial walk-outs, and other measures generally employed to impose a ban on the effective use of manpower. For example, it was customary for a crane-driver to be allocated to a crane for a day. If no work was available for that crane, he could not be transferred to operate another crane. The re-imposition of such sanctions could have a restrictive effect on production. The usual range of sanctions† was occasionally employed by the shop stewards at Fairfields. Despite the use of sanctions the stewards were very much aware of their role in the proving ground and were definite in their order of priorities for the future.

Table I.14

What would you like to see emerge from the company?

	Ranked
Security of employment	1
Increased wages	2
Pensions, a sick-pay scheme, etc.	3

Given the historical situation in the industry, the first two choices were expected. The third choice reflects the workers'

*The only exception to this being the recognition of national wage awards.

† See 'The role of shop stewards in British industrial relations', *Research Paper I*, Royal Commission on Trade Union and Employers' Associations, Section E, HMSO, 1966.

desire to share some of the benefits enjoyed by some workers in other industries. The company were later to introduce a pension scheme for the yard workers, and in some cases guarantees of employment were given, for example, in the ASB agreement. When the stewards had indicated what they expected from the future, they then indicated what priorities the management should have in mind.

Table I.15

What do you think the company should do first?

	Ranked
Eliminate wage differentials	1
Obtain more orders	2
Make production more efficient	3

In establishing these priorities, the stewards favoured the reverse order to that which most managements (and, indeed, economists) would adopt. There was little doubt that wage structure was a potent cause of discontent in the yard, and, in the opinion of the shop stewards, was one of the three major problems facing the company.

Table I.16

What are the biggest difficulties facing the company?

	Ranked
Old traditions and past practices	1
Wage differentials	2
Implementation of methods and planning	3

The stewards felt that most of these difficulties could be overcome by greater productivity – and this was dependent among other things on the improvement of methods and planning of production. In June 1966 the shop stewards' opinions on the future of the company are shown in the following table.

Table I.17

*How do you assess the chances of this shipyard being
successful and being in business by 1970?*

	Number
Good	24
Fair	13
Certain	6
Poor	1
Don't know	1

The stewards were aware of the significance of the proving
ground to their own future and that of the industry. Despite
outbreaks of militancy and occasionally strikes, they gave their
cooperation to management and worked for the improvement
of labour relations in the industry.

Foremanship Survey

THIS survey was made during August 1967. There were 160 foremen or 'foreman status' employees in the company at that time. Only those foremen with direct 'line' authority were interviewed, i.e. those of foreman rank in the offices were excluded. In all, 143 foremen completed the questionnaire in the presence of a research worker.

PART A

Table II.1 shows that the largest group of foremen had held their positions for less than five years.

Table II.1

Length of service as foremen

Years' service	Number
Under 5	91
6–10	19
11–15	9
16–20	20
21–25	2
26–30	2
	143

Table II.2 shows that roughly one-third of the total interviewees had been with the company less than five years before being promoted to the rank of foreman.

236

Table II.2

Length of service before attaining foremanship

Years' service	Number
Under 5	47
6–10	18
11–15	16
16–20	26
21–25	8
26–30	20
Others	8
	143

This is not surprising given the rapid increase in staff which accompanied the formation of the new company.* Both the tables exclude the seventeen foremen who were transferred into the new company when Fairfield-Rowan went into liquidation. The following tables refer to the 109 foremen exercising 'Line Authority'.

As was anticipated, the age distribution of the foremen tended to 'bunch' towards the centre and upper age brackets.

Table II.3

Age distribution of foremen at Fairfields

Age	Number
20–29	1
30–39	24
40–49	45
50–59	26
60–65	11
65+	2

The same pattern of distribution is seen in the table dealing with the years of service given to the shipbuilding industry.

*The 'company' is taken to refer to the old company (before 1966) or the new company (after January 1966) as may be appropriate.

Table II.4

Years worked in the shipbuilding industry

Years	Number
0– 5	4
6–10	5
11–20	28
21–30	39
31–40	23
41 +	10

The above table makes it clear that most of the foremen had not moved to other industries. The accumulation of members in the intermediate brackets suggests that most of the foremen will remain for the remainder of their working lives in the industry. The next table suggests that most foremen retain an identity with Fairfields.

Table II.5

Length of unbroken service at Fairfields

Years	Number
0– 5	36
6–10	11
11–20	36
21–30	11
31–40	14
41–50	1

Before going into industry the foremen had been educated as follows:

Table II.6

Grade of school attended

Grade	Number
Junior	17
Secondary	65
High School	27

Of the 109 foremen, ninety-nine had completed apprentice-ships. Of the seventeen foremen who had only attended junior schools, six had attended further education classes. Of the six foremen, two had been sent by their firms and the other four had gone from 'personal inclination'. Of the sixty-five foremen who had attended secondary school, twenty-one had later attended further education classes, the majority (eighteen) through 'personal inclination'.

Of the ninety-nine foremen who had completed apprentice-ships, seventy-six had served their apprenticeships in the ship-building industry. Since their first appointments as foremen only twenty-two of the foremen had subsequently held non-supervisory positions.

Table II.7

Since your first appointment as foreman, have you held any non-supervisory position?

	Number
Yes	22
No	87

The degree of industry-stability shown in Tables II.1 and II.2 is reflected in the small numbers of foremen who had held similar positions in other industries.

Table II.8

Have you held a foremanship outside the shipbuilding industry?

	Number
Yes	15
No	94

Eight of the fifteen foremen who had held similar positions in other industries thought that foremen should move from firm to firm in order to gain experience. However, of the total number of foremen, only fifty-two thought that it was necessary to gain wider industrial experience.

Table II.9

Should a foreman move from firm to firm to gain experience?

	Number
Yes	52
No	57

The foremen ranked the following factors in order of importance to the foremen's job.

Table II.10

	Ranked
Knowledge of job	1
Ability to take quick decisions	2
Firmness	3
Tact and understanding	4
Ability to get on with people	5
Knowledge of trade-union procedure	6

Of the foremen only four did not think that newly appointed foremen should be given any training. Of the factors listed in Table II.10, the foremen thought that the following (ranked in order of priority) could be included in a foremen's course.

Table II.11

What should be included in a foremanship course?

	Ranked
Knowledge of trade union procedure	1
Knowledge of the job	2
Tact and understanding	3
Ability to take quick decisions	4
Ability to get on with people	5
Firmness	6

Quite obviously all but the first two ranked factors would be difficult to teach – one could only hope to eradicate the worst characteristics of the individual foreman. However, it is interesting to note the desire to learn something of trade-union practice and procedure, particularly when this was ranked last in Table II.10. With regard to training of foremen of the 105 foremen who thought that they should be given some teaching, ninety-three said that training 'would have helped them' whereas twelve thought that foremanship was best learned 'on the job'.

Table II.12

Do you think that some training would have helped you, or is foremanship best learned on the job?

	Number
Some training would have helped	93
Best learned on the job	12

Of the four foremen who did not believe that training was necessary for newly appointed foremen, one thought that training might have helped him.

Table II.13 indicates the amount of industry-loyalty found among this sample of foremen.

Table II.13

If you were applying for your first foremanship, would you choose the shipbuilding industry as a place to work?

	Number
Yes	79
No	30

Of the seventy-nine answering 'yes' in Table II.13, sixty-one said that they would not accept a similar job with equal pay and status outside the shipyards. Even with their experience of

241

the shipyards, the majority of foremen would still prefer to remain in the industry.

Table II.14

If you were applying for a job as foreman, where would you prefer the job to be?

	Number
In the shipbuilding industry	81
In another industry	28

PART B

The largest proportion of foremen were members of trade unions.

Table II.15

Are you a member of a trade union?

	Number
Yes	97
No	12

The high level of union membership was attributable to two main factors: the need for protection against injustices and the possibility that union membership was compulsory for their job.

Table II.16

Do you feel that union protection is less important to you as a foreman than it was before you were appointed to your present position?

	Number
Yes	46
No	62
No answer	1

The implications in the above table are reflected in the following figures.

Table II.17

Why did you join a trade union?

	Ranked
Membership was necessary to take up the job	1
You believe in trade unionism	2
You were expected to be a member	3
Protection against possible injustices	4

Therefore, although believing that 'protection against possible injustices' was still of importance to foremen, it was only ranked last in the reasons for joining a trade union. The necessity of union membership to fulfil the job of foreman is particularly noticeable in the steel-work trades, where only members of the Amalgamated Society may supervise members of the same society. Union membership also tended to be transferred to the 'staff sections' of the union where these existed.

Table II.18

Principal unions involved at Fairfields

	Number
ASB	49
ASSET	16
ETU	11
PTU	7
Others	14
No answer	12

Eighty-one of the foremen had remained in the same union when they were appointed as foremen. The period of union membership among foremen was as follows.

Table II.19

How long have you been a member of your present union?

Years	Number
0– 1	7
2– 5	11
6–10	4
11–15	14
16–20	22
21–25	11
25+	28

It is not surprising that practical experience of trade unionism was regarded by seventy-one of the foremen as being necessary for their position.

Table II.20

Is practical experience of trade unionism necessary for the position of foreman?

	Number
Yes	71
No	38

Approximately one-third of the foremen had taken some part in union affairs.

Table II.21

Have you held any of the following offices or similar positions in any trade union?

	Number
Shop steward	33
Branch official	9
District representative	–
Other positions	7

The foremen's appreciation of the need for some practice of, or some education in union practice was indicated in Table II.11 and supported in the following.

Table II.22

*Should trade-union organization and practice be a basic
part of any course on foremanship?*

	Number
Yes	84
No	25

PART C

Only nine foremen had received their initial appointments in other industries.

Table II.23

Where did you receive your first appointment as foreman?

	Number
Fairfields (Glasgow) Ltd	47
Fairfields S. & E. Co. Ltd	39
Fairfield-Rowan Ltd	3
Another shipyard	10
Another industry	9
No answer	1

However, it is interesting to note that a majority of the foremen had been appointed without making formal application for the job.

Table II.24

How were you appointed as foreman?

	Number
Applied for the position	41
Appointed without application	68

The large number who had been appointed without formal application suggests that appointments were generally at the discretion of the managers and were not administered through the personnel department.

Table II.25

Before your appointment at Fairfields, who were you interviewed by?

	Number
Personnel department	22
Manager	96
No interview	3

The lack of balance of the figures suggest that personnel department and managers were synonymous in some foremen's eyes. However, once an appointment was made there was little delay before the man began his duties.

Table II.26

What was the time-lag between your appointment and beginning your duties?

	Number
Under one week	53
2 – 3 weeks	42
More than four weeks	12
No answer	2

The greatest number of foremen had not received any training, either technical or managerial, before taking up their appointments.

Table II.27

Were you given any technical training before beginning your foremanship?

	Number
Yes	15
No	94

Table II.28

Were you given any management training before beginning your foremanship?

	Number
Yes	14
No	95

However, since the men had been made foremen, just under one-half of them had received some type of training.

Table II.29

Have you received any training since beginning your foremanship?

	Number
Yes	49
No	60

As shown in Table II.12, most of the foremen thought that some training would have helped them in their jobs.

The majority of foremen considered the system of foreman selection at Fairfields to show no bias, and they also considered that their prospects of promotion at Fairfields were 'better than' or at least 'the same as' prospects in other shipyards.

Table II.30

Do you think that the system of selecting and appointing foremen at Fairfields is:

	Number
Fair	98
Biased	4
No answer	7

Table II.31

How would you describe your prospects of promotion in Fairfields compared with your prospects in another shipyard?

	Number
Better	56
Same	49
Worse	2
No answer	2

Over half of the foremen did not consider that a move to another industry would improve their promotion prospects.

Table II.32

How would you evaluate your prospects for promotion in another industry?

	Number
Better	18
Same	68
Worse	21
No answer	2

The foremen were clear what they required from their future careers – job security and higher salaries.

Table II.33

Which of the following factors do you consider to be of most importance to you in your future career?

	Ranked
Job security	1
Higher salary	2
Improved working conditions	3
Higher status	4
Improved pension and sickness benefits	5

A surprisingly large number of foremen believed that the above factors could be more quickly obtained at Fairfields than in any other shipyard.

Table II.34

*Do you think that you are more likely to attain some or
all of the above factors more quickly in this company
than in any other shipyard?*

	Number
Yes	102
No	7

Perhaps the above table was one of the reasons why so small
a number of foremen believed that they were under-paid relative
to foremen in other yards.

Table II.35

*To the best of your knowledge how does your present
salary compare with foremen of similar qualifications
and responsibilities in other shipyards?*

	Number
Above	44
About equal	49
Below	9
No answer	7

Table II.34 again reinforces the foremen's idea that they are
part of a unique 'experiment' at Fairfields rather than part of
the usual industrial firm.

Table II.36

Do you consider your position at Fairfields to be:

	Number
Just another job	1
An important part of an industrial 'experiment'	103
A 'high risk' job	5

Perhaps the high degree of company and industry loyalty
coupled with their awareness of their role in an 'experiment',
reduced the mobility of the men.

Table II.37

*If you were offered a job of equal salary and status in an
industry outwith the shipyards and near to Glasgow,
would you be inclined to accept it?*

	Number
Yes	36
No	73

The same loyalty that is given to the industry is obviously
given to the company.

Table II.38

*If you were offered a job of equal salary and status in
another shipyard would you accept it?*

	Number
Yes	6
No	103

PART D

This section was devised to throw some light on the relationship of the foremen with the shop stewards and how they viewed
the role of shop stewards. The foremen felt that regular departmental meetings to discuss matters affecting the men and management would be useful. This has generally been recognized
by the advisory committee procedures.

Table II.39

*Do you think that regular departmental group meetings
between foremen and shop stewards to discuss problems
common throughout the department would be of value?*

	Number
Yes	96
No	11
No answer	2

The majority of foremen considered the shop steward did not make their jobs more difficult, and were in fact, 'a necessary part of the industrial work-place'.

Table II.40

Is your job made more difficult by the existence of shop stewards in your department?

	Number
Yes	13
No	96

Table II.41

Do you consider shop stewards to be a necessary part of the industrial work-place?

	Number
Yes	107
No	2

During the two years before this survey great changes had taken place in the yard. Despite these changes, the foremen felt that there had been a general improvement and certainly no deterioration in the relationship with the shop stewards.

Table II.42

Do you consider your relationship with the departmental shop steward to be:

	Number
Better than two years ago	50
Same as two years ago	47
Worse than two years ago	7
No answer	5

The majority of foremen considered that too much attention was being paid to shop stewards by higher management.

Table II.43

Do you think that shop stewards are given too much attention by management?

	Number
Yes	78
No	31

The following ways were indicated as being part of the reason in which shop stewards were given 'too much attention'.

Table II.44

Reasons why shop stewards receive too much attention

	Ranked
Too much time is allowed for meetings	1
Too much importance is given to shop stewards' views	2
There is too much direct consultation with shop stewards	3
There is too much consultation on non-industrial-relations matters	4

Sixty-two foremen said that they consulted their departmental shop stewards on matters other than grievances or disputes.

Table II.45

With the exception of grievances and disputes, do you ever consult your shop stewards in an advisory capacity?

	Number
Yes	62
No	46
No answer	1

Of the sixty-two foremen who consulted their shop stewards for advice, twenty-seven said that their shop stewards always approached them with problems, thirty-one said that they sometimes did, and only four that they never did. Of the forty-six who did not seek shop stewards' advice, their shop stewards approached them 'always' (eleven), 'sometimes' (twenty-nine) and 'never' (six).

The frequency with which the sixty-two foremen consulted their shop stewards was as follows:

Table II.46

In the last three months how often have you consulted your shop steward?

	Number
Never	7
2–5 times	38
6–10 times	10
More than 10 times	7

In general, the majority of the foremen thought that the shop stewards spent less than ten hours per week on shop stewards' business.

Table II.47

How much time each week do you think that your department's shop steward spends on union business which takes him 'away from the job'?

	Number
Under 5 hours	38
6–10 hours	28
11–15 hours	12
16–20 hours	27
No answer	4

Regarding higher management's dealings with shop stewards, only nineteen foremen considered they 'always' neglected foremen as the most direct link with shop stewards.

Table II.48

*Does higher management tend to neglect foremen as
the most direct link with shop stewards?*

	Number
Always	19
Sometimes	79
Never	10
No answer	1

With regard to the operation of the procedure agreement, most of the foremen felt that the first stage in procedure, i.e. discussion with the foreman, is adhered to.

Table II.49

*Do you think that clause 7(a) (i) of the procedure
agreement is adhered to?*

	Number
Yes	58
No	12
Sometimes	35
Don't know	4

Approximately one-quarter of the foremen did not know (one year after the signing of the agreement) that such a booklet dealing with the procedure agreement was available.

Table II.50

Did you know that such a booklet existed?

	Number
Yes	85
No	24

Table II.51

Have you a personal copy of this booklet?

	Number
Yes	70
No	39

Table II.52

Do you have access to the booklet?

	Number
Yes	80
No	29

In view of the fact that approximately one-third of the foremen did not have a copy of the booklet, it is not surprising that the shop steward was considered to have a better knowledge of union-management negotiations than did the foremen.

Table II.53

Do you feel that the shop steward is better informed than the foremen on current union-management negotiations?

	Number
Yes	93
No	16

PART E

This small section relates to the general aspects of the foremen's relationships with their managers. The foremen were asked to assess their influence on their manager – only eleven described this as 'negligible'.

Table II.54

What do you think is the measure of your influence on your manager?

	Number
Considerable	31
Moderate	64
Negligible	11
Nil	2
No answer	1

The majority of foremen felt that their manager was 'good' at communicating information.

Table II.55

Do you consider that your manager is good at communicating information, instructions, decisions to you?

	Number
Yes	87
No	22

The same pattern was evident with communication of general company affairs.

Table II.56

Do you consider that you are kept up-to-date on general company affairs?

	Number
Yes	82
No	27

The foremen listed the following in order of priority, to be necessary to maintain an up-to-date knowledge of company affairs.

Table II.57

*Areas of information necessary to fulfil
properly the role of foremen*

	Ranked
General company policy	1
Departmental cost targets	2
Disciplinary procedure	3
Changes in work rules	4

The largest number of foremen felt that their performances were being reviewed by their managers, and a majority felt that such reviews were made on a regular basis.

Table II.58

*Do you think that foremen's performances are being
judged by senior management?*

	Number
Yes	83
No	13
Don't know	13

With regard to reviews of performance, 105 of the foremen considered the prospect of promotion to be an incentive to foremen.

Most of the foremen had tried to persuade a manager to change a decision and more than half would describe their persuasion as successful.

Table II.59

*Have you ever tried to persuade your manager that he
has made a wrong decision?*

	Number
Yes	85
No	25
No answer	1

The foremen ruled the following factors as preventing them from persuading the manager that he had made a wrong decision.

Table II.60

*Why didn't you approach your manager when you
felt that he had made a wrong decision?*

	Ranked
I am not paid to question managers' decisions	1
The manager will not accept criticism	2
The manager is not easily approachable	3
I am afraid of manager's disapproval	4

Ninety foremen considered themselves 'well informed' on company policy and only nineteen did not. Of the ninety, fifty-three thought that communications were better in this firm than in others, and twenty-three foremen thought that they were 'about the same'. Only three foremen considered communications in this firm to be 'worse' than elsewhere. The remaining eleven foremen had not worked in other firms.

The foremen were largely of the opinion that even 'though the pace of industry increased there would be no need for an age bar on foremen's jobs'.

Table II.61

*As the pace of industry grows, should there be an age
bar of forty on foremen's jobs?*

	Number
Yes	11
No	98

The foremen felt that the most important aspects of their jobs centred on production targets, cost and quality considerations.

Table II.62

Aspects of the foremen's job ranked in order of importance

	Ranked
To meet and improve on production targets	1
To reduce costs but maintain quality	2
To get men to work harder	3
To maintain morale	4
To maintain good relations with the men	5

In order to fulfil their roles adequately, only fifteen foremen considered that they were not getting the support they required from the managers.

Table II.63

Is your manager giving you the support you require to carry out your job?

	Number
Yes	94
No	15

The following possible reasons for the manager's failure to provide support for his foremen are ranked in order of importance.

Table II.64

Reasons for failure of manager to give support to foremen

	Ranked
Failure to communicate instructions and information	1
Failure to support disciplinary action	2
Failure to trust judgement of foremen	3
Failure to keep foremen informed of changes in company policy	4

Quite clearly any manager's failure to communicate instructions and/or information to his foreman will reduce the foreman's knowledge of company affairs, the importance of which is referred to in Table II.57.

Although the abolition of the position of head foreman was regarded by forty-one foremen as making their job 'more difficult', fifty-six foremen saw 'no change' or increase in the difficulty of their job. Any increase in difficulties of the foreman's role was not in the foreman's accessibility to his manager.

Table II.65

When you require your manager's assistance, when can you usually see him?

	Number
Immediately	63
Within a few hours	43
Within a few days	1
Only with difficulties	2

Under the new company, with an increased amount of work being placed on foremen, a majority of them did not consider that too much of their time was being spent at meetings.

Table II.66

Do you think that you attend too many meetings?

	Number
Yes	33
No	76

This section covers some aspects of communications within the company but also covers the foremen's reactions to the ETPS.

Although sixty-one foremen thought that communications at Fairfields were better than in 'any other firms in which you have been employed', some duality of command still existed which usually manifested itself in conflicting instructions.

Table II.67

Do you receive conflicting instructions from senior managers?

	Number
Often	8
Sometimes	69
Never	31
No answer	1

The brief of foremen was important because they considered that the successful application of the scheme depended on themselves.

However, despite the occasional confusions in communications a large number of foremen have noted an improvement.

Table II.68

During the last twelve months do you consider that communications within the company have:

	Number
Improved	75
Worsened	4
No change	26

Although communications have improved, the 'grapevine' is still evident.

Table II.69

Do you obtain information from the 'grapevine'
when you feel it should have been passed down
the 'line' to you?

	Number
Often	28
Sometimes	73
Never	8

A large number of the foremen felt that an extension of the 'briefing' system would ease communication difficulties.

Table II.70

Would an extension of the 'briefing group' system
help to ease any communication difficulties?

	Number
Yes	94
No	15

The foremen considered deficiencies in communications to be the result of individual errors rather than any inherent defects.

Table II.71

Do you think that any deficiencies in the communications
system are caused by individuals or defects in
the system itself?

	Number
Individuals	94
System	13

The ETPS has been introduced only two months prior to this questionnaire being issued. The Scheme was a complete departure from any of the incentive schemes previously used in the yard. Only one-third of the foremen felt that they had not received sufficient briefing on the scheme before its implementation.

Table II.72

Do you think that your briefing on ETPS
was sufficient to allow you to supervise its
implementation in your section?

	Number
Yes	70
No	37

Table II.73

Whose responsibility is it to ensure the successful
application of the scheme?

	Number
Foremen	77
Industrial engineer	32

The foremen's sense of responsibility for the scheme is shown in their desire for more training and details on the scheme. Of the seventy foremen who said that they had received 'sufficient' briefing on the scheme, thirty-six felt they still needed more time to understand the details of the scheme. This feeling is borne out in the following table.

Table II.74

Do you feel you require more time and training to really
understand the details of the ETPS?

	Number
Yes	65
No	43
No answer	1

The foremen in their administration of the scheme have been able to obtain the assistance of the industrial engineers.

Table II.75

*Since the beginning of the scheme have you been able to
receive the guidance and assistance you require from
your industrial engineer?*

	Number
Yes	86
No	16
No answer	7

The foremen believed that the scheme was likely to succeed.

Table II.76

*Do you think such a scheme can operate successfully
in a shipyard?*

	Number
Yes	102
No	7

Since the scheme had been introduced, the foremen believed
that output per man had either 'increased' or 'greatly increased'. Only thirty foremen believed output to have 'remained the same'. None considered output to have gone down.
On balance, the foremen believed that the increased output had
come from the men working more minutes in every hour rather
than more intensive working.

Table II.77

Do you think that the men have reacted to the ETPS by:

		Number
Working more minutes in each hour	Yes	82
	No	14
Working more intensively in each minute worked	Yes	58
	No	20

After the introduction of the scheme it is not surprising that the foremen considered they should have some knowledge of work study.

Table II.78

Do you think a foreman should have a knowledge of work study?

	Number
Yes	97
No	12

PART G

This section sought to obtain the foremen's opinion on the 'experimental' aspect of the yard's survival and to assess its chance of survival. The survey was taken approximately eighteen months after the inception of the new company.

Table II.79

Do you think that the 'experiment' will make the yard viable and profitable?

	Number
Certain	52
Probable	54
Doubtful	3
Unlikely	—

The foremen ranked the following factors as influencing the 'certainty' or 'probability' of viability.

Table II.80

Factors contributing to the success of the 'experiment':

	Ranked
Managerial ability	1
Better understanding between management and men	2
Worker's desire to avoid another closure	3
Government influence	4

From the above table it is interesting to note that emphasis has been given to the 'positive' aspects of the new 'experiment' rather than, say, the negative of government influence. The 'experimental' aspect is again stressed by the description of the changes made by the new company.

Table II.81

Since the Fairfields 'experiment' began would you describe the changes made by the company as:

	Number
Major	73
Important	34
Minor	1
No answer	1

After eighteen months of the 'experiment', no foremen were opposed to it, while a majority were enthusiastic.

Table II.82

How would you describe your attitude towards the 'experiment'?

	Ranked
Enthusiastic	82
Accept it	27
Disinterested	–
Opposed to it	–

However, in the event of failure, the foremen believe that it would be unrealistic to expect another body or even the Government to again save the yard.

Table II.83

If the 'experiment' was to fail do you think that the Government or some other body would 'save' the yard again?

	Number
Yes	16
No	85
Don't know	8

A majority of foremen thought that it would be easier to carry out their jobs in a more 'traditional' environment than in Fairfields.

Table II.84

Would you consider your job to be more easily carried out in a 'traditional' shipbuilding environment rather than in an environment of 'experiment'?

	Number
Yes	64
No	44
Don't know	1

One hundred and one of the foremen anticipated that the results of the 'experiment' would be of benefit to the foremen. One aspect of the new company has been the attendance of the whole yard at cinema meetings. In general, the foremen felt that these meetings made them 'more enthusiastic' about their jobs.

Table II.85

*Did the meetings make you feel more enthusiastic about
your job?*

	Number
Yes	87
No	14
No answer	8

But the foremen, although themselves 'enthused' after the meetings, noted only a 'slight improvement' in the work performance of the men.

Table II.86

*Did the meetings have any subsequent effect on the
work performance of the men?*

	Number
Much improved performance	11
Slight improvement	74
No effect	15
No answer	9

However, in general the foremen considered that the cinema meetings had not been a waste of time.

Table II.87

*Do you consider that the cinema meetings have been
'a waste of time'?*

	Number
Yes	10
No	90
Don't know	9

SUMMARY

This survey was made during August 1967. It was made to obtain a wide range of information on foremen at Fairfields; their backgrounds, their opinion on higher management, on communications, on the new methods at the yard, and on their role in an industrial 'experiment'.

What is most apparent in SECTION A is the strong links that the men have with the shipbuilding industry and particularly with one firm. In Table II.8 it is seen that only fifteen out of the 109 foremen who completed the questionnaire had held a foremanship outside the shipbuilding industry. Even after long service in the industry and particularly with Fairfields (Tables II.1 and II.2), seventy-nine of the foremen would still choose to take a first foremanship in the industry if they were setting out on their careers again (Table II.13). Over 56 per cent of the foremen had been with Fairfields for more than eleven years, and 24 per cent had served for twenty-one years.

The high degree of skill in the industry is reflected in the fact that ninety-nine of the foremen had completed apprenticeships. The craft-pride doubtlessly is one factor influencing their selection of 'knowledge of the job' as the prime asset of the foreman (Table II.10). It is obvious that there is a low degree of mobility among these foremen. Only nine had received their first jobs as foremen outside the industry (Table II.23). Tables II.37 and II.38 indicate that very few of the Fairfield foremen (six) would accept a similar job in another shipyard, whereas thirty-six might, in given conditions, be attracted from the industry. This is noticeable insomuch as the men cannot usually be expected to move to a situation less favourable than they occupy at present. Since their appointment to their initial foremanship, only twenty-two foremen had subsequently held non-supervisory posts.

This first section produces a picture of the foreman who is craft-trained, immobile between yards or industries, and one who seems unaffected by the specific troubles of the industry in the last seven years.

SECTION B shows that there is a high degree of union membership among the foremen; only twelve foremen were not union members. As one would expect, union membership is by trade where 'staff sections' exist, otherwise ASSET claims a number of members (Table II.18). Most of the foremen were union members because they had to be so to fulfil their jobs (e.g. ASB foremen) or because they 'believed in trade unionism' (Table II.17). Just over one-third of the foremen had held some union position before becoming a foreman (Table II.21). However, even with this experience the foremen as a group felt that some aspects of trade unionism should be taught on a 'foremanship course' (Tables II.11 and II.22).

SECTION C clearly indicates that the foremen felt that the selection of foremen at Fairfields was 'fair' (Table II.30). The foremen also considered their promotion prospects at Fairfields vis-à-vis other yards and other industries to be 'good' (Tables II.31 and II.32). There was also the belief that salaries at Fairfields were 'equal to' or 'above' those paid in other yards (Table II.35). These factors also cause a reduction in foreman mobility between firms.

Only a few foremen had received any training before taking up their foremanship. However, since appointment over half of them had still not received any training (Table II.29). The rapidity of events at Fairfields in the eighteen months prior to the survey has obviously made any systematic training of foremen difficult.

SECTION D indicates some of the foremen's attitudes to the shop stewards. The latter's position is clearly recognized by the foremen in Table II.41; but in the context of Fairfields, the foremen feel that the shop stewards are being given too much attention by senior management (Tables II.43 and II.44). In particular the foremen believe that too much time is being allowed for meetings and that quite a lot of time is taken by the shop steward 'away from his job' (Tables II.47). However, despite these criticisms and the upheavals of the prior eighteen months, Table II.42 shows that fifty foremen considered themselves over the last two years to have improved relations with their departmental shop stewards, while forty-seven thought there had been no deterioration, which accords with the views of the shop stewards (Appendix 1, Table I.10).

One surprising feature of this section was the fact that twenty-four foremen said that they did not know that a booklet containing the procedure agreement was available, whereas five more did not think that they had access to the booklet (Tables II.50 and II.52). It is perhaps not surprising that the shop stewards were regarded as being better informed on union-management relations.

SECTION E indicates that in general, managers are 'good' at communicating information and instructions to the foremen (Table II.55). Areas of general weakness may be eradicated by expansion of the 'briefing group' system for general announcements. The foremen thought that by and large they were kept up-to-date on general company affairs (Table II.56). This they regard as being very important to enable them to fulfil their jobs properly (Table II.57). It was, however, disappointing to note that the foremen took a negative action to doubtful instructions (Table II.58). As the foremen had easy access to their managers in most cases, this attitude is inexplicable. However, the foremen felt that they were supported by their manager in most situations (Table II.63) to enable them to meet cost, quality, and production targets which they regard as the most important parts of their jobs (Table II.62).

SECTION F shows that although there is evidence of the existence of duality of command (Table II.67) the foremen believed that during the last twelve months communications within the company have 'improved'. Weaknesses in the system of communication are thought to be the result of individuals rather than defects in the system itself. However, the 'grapevine' is still very much in evidence as a source of information (Table II.67) and it is considered that some extension of the 'briefing system' would be helpful (Table II.68).

The foremen firmly believe that the success of the ETPS is their responsibility (Table II.73) and they would appreciate more time to obtain detailed knowledge of the scheme (Table II.74). A large number of foremen felt that they had received all the help they had needed from the industrial engineers

271

(Table II.75). Only seven foremen thought that the ETPS was unlikely to succeed in a shipyard. The foremen thought that the ETPS had resulted in increased output from the men in their departments. Since the inception of the scheme it is not surprising that ninety-seven of the foremen felt that they should have a knowledge of work study (Table II.78).

SECTION G questioned the foremen's view and appreciation of the 'experiment'. Table II.79 indicates that only three foremen felt that experiment was a 'doubtful' means of making the yard viable and profitable. One hundred and six foremen were of the opinion that the experiment was 'certain' or 'probable' to succeed. It was thought that 'managerial ability' and the 'improvement in industrial relations' were two important aids to a successful outcome (Table II.80). The majority of the foremen described their attitude as 'enthusiastic' towards the experiment (Table II.82). The majority of the foremen seemed to realize that in the event of the experiment failing, there was little chance of the yard being 'saved' by the Government or some other group (Table II.83).

There seemed a general opinion that the cinema meetings had not had much effect on the work performance of the men (Table II.85), but eighty-seven of the foremen said that they felt 'more enthusiastic' about their jobs after the meetings (Table II.83). Generally, the foremen seemed to be well aware of their part in an industrial experiment (Table II.36), and only eight thought that it would not result in 'improved benefits' for foremen.

Index

273

INSTITUTE OF ECONOMICS
AND STATISTICS
OXFORD